JUST PREACHING

JUST PREACHING

Prophetic Voices for Economic Justice

edited by André Resner, Jr.
for Family Promise

CHALICE
PRESS

ST. LOUIS, MISSOURI

Family Promise can be contacted at: 715 Summit Avenue, Summit, NJ, 07901 (www.familypromise.org).

Biblical quotations, unless otherwise noted, are from the *New Revised Standard Version Bible*, copyright 1989, Division of Christian Education of the National Council of the Churches of Christ in the United States of America. Used by permission. All rights reserved.

Scripture quotations marked NKJV are taken from the *New King James Version.* Copyright © 1979, 1980, 1982 by Thomas Nelson, Inc. Used by permission. All rights reserved.

Scripture quotations marked (NIV) are taken from the HOLY BIBLE, NEW INTERNATIONAL VERSION®. NIV®. Copyright © 1973, 1978, 1984 by International Bible Society. Used by permission of Zondervan Publishing House. All rights reserved.

Cover art: © Getty Images
Cover and interior design: Elizabeth Wright

This book is printed on acid-free, recycled paper.

Visit Chalice Press on the World Wide Web at
www.chalicepress.com

10 9 8 7 6 5 4 3 2 1   03 04 05 06 07 08

Library of Congress Cataloging-in-Publication Data

Just preaching : prophetic voices for economic justice / edited by André Resner, Jr.
    p. cm.
Includes bibliographical references and index.
  ISBN 0-8272-1715-3 (alk. paper)
  1. Distributive justice–Religious aspects–Christianity–Sermons. 2. Sermons, American. 3. Distributive justice–Religious aspects–Christianity. 4. Topical preaching. I. Resner, André. II. Title.
  BR115.E3J87 2003
  261.8'5–dc21

                                                    2003009725

Printed in the United States of America

Contents

PART 3: God's Stake in Just Preaching

PART 4: Is It Just America? Poverty and Homelessness in the Homeland

PART 5: Children, Poverty, and the Just Word

PART 6: The Voice of the Poor

Acknowledgments

Family Promise would like to thank the following people:

Rev. Dr. André Resner, Jr., for doing the theological and editorial heavy lifting necessary to coax, cajole, and craft the work of thirty-two diverse contributors into a coherent whole.

Karen Olson for her unflagging vision of what this book—and this world—could become and for her understanding that the end of poverty must be preached.

James Winans for keeping this project on track and for his keen insight, attention to detail, and passion for justice.

Rev. Laura Benson for reviewing scores of submissions and offering helpful insights and suggestions.

Rev. Dr. William Willimon for believing in this project and for encouraging clergy across the country to share their sermons.

The Lilly Endowment for the ongoing commitment to education, community development, and the enrichment of the religious lives of Americans and for the generous financial support that made this book a reality.

Rev. Dr. Jon L. Berquist and Chalice Press for their recognition of the worth of this book and for their singular vision and dedication in publishing it.

The clergy of the Interfaith Hospitality Networks nationwide, especially the dozens who submitted sermons for this volume, for all the work they do alongside and on behalf of homeless families. Their leadership is vital to the success of the Interfaith Hospitality Networks and a critical part of the work against homelessness and poverty nationwide.

Contributors

Dale P. Andrews is the Frank H. Caldwell Associate Professor of Homiletics and associate professor of homiletics and pastoral theology at Louisville Seminary. He is an ordained minister in the A.M.E. Zion Church and has served several congregations in Connecticut and New Jersey. Andrews is the author of *Practical Theology for Black Churches: Spanning the Chasm between Black Theology and African American Folk Religion* (Westminster John Knox Press, 2002).

Diana Brown is the director of Christian education at First Baptist Church in Teaneck, New Jersey. She received her Master of Divinity from New Brunswick Theological Seminary with a concentration in urban ministry. Her thesis is entitled "The Black Church: Reconnecting the Disconnected, Tearing Down the Walls of Economic Class." Brown is also a nursing director with the New Community Corporation in Newark, New Jersey, the nation's largest community development corporation.

Walter Brueggemann is the William Marcellus McPheeters Professor of Old Testament at Columbia Theological Seminary. A member of the United Church of Christ, Brueggemann is the author of hundreds of articles and more than fifty books, including *Peace* in the Understanding Biblical Themes series (Chalice Press, 2001) and *Testimony to Otherwise: The Witness of Elijah and Elisha* (Chalice Press, 2001), as well as *The Covenanted Self: Explorations in Law and Covenant* (ed. Patrick D. Miller; Fortress Press, 1999), *Texts That Linger, Words That Explode: Listening to Prophetic Voices* (ed. Patrick D. Miller; Fortress Press, 2000), and *Deep Memory, Exuberant Hope: Contested Truth in a Post-Christian World* (ed. Patrick D. Miller; Fortress Press, 2000).

Walter Burghardt, S.J., is a senior fellow at Woodstock Theological Center in Washington, D.C. Burghardt founded and directed the "Preaching the Just Word" retreat and workshop aimed at improving preaching on justice issues. He was named one of the twelve most effective preachers in the English-speaking world by Baylor University. Among Burghardt's books are *Preaching the Just Word* (Yale University Press, 1996) and *Let Justice Roll Down Like Waters: Biblical Justice Homilies throughout the Year* (Paulist Press, 1998).

Jim Burklo is a campus minister at the United Campus Christian Ministry at Stanford University in Palo Alto, California, and minister of the College Heights United Church of Christ in San Mateo. He is a graduate of San Francisco Theological Seminary and an ordained minister of the United Church of Christ. Burklo is a supporter of the San Mateo County Interfaith Hospitality Network (IHN). He is the author of *Open Christianity: Home by a Different Road* (Rising Star, 2000) and host of the Web site OpenChristianity.com.

Brian Byrne is the senior minister at East Congregational United Church of Christ in Grand Rapids, Michigan. He is a graduate of the Chicago Theological Seminary and an ordained minister of the United Church of Christ. Byrne is a former board member of the IHN of Indianapolis and is the former board chairperson of the Greater Grand Rapids IHN. For the past three years, he has traveled nationally, meeting with and speaking to congregations interested in developing IHNs in their communities.

James M. Childs, Jr., is the Joseph A. Sittler Professor of Theology and Ethics and Director of Academic Development at Trinity Lutheran Seminary in Columbus, Ohio. Among the books he has authored are *Greed: Economics and Ethics in Conflict* (Fortress Press, 2000) and *Preaching Justice: The Ethical Vocation of Word and Sacrament Ministry* (Trinity Press International, 2000). Childs is a member of the Evangelical Lutheran Church of America.

William R. Coats is the rector of St. Clement's Episcopal Church in Hawthorne, New Jersey. St. Clement's is a host congregation of the Passaic County IHN. Coats served as a university chaplain for fourteen years and as a parish priest for the past twenty-four years. He is the author of the book *God in Public* (Eerdmans, 1974).

William Sloane Coffin gained national attention in the 1960s as one of seven "Freedom Riders" arrested and convicted in Montgomery, Alabama, while protesting local segregation laws. He has served as chaplain at Yale University, senior minister of the Riverside Church in New York, and president of SANE/FREEZE: Campaign for Global Security, the largest peace and justice organization in the United States. An active writer and preacher, he is the author of the recent *The Heart Is a Little to the Left: Essays on Public Morality* (University Press of New England, 1999).

Pamela D. Couture is associate professor of pastoral theology at Colgate Rochester Crozer Divinity School. She teaches in the areas of pastoral care, theology, United Methodism, and women and gender studies. She is the author of *Seeing Children, Seeing God: A Practical Theology of Children and Poverty* (Abingdon Press, 2000) and *Blessed Are the Poor? Women's Poverty, Family Policy, and Practical Theology* (Abingdon Press, 1991). Couture has been educational consultant to the United Methodist Bishops' Initiative on Children and Poverty since 1996.

Marian Wright Edelman, founder and president of the Children's Defense Fund (CDF), has been a lifetime advocate for disadvantaged Americans.

CDF is the leading child-advocacy organization that seeks to ensure every child a healthy start, a head start, a fair start, a safe start, and a moral start in life. Edelman has received many awards, including the Presidential Medal of Freedom, the nation's highest civilian award, and a MacArthur Foundation Prize Fellowship. She is also the author of five books, including *Families in Peril: An Agenda for Social Change* (Harvard University Press, 1986).

Steven Egland is pastor of Prince of Peace Lutheran Church in Spokane, Washington. Prince of Peace is a host congregation of the IHN of Spokane. An ordained pastor of the Evangelical Lutheran Church in America, Egland has served congregations in Idaho and Iowa, was a chaplain with the United States Navy, and served eight years as a missionary pastor in Tanzania, East Africa.

Bob Ekblad is the founder and director of Tierra Nueva and The People's Seminary. Tierra Nueva is an ecumenical ministry with peasants in rural Honduras and Mexico and with immigrants, inmates, and permanent Hispanic residents in western Washington. The People's Seminary, a natural extension of Tierra Nueva, is an ecumenical learning center for scripture study and theology, rooted in solidarity with people on the margins. Ekblad is an ordained minister of word and sacrament in the Presbyterian Church (USA). He is an adjunct professor at Regent College, where he teaches a course entitled "Reading the Bible with the Damned."

James Forbes is senior minister of the Riverside Church in New York, one of the largest multicultural churches in the nation, and Harry Emerson Fosdick Adjunct Professor of Preaching at Union Theological Seminary in New York. An ordained minister in the American Baptist Churches and the Original United Holy Church of America, Forbes served congregations in Virginia and North Carolina prior to becoming a professor at Union Seminary in 1976. Forbes was named one of the twelve most effective preachers in the English-speaking world by Baylor University. He is the author of *The Holy Spirit and Preaching* (Abingdon Press, 1989).

Francisco O. García-Treto is professor of religion at Trinity University in San Antonio, Texas. His teaching areas are Old Testament literature, history, and religion; Judaism; and Islam. García-Treto is an ordained minister of word and sacrament in the Presbyterian Church (USA) and has contributed in recent years to the theological discussions in liberation and *mujerista* theologies.

Mary Catherine Hilkert, O.P., is associate professor of theology at the University of Notre Dame. An expert on the thought of Edward Schillebeeckx, she is coeditor of *The Praxis of the Reign of God: An Introduction to the Thought of Edward Schillebeeckx* (Fordham University

Press, 2002). Hilkert has published extensively on the relationship between theology and preaching, including her book *Naming Grace: Preaching and the Sacramental Imagination* (Continuum, 1997).

Lewis H. Kamrass is the senior rabbi of Isaac M. Wise Temple of Cincinnati, Ohio, where he has spent his entire rabbinate of seventeen years. His tenure has been marked by significant congregational involvement in social action, and Wise Temple is a host congregation in the IHN of Greater Cincinnati. Kamrass has served for sixteen years as instructor in the theology department of Xavier University, as well as on the adjunct faculty at his alma mater, Hebrew Union College, teaching rabbinical students.

Charles A. Kroloff is the senior rabbi of Temple Emanu-El in Westfield, New Jersey. Temple Emanu-El is a host congregation of the Union County IHN. Kroloff has served in a variety of positions, including president of the Central Conference of American Rabbis, president of the Coalition of Religious Leaders of New Jersey, and commissioner of the New Jersey State Bioethics Commission. He is the author of *54 Ways You Can Help the Homeless* (Macmillan, 1993) and *When Elijah Knocks: A Religious Response to Homelessness* (Behrman House, 1992).

Kim Latterell is senior pastor of the Zion Lutheran Church in Loveland, Colorado, where he has been since 1987. Zion Lutheran is a host congregation of the Loveland-Berthoud IHN. Latterell earned his Master of Divinity at Luther Theological Seminary in St. Paul, Minnesota, and is ordained in the Evangelical Lutheran Church of America.

Roger Lovette is a minister in the Baptist Church (CBF). Lovette has served congregations in Kentucky, Virginia, South Carolina, Tennessee, and Alabama. The congregation Lovette most recently served, Baptist Church of the Covenant in Birmingham, Alabama, is a host congregation in the Birmingham IHN. Lovette is the author of five books, including *For the Dispossessed* (Pilgrim Press, 1973).

Cliff Lyda is pastor of the Highlands Presbyterian Church (USA) in Gainesville, Florida. Lyda earned his Master of Divinity at Southwestern Baptist Theological Seminary in Fort Worth, Texas. He has served congregations in Florida for twenty-four years and serves as president of ACTION Network, a faith-based community organizing group. Highlands Presbyterian Church is a host congregation of the IHN of Greater Gainesville. The IHN day center is located in the congregation's building.

Victor McCracken served as minister of adult education for the Oak Hills Church of Christ in San Antonio, Texas. He earned his Master of Divinity at Abilene Christian University and is now a Ph.D. candidate in ethics at Emory University.

Marvin A. McMickle is pastor of Antioch Baptist Church in Cleveland, Ohio. He is also professor of homiletics at Ashland Theological Seminary. McMickle is founder of the AGAPE Project, a testing and prevention program focusing on HIV/AIDS. He is the author of four books, including *From Pulpit to Politics: Reflections on the Separation of Church and State* (Williams Custom, 1998), *Preaching to the Black Middle Class: Words of Challenge/Words of Hope* (Judson, 2000), and *Encyclopedia of African American Christian Heritage* (Judson, 2002).

Patrick D. Miller, Jr., is the Charles T. Haley Professor of Old Testament Theology at Princeton Theological Seminary. He is the editor of *Theology Today* and coeditor of the Interpretation Commentary series and the Westminster Bible Companion series. Miller has also served as president of the Society of Biblical Literature and dean of the faculty at Union Theological Seminary in Virginia. A member of the Nassau Presbyterian Church (USA), Miller is the author many books, including, *They Cried to the Lord: The Form and Theology of Biblical Prayer* (Fortress, 1994).

Karen Olson is the founder and president of Family Promise, the parent organization of the Interfaith Hospitality Networks, which involve more than ninety thousand volunteers who provide shelter, meals, and assistance to homeless families. A former manager at Warner Lambert, Olson has been working on behalf of the poor and homeless since the early 1980s. Olson has received numerous awards for her work, among them the 1992 Annual Points of Light Award from former President George H. W. Bush, the New Jersey Governor's Pride Award in Social Services, and the Jefferson Award from the American Institute for Public Service.

Bryan O'Rourke is pastor of the Church of St. Mark (Roman Catholic) in St. Paul, Minnesota, the parish of his youth. O'Rourke was previously pastor of St. Mary of the Lake Church in Plymouth, Minnesota, a host congregation of the IHN of Minneapolis. O'Rourke was ordained in 1966. For seventeen years, he worked as a therapist in the field of chemical addiction, four years of which were spent working with priests in a treatment center in England.

Ann R. Palmerton is an ordained minister of word and sacrament in the Presbyterian Church (USA). She serves as associate pastor of pastoral care and social outreach at the Broad Street Presbyterian Church in Columbus, Ohio. Palmerton's work on the former "Justice for Women" committee of the Presbyterian Church (USA) served to call her into advocacy on behalf of those on the margins. Her sermon "Lifestyles of the Rich and Famous" is forthcoming in the *Journal of Religion and Abuse.*

André Resner, Jr., is senior pastor of the Lamington Presbyterian Church (USA) in Bedminster, New Jersey. Lamington Presbyterian Church is a support congregation for the IHN of Somerset County. Resner also serves as adjunct professor of preaching at New Brunswick Theological Seminary and convenes the Pedagogy Work Group for the Academy of Homiletics. He is the author of the book *Preacher and Cross: Person and Message in Theology and Rhetoric* (Eerdmans, 1999).

Melanie Morel Sullivan is the pastor of the Unitarian Universalist Church of Chattanooga, Tennessee. Her congregation is a host congregation of the IHN of Greater Chattanooga, and Sullivan has served on the IHN board of directors. Sullivan also served as president of the Southeast Unitarian Universalist Ministers' Association in 2000–2002 and president of the Unitarian Universalist Christian Fellowship in 2001–2002.

Barbara Brown Taylor is an Episcopal priest in the diocese of Atlanta. Ordained in 1983, she served urban and rural parishes in Georgia for fifteen years. Taylor is currently Butman Professor of Religion and Philosophy at Piedmont College in Demorest, Georgia, and adjunct professor of Christian spirituality at Columbia Theological Seminary in Decatur, Georgia. Taylor was named one of the twelve most effective preachers in the English-speaking world by Baylor University. She is the author of ten books, including *Speaking of Sin: The Lost Language of Salvation* (Cowley, 2000).

Thomas K. Tewell is senior pastor for the Fifth Avenue Presbyterian Church (USA) in New York. He serves on the board of trustees at Princeton Theological Seminary, where he earned his Master of Divinity degree. Tewell earned his Doctor of Ministry degree from Drew University Theological School in Madison, New Jersey. He was pastor of a founding congregation of the first IHN in Union County, New Jersey. Tewell has also served pastorates in Pennsylvania and at the 5,000-member Memorial Drive Presbyterian Church in Houston, Texas.

Margaret Moers Wenig is rabbi emerita of New York's Beth Am, The People's Temple. Wenig is an instructor in liturgy and homiletics at the New York school of Hebrew Union College–Jewish Institute of Religion. Wenig's sermons are widely published in journals and anthologies, and she has written the first textbook for the teaching of homiletics in a modern rabbinical seminary.

Preface

For more than fourteen years, volunteers in the Interfaith Hospitality Network have provided compassionate assistance to homeless families. The volunteers have prepared meals, moved cots, searched for housing, driven vans, tutored children, donated clothing, and helped write résumés. Ninety thousand volunteers in three thousand congregations nationwide are now involved in these greatly needed acts of service.

For the volunteers of the Interfaith Hospitality Networks, homelessness is no longer merely a headline in a newspaper. It is no longer just a glimpse of a ragged stranger who passed them on the street. These volunteers see real families search in vain for decent apartments at rents they can afford to pay. They see people working full time at minimum-wage jobs who are unable to provide their families' basic needs—even when they hold two full-time jobs. They see children struggle to learn in overcrowded classrooms with outdated textbooks and with little hope for their future.

They have seen that their efforts alone are not enough.

As important as it is to provide a safe refuge and homecooked meals and all the care and support that we can muster, that is not enough. The root causes of poverty persist: jobs that don't pay a living wage; housing that is inadequate, unsafe, or priced out of reach; and the lack of quality healthcare, childcare, and education. If these realities go unchanged, families will continue to be thwarted when they attempt to escape homelessness and want.

Some volunteers, spurred by their experiences, have begun to mobilize their congregations to go beyond acts of service to acts of justice. More and more people of every creed are awakening to the facts of systemic injustice. More and more clergy of every faith must speak out against these injustices.

To help in this effort, Family Promise (the parent organization of the Interfaith Hospitality Networks) has created *Just Preaching*. We envisioned a collection of sermons that would inspire clergy of every faith to preach frequently and effectively on matters of poverty and economic justice.

The range of essays and sermons in *Just Preaching* reflects the range of need and the range of potential action. Low-income people have immediate needs that a congregation can alleviate by organizing food pantries, tutoring children, and the like. However, the underlying causes of poverty can only be alleviated by people who are ready to work passionately for systemic change, holding their elected officials responsible and campaigning for just policies and legislation. Recognizing this range of need, we've included in *Just Preaching* some sermons that emphasize immediate aid and service, some that advocate for social justice, and others that fall along the spectrum in between.

Our hope is that the essays and sermons in this volume will be a powerful resource for you, a place to turn to again and again for information and inspiration, a place to turn to as you raise your voice on behalf of the poor and homeless in this country.

As your preaching inspires members of your congregation to move from acts of service to acts of justice, they will want to learn more about the systemic problems and about opportunities for action. To help you help your congregation move toward action, Family Promise has developed *Just Neighbors,* an educational and motivational program that examines the underlying causes of poverty and homelessness and the policy changes that could reverse their effects.

In the Appendix that begins on page 223, you will find a description of the *Just Neighbors* program.

In the Appendix that begins on page 221, you can read more about Family Promise and its various programs, including the Interfaith Hospitality Network.

Karen Olson,
President, Family Promise

Introduction

Several years ago I was listening to master homiletician and preacher Fred B. Craddock at a forum on preaching. He spoke to us about the power of the preached word, motivating us to our call and task. He knew that we, like most preachers, doubt from time to time whether our preaching does anything significant enough to justify the time and energy that goes into it. Fred reassured us that much more goes on in our preaching than we know, that God is truly at work in the proclaimed word so that "it shall not return to me empty, but it shall accomplish that which I purpose" (Isa. 55:11). Then came a story. A preacher stood at the back door of the church one Sunday, shaking hands with his departing parishioners. Same old routine, same old comments about the worship, about the sermon. "Good job, preacher." "Thank you for your sermon, pastor." "How 'bout them Cowboys, Bill?" Then someone approached with a different look on his face. It was a person well known to the preacher, but the look on the man's face was new. When it was the man's turn to speak to the preacher he said very slowly and sternly, "This changes everything." The preacher didn't know what the man was talking about, but he was genuinely concerned: "What, Jim?" "What you said in the sermon…if it's true what you said, it changes everything…What I mean is that, well, none of us here can just go home and do what we thought we were going to do this afternoon. We're not here just for that…for the lawn mowing or the 4:00 football game. Our world is not right. Our society right here in America is spinning off its axis for so many who cannot do anything about it. Preacher, *you're right:* We are called to put in place here and now God's reign and God's care for the planet and for every person. *Everything has changed.*" The preacher, getting a little worried about Jim and his reaction to the sermon found himself saying before he realized it, "Now, Jim, don't get so worked up. I was *just preaching.*"[1]

That one little phrase sums it all up. Most preachers are *just preaching,* just trying to make it through another week's sermon-dispensing requirement. Most church-, synagogue-, and temple-goers come to the assembly and, more weeks than not, find themselves *just listening* to another sermon. Craddock reminds us of the possibilities present in these settings for *just preaching* and *just listening* to take on double meaning. Though preacher and hearers may be *just* preaching and listening as usual, by the grace of God, our perfunctory motions become prophetic instances of *just proclamation and hearing*–preacher and hearer alike convicted, empowered, and sent out for just actions in the world.

These moments when God trumps our preaching and listening lethargy are wonderful and even reassuring, as Craddock stressed, but is there a way for our preaching to be more intentionally *just?* The writers in this book believe so. Every author herein believes that *just preaching* can be more than a trump card that God is forced to play. Just preaching is the collaborative effort of preachers speaking for God, yes, but also speaking for "the widow, the orphan, and the stranger" in our land.

Just preaching is a deliberate redressing of the preaching task from the perspective of justice. Why justice? Because it has been and continues to be the greatest need in human, but also divine, history. A faith driven by the biblical vision realizes that in a world that continues to compromise fair treatment of human beings based on color, ethnicity, or socioeconomic status that God, and all of God's creation, is being compromised at the same time.

No one has voiced this relation of justice to God more powerfully than Jewish theologian Abraham Heschel. After asking why God should care so much about justice being done for the most vulnerable—the widow, the orphan, and the stranger—Heschel asserts this answer:

> Perhaps the answer lies here: righteousness is not just a value; it is God's part of human life, *God's stake in human life.* Perhaps it is because the suffering of [humankind] is a blot upon God's conscience; because it is in relations between [one person] and [another person] that God is at stake...People act as they please, doing what is vile, abusing the weak, not realizing that they are fighting God, affronting the divine, or that the oppression of [any person] is a humiliation of God.[2]

The Proverbs writer said, "Those who oppress the poor insult their Maker, but those who are kind to the needy honor [God]" (Prov. 14:31). Human community living in harmonious, right, and healthy relationships is what God had in mind before creation began. God's continued desire and struggle within human history is for this end. Heschel continues: "Life is clay, and righteousness the mold in which God wants history to be shaped. But human beings, instead of fashioning the clay, deform the shape."[3]

Just relations—and systems that promote fairness and equity among all people—are not simply a value of God and of all who would call themselves God's people: these constitute faith's supreme value. It is *the* value out of which all other values are to be understood. In fact, it may be too little to call it *a value*, especially in view of the divine desire and demand for it. God's desire for justice can be called nothing less than an obsession:

> Justice is not an ancient custom, a human convention, a value, but a transcendent demand, freighted with divine concern. It is not only a relationship between [one person] and [another], it is an *act*

involving God, a divine need. Justice is [God's] line, righteousness [God's] plummet (Isa. 28:17). It is not one of [God's] ways, but in all [God's] ways. Its validity is not only universal, but also eternal, independent of will and experience.[4]

To be human and to be awakened to faith in the God who created us are at the same moment to be awakened to our role in carrying out God's most desired ends for creation. That means above all putting into place and keeping in place the kind of just relations and structures that mirror God's concerns for right relations. It also means to develop eyes to see and a heart to feel when and where situations and systems of injustice have arisen and exist and to work toward the deconstruction of such situations and systems. To set one's life to do so is not to do anything special, really. It is simply to get in step with the rhythm of God's designed dance for all creation. "People think that to be just is a virtue, deserving honor and rewards; that in doing righteousness one confers a favor on society. No one expects to receive a reward for the habit of breathing. Justice is as much a necessity as breathing is, and a constant occupation."[5]

If this is true for all God's creatures, it is true for preachers too. But preachers stand in relation to the need and demand for justice in a unique way. For they are the dominant voice within their faith communities and within their wider social contexts. Preachers are called first to be actors toward justice, just as all people are who are gripped by the need for justice and God's desire for it, but preachers are also called to use their voices to sound out the call, the demand, the grace of entering into God's struggle for justice in the world. Thus the second major concern of this book: *How do preachers, in their preaching, become good stewards of God's concern and desire for justice?*

This book, through essays and sermons, is a down payment on a vision for what a preaching paradigm driven by the concern for justice might look like. With that as the agenda, you will see herein that just preaching is prophetic, pastoral, and political, with very specific goals:

- the indictment of those responsible for injustice and its continuance
- the motivation and empowerment of hearers to do just acts of accompaniment with the marginalized
- the motivation and empowerment of hearers to advocate for systemic change

In a world where preachers are *just preaching* and hearers are *just listening,* sermons seem to have little social or political impact. The writers of this book believe that preachers and congregations can become the people, the place, and the source of widespread social, political, and humanitarian reform. *Just preaching* is a renewed call to preachers in all faith communities to focus our energies and attention to one matter—*justice*—that we believe is of intimate concern to God and of ultimate need in our world. It is an old axiom of preaching that if one aims at nothing in particular in one's preaching, one is almost assured of hitting it. Just preaching takes dead aim. It could change everything.

André Resner, Jr.

PART 1

Economics and the Just Word

If the problem of history were that the poor kept taking advantage of the rich, the God we know from the Bible would surely rise up on behalf of the marginalized wealthy. In fact, we catch a glimpse of just such a surprise twist in Luke's gospel of the marginalized when Jesus singles out Zacchaeus, the seemingly rich yet truly impoverished man in Luke 19:1–10. For Luke the "poor" aren't necessarily those without material possessions; they are those who live their lives without God and God's concerns as their primary reference point for life. Luke's poor are those who fail to see all the resources of their lives–whether few or many–as instruments of God's just concerns.

This is why the truly poor, from a biblical perspective, are typically the world's rich. Those well endowed with this world's things typically close themselves off from both God and humanity. And though we can say in apocalyptic terms that such a closing off impoverishes them, such a word often rings hollow for those who suffer in the present. The prophetic word of scripture tempers the apocalyptic word by stressing God's passion that present-tense social systems be set right.

The Jewish and Christian scriptures tell us about a God who impartially cares for all people, yet whose ear and heart turn with ever special concern toward those who are most at risk, those who are most vulnerable in the world of human relations politically, economically, and religiously. God has a stake in just dealings in human society because God is the author of the human being, and each bears God's own image.

Each author and preacher in this section shines an unrelentingly bright light on economic injustice and its effect on society and human relations, effects that are deepening an increasingly disastrous divide in the human community.

1

Preaching in the Face of Economic Injustice

MARVIN A. MCMICKLE

Those who seek to preach from the Bible in the twenty-first century must do so with an awareness of the issues of poverty and economic disparity that everywhere grips our nation and the world. Whether one looks at the ghettoes of urban America, the slums of Rio De Janeiro in Brazil, the shantytowns of South Africa, or the squalid refugee camps in Palestine and elsewhere, the reality of economic disparity is apparent. Biblical faith is not silent about this problem, but for far too long those who have been called upon to preach and interpret that faith in the present world have been too silent about these matters. God has spoken on the matter, but far too many pulpits across the country and around the world have failed to echo the message.

No one has stated this problem in clearer terms than did James Madison writing in the Federalist Papers #73. He said, "The most common and durable source of factions has been the various and unequal distribution of property. Those who hold and those who are without property have ever formed distinct interests in society."[1] That observation made near the end of the eighteenth century is no less relevant at the turn of the twenty-first century. It is not possible to comprehend correctly the factions and tensions that scream out to us from street corners, headlines, and twenty-four–hour news without coming to grips with the persistent problems of poverty and economic disparity. Similarly, it will be argued here that it is not possible to preach faithfully from the Old or New Testament at this point in history without addressing these issues from the perspective of the scriptures. In light of that, I will organize my thoughts around the biblical characters and messages of Amos, Ezekiel, and Lazarus.

Amos as a Model for Addressing Issues of Economic Injustice

In an article entitled "The Prophet Amos as a Model for Preaching on Issues of Social Justice," I suggested that the causes and consequences of economic disparity are at the core of that prophet's message.[2] "Amos railed against the staggering income gap that divided the rich and the poor. More importantly, he condemned the various forms of economic injustice that both created and sustained that imbalance."[3] Amos harshly condemned the rich who were busy enjoying a luxurious lifestyle and who took no notice of, no interest in, and who assumed no responsibility for the misery that many people around them had to endure every day. Consider these four passages:

> For three transgressions of Israel,
>> and for four, I will not revoke the punishment;
> because they sell the righteous for silver,
>> and the needy for a pair of sandals. (2:6)

> Alas for those who lie on beds of ivory,
>> and lounge on their couches,
> and eat lambs from the flock,
>> and calves from the stall...
>> but are not grieved over the ruin of Joseph! (6:4, 6)

> Hear this word, you cows of Bashan
>> who are on Mount Samaria,
> who oppress the poor, who crush the needy. (4:1)

> Hear this, you who trample on the needy,
>> and bring to ruin the poor of the land...
>> and practice deceit with false balances. (8:4–5)

The words of Amos spoken in the eighth century B.C.E. are painfully pertinent as twenty-first-century preachers consider the content of their sermons in the context where millions in this nation and billions around the world live in absolute, abject poverty. It is important to note that poverty is not simply a fact of life. Poverty is a grinding and degrading way of life that drains the hopes and breaks the spirit of those who are within its grasp. Poverty takes the form of an inadequate diet that frequently results in sickness. That sickness is complicated by an absence of available and/or affordable healthcare. The best cure for poverty is a job. However, the poor find it difficult to secure employment, because so many employers are moving their operations out of the cities where the poor are clustered.

They then open new factories or offices in second-ring suburbs or in even more remote rural areas that are not served by public transportation.

Poverty as a way of life has other contributing dimensions. The poor provide for their housing either by living in cramped and dangerous public housing units or by paying rent, often exorbitant rent, because they cannot accumulate enough money for a down payment on a home. As a result, the poor never have the economic leverage of equity, tax deductions, and second mortgages that are available to those who become homeowners. Quite often the poor do not have a standard checking account but use instead various check-cashing services that charge exorbitant rates and fees for every transaction. These issues look and sound like the society Amos so strongly condemned in the eighth century B.C.E. Those who seek to be faithful preachers of the biblical message dare not fail to see and speak to these same issues in the twenty-first century.

Poverty as a way of life is not limited to our concern for those who cannot find employment and thus are relegated to some form of public assistance. The far more subtle and shameful face of poverty involves the working poor. This would include migrant workers, temporary employees, and nonunionized workers with no job security or bargaining strength. Sadly, many of the working poor are single females who are heads of households. Thus, the hardships of poverty affect not only them but their young children as well. As I stated in the article on preaching from Amos:

> They lead the most anxious lives of any persons in America. They work hard but never get ahead. They usually work more than one job just to make ends meet. They fear sickness, first because they have no medical insurance to cover the costs of prescription drugs and surgical procedures, and secondly because if they miss too many days from work they will lose one or more of their jobs. Why do people have to live under such conditions in the richest country in the world?[4]

Preaching That Attacks the Public Policies That Contribute to Poverty

Those who would preach in ways that call attention to the problems of poverty and economic disparity must understand that most of what we presently hate about these problems can be resolved by creative and courageous changes in some of our nation's public policies. Preachers should not feel content simply to assail the problems. Amos showed Israel the way out by calling it back to the fundamental teachings of the law of Moses and to its responsibilities as a "covenant community." We must speed up the solution to problems by identifying the policy solutions that can move our society toward liberty and justice for all. Preachers can help to build a national consensus for such policies.

Minimum Wage

The perpetual income gap of which James Madison spoke is the chief means by which America has become the richest country in the world. In fact, several historians argue that one of the roles of the United States Constitution during its first one hundred years was to allow a small economic elite to preserve their wealth, whether it took the form of real property, slaves, or other assets.[5] Until such practices were outlawed, America's wealth was created through the use of slave labor, child labor, sweatshop labor, twelve-to-sixteen-hours-a-day factory labor, and low-wage and minimum-wage labor. It can be argued today, just as it was argued in the days of Amos, that much of the wealth of this nation is the result of the exploitation and unfair compensation of workers. That exploitation is felt both in this country and in countries around the world where goods are produced for the United States markets.

In cities across America, efforts are underway to adopt what is called a Living Wage Ordinance.[6] It is shocking to see that the stiffest resistance to the adoption of such ordinances comes from corporate executives who earn millions of dollars in salary and stock options, but advance arguments for why they cannot afford to pay a living wage and benefits to their workers. What will twenty-first-century preachers say about this shameful reality?

Urban Sprawl

It is almost impossible to calculate how much of our nation's resources are being invested in constructing the houses, highways, and infrastructure that are allowing more and more Americans to escape the central cities. Every day more and more families of all racial and cultural groups are moving into glistening new communities with larger homes and green spaces. That movement in and of itself is not the problem. That is the closest that most Americans can now come to the search for the new frontier that has been the hallmark of the American experience.

The challenge presented by urban sprawl is what is left behind in the cities that most people of middle-class income have abandoned. There is growing within this country an impoverished underclass that is becoming increasingly detached from the values and aspirations of mainstream America. This underclass represents "the least of these" that Jesus spoke about in Matthew 25:40, 45. When we turn our backs and run away from them, we are doing it to Jesus as well. And the problem is made all the more dramatic by the fact that not only families and households and businesses are fleeing the cities for greener pastures. Far too many churches and synagogues have done the same thing. The leaders of those congregations seem to be more interested in following their members into the suburbs than in leading their members into a meaningful ministry that engages and works to resolve the problems that have taken root in our cities.

The Prison Industry

Preachers should speak harshly about this society that has allowed prison construction to become a boom industry and where nearly two million persons (male and female) are now incarcerated. In most states, it costs $35,000 annually to maintain a person in a state-run correctional facility. The cost of one year in prison exceeds the cost of tuition and room and board at the most elite private universities in the country. Can we not redirect the use of that $35,000 to more constructive and efficient ends? Add to this dollar amount the indisputable fact that most people in prison are nonviolent drug offenders who might be better served by treatment than by incarceration. Then consider that most drug offenders are products of dysfunctional inner-city schools and are typically unemployed and unemployable because they lack any skills for the twenty-first-century job market. It has been argued here that the existence of poverty and economic disparity are the results of policies that were put in place to protect the economic elite. I am also arguing that the path to a more equitable distribution of national wealth involves preaching that identifies and examines those policy changes that can help bring to life the biblical vision of a just society.

The Lack of Access to Healthcare

Forty-five million people living in this country have no medical insurance except the very limited benefits of Medicare and Medicaid. There are senior citizens who must make the daily choice of (a) heating, (b) eating, or (c) treating. This unfortunate trio of choices suggests that far too many elderly persons who live on fixed incomes must choose between heating their homes in the winter, buying food that allows for a healthy diet, or purchasing the prescription drugs that have become a necessity in the practice of modern medicine. The people who are forced to make those choices every day also sit in the pews of churches and synagogues across the country. Will their pastors, priests, and rabbis speak to the public policy changes that can affect the lives of their congregants?

The problem of poverty exacerbates the problem of access to healthcare in other ways. In many urban areas the trauma centers and emergency rooms are being shut down. Meanwhile, the corporations that now manage so much of the healthcare of the nation are building their new clinics and instant-care facilities outside the central city. This is also an issue of access for persons living in poverty. So too is the absence of an adequate number of doctors both in the inner cities and in the poverty-ridden rural areas of the nation. As a result of all these access factors, people living in poverty rarely if ever practice preventative medicine. They typically wait until their condition is so severe that it requires emergency-room treatment, which is the most expensive medical care of all. If that emergency room is more than a few minutes away, they may be dead on arrival.

The Domestic Costs of Militarism

In a country that cannot or will not provide decent housing or adequate medical treatment for all its citizens, preachers and people of faith generally must consider the morality of defense spending in this country. In the wake of the tragic terrorist events of September 11, 2001, it might sound unpatriotic to question any aspect of national defense. Members of the Bush administration went so far as to say on national television that "now is no time for that kind of talk." However, those who occupy pulpits across the country cannot dare take their lead from political appointees concerning when they will speak on issues of justice and morality.

Long before the terrorist attacks, the nation was being urged to view a missile defense system called Star Wars as the key to our national security, at a minimum cost of $300 billion. Even if you ignore the violations of treaties, the risks of weapons proliferation, and the fact that this system would not have prevented anything that happened on September 11, consider how that $300 billion could work to resolve the issues of poverty and economic disparity.

In 2003, our national political leadership went to war against Iraq, with first-year costs estimated at $75 billion. What urgent domestic programs will be delayed or permanently defunded to pay for this war? Even before the war, U.S. gasoline prices had already risen to record levels. Oil companies had already gouged the public at the gas pump and increased their profits. Who will be most negatively impacted by these price increases? It will be the poor, the working poor, and those in our society who are just barely making ends meet. In the face of all these problems, and as we are aware of the policies that can begin to resolve them, it is not acceptable for preachers to go through the formalities of worship while ignoring the very real pains that are daily being inflicted on people all around them. This is especially true because so often those pains can clearly be viewed through the windows of the churches and synagogues where they prepare their sermons.

Returning to the oracles of Amos, that prophet declared that God would not be pleased with people who professed religious faith but lacked compassion for the needy and the oppressed. Thus, this fiery prophet declared:

> Seek good and not evil,
>   that you may live;
> and so the LORD, the God of hosts, will be with you...
> Hate evil and love good,
>   and establish justice in the gate;
> it may be that the LORD, the God of hosts,
>   will be gracious to the remnant of Joseph. (5:14–15)

The frustrating dichotomy between Israel's careful observance of the rituals of their religion and their failure to exhibit the righteousness that the law was meant to bring forth led Amos to declare what may be his most famous words:

> I hate, I despise your festivals,
>   and I take no delight in your solemn assemblies…
> Take away from me the noise of your songs;
>   I will not listen to the melody of your harps.
> But let justice roll down like waters,
>   and righteousness like an ever-flowing stream. (5:21, 23–24)

Ezekiel and God's Reminder of Accountability

If Amos serves as the model of what we should be doing and saying as preachers in the twenty-first century, Ezekiel offers the challenge for why we should be doing this work of addressing the problems of poverty and economic disparity. In chapters 3 and 33 God tells the prophet, that he has been made a sentinel for the house of Israel. God continues:

> If I say to the wicked, "You shall surely die," and you give them no warning, or speak to warn the wicked from their wicked way, in order to save their life, those wicked persons shall die for their iniquity; but their blood I will require at your hand. (3:18)

> But if you warn the wicked to turn from their ways, and they do not turn from their ways, the wicked shall die in their iniquity, but you will have saved your life. (33:9)

The problems associated with poverty and economic disparity are having a divisive effect on our nation and our world. It is much easier for the preacher to ignore these issues and focus solely on safe subjects such as liturgical seasons and denominational points of emphasis. The fact is, however, that God is calling on preachers to stand up and speak out on these issues that impact the lives of their parishioners and that impact the quality of life available to millions throughout the country and around the world. The ultimate measure of the effectiveness of our preaching is not the number of people who say they "enjoyed" the sermon as they file past us in the receiving line at the end of the worship service. The ultimate measure of our effectiveness is whether we have "sounded the trumpet" as mentioned in Ezekiel 33:3 and by Paul in 1 Corinthians 14:8, warning both our immediate listeners and the wider nation of the dangers that we see approaching.

Lazarus and the Preacher's Response to Poverty and Economic Disparity

In Luke 16:19–31, Jesus offers a parable that further informs the biblical preacher in terms of an appropriate response to the problems of poverty and economic disparity. The story is framed by two men who occupy two widely different positions within their world: "There was a rich man who was dressed in purple and fine linen and who feasted sumptuously every day…and at his gate lay a poor man named Lazarus, covered with sores." To quote again the words of James Madison, these two men embodied the "various and unequal distribution of wealth."[7] It is reasonable to assume that these two men encountered each other every day as the rich man entered and exited from his home, passing poor Lazarus, who sat by the gate and would gladly have eaten whatever crumbs had fallen from the rich man's table.

I read this passage as a continuing indictment on the biblical community. In my book *Preaching to the Black Middle Class,* I suggest that as every Sunday morning black worshipers drive into the city from the suburbs, the only thing that is as important to them as the beauty of the sanctuary is the size and proximity of the parking lot so their cars will be secure for their quick exit from the inner-city locations where their churches are located. Every Sunday, Lazarus is sitting at the gate in the form of the homeless, the derelict, the drug or alcohol addicted, the impoverished, the hungry, and the unwed teenage mother. More often than not, those black middle-class Christians just walk past Lazarus as they come in and out of the house of God. No more notice or responsibility for Lazarus is taken now than when Jesus told the parable.[8]

The attitude of too many preachers and people in synagogues and churches is captured in a litany referenced by James H. Cone in an essay entitled "The Servant Church." May those who preach a biblical message of justice and mercy never be guilty of the indictment found in these words:

I was hungry and you formed a humanities club and you discussed my
    hunger. Thank you.
I was imprisoned and you crept off quietly to your chapel in the
    cellar and prayed for my release.
I was naked and in your mind you debated the morality of my
    appearance.
I was sick and you knelt and thanked God for your health.
I was homeless and you preached to me of the spiritual shelter of the
    love of God.
I was lonely and you left me alone to pray for me. You seem so holy;
    so close to God. But I'm still very hungry and lonely and cold.
So where have your prayers gone? What have they done? What
    does it profit a man to page through his book of prayers when
    the rest of the world is crying for his help?[9]

Preaching's Purpose

Thoughts on Message and Method

ANDRÉ RESNER, JR.

At the outset of a discussion of *just preaching*, preachers may immediately discern a problem: the paradigms for preaching do not help preachers preach on justice as well as they might. One might even argue that methods for preaching arose over time and became fixed in our pedagogical systems for teaching preachers (universities and seminaries) and that they themselves work against the call and need for justice. Such a state illustrates another systemic "hardness of heart" within the very place that preachers are supposed to be learning how to confront powers that stand against what God desires.[1] I believe that the topic of preaching on justice raises the profound question of *how we preach*. When justice drives preaching, an alternative paradigm for preaching presents itself—one that is faithful to the biblical heritage, on target for today's pressing issues pertaining to justice, and philosophically legitimate.

To see the difference that justice as a point of departure makes for preaching, it is necessary to look briefly at the traditional approach to preaching and why it hamstrings preachers from preaching more effectively on justice. Books on preaching typically focus on the nuts and bolts of sermon preparation: (1) exegesis of a biblical passage (typically by means of the historical-critical method); (2) reduction of exegetical results down to one or more "points" and the choice of a central "theme/focus" and "aim/function"; (3) organization of one's goals for the sermon into a logical sequence; and (4) the "fleshing out" of one's goals by means of stories or "illustrations" that help hearers to visualize the sermon's message and so make it more accessible to them. This is the point in the process where the imagination is called on to make analogies between the biblical message and the current situation of one's hearers. It is the place where the exegesis

11

of the biblical text and one's congregational and societal context are said to overlap and feed into one another.

Most recommended approaches to preaching try to keep under control the flow from contemporary context back to the text so that the biblical text's message can remain pure and untainted by our impositions. The danger in allowing our concerns to spill onto the text, we have been warned, is "eisegesis," the reading into the biblical text of our presuppositions and prejudices. Eisegesis has traditionally been labeled interpretation's (and preaching's) unforgivable sin. Randy Nichols was the first person I heard say that all exegesis for preaching is essentially eisegesis.[2] As if that weren't disturbing enough, he then said that eisegesis was a good thing for preaching.

It was a kind of shock-homiletics for me when I first heard it, but Nichols was right. Good therapist that he is, Randy was trying to help homileticians and preachers tell the truth about themselves and their interpretive practices. And though that truth may seem like a secret sin about which historical-critical biblical scholars would want preachers to confess and repent, Nichols was inviting preachers to come out of the hermeneutical closet.

Just preaching provides an opportunity for preachers and homileticians to "come clean" about the use of scripture and even to assert the legitimacy of their textual practices, even in their differences from others' uses of the biblical texts. Exegesis for preaching is an inherently different enterprise than exegesis for other purposes. Exegesis for preaching engages interpreters in unique readings and uses of texts for which preachers need not apologize to those who use the biblical texts for other purposes. In fact, if anyone should have to give an account for their (mis)use of the biblical texts, it ought to be those who have used them with methods and in situations that bracket out faith and God, that claim scientific objectivity, and that claim hegemonic meanings, when the texts themselves were written from faith and to faith, the very thing for which preachers continue to read and use them.

Some recent approaches to preaching reflect Hans-Georg Gadamer's phenomenological hermeneutics, which attempt to help interpreters become more aware of the hermeneutical importance of all that they bring to the text.[3] According to Gadamer, unacknowledged presuppositions and prejudices are perhaps the greatest danger to hearing the text. Interpreters who hide behind ostensibly pure uses of scientific method are actually the most proficient at smuggling in their presuppositions and prejudices as simply "what the Bible says." Understanding texts for the purpose of applying them in contemporary situations is actually an eventful experience, an interplay between a person who reads the text—and all that person is and brings from his or her life and situation—and the text itself—and all that it brings from its historical, literary, and esthetic matrix. The understanding of the self and the text in conversation and the application of the text to the interpreter's context become an unpredictable and nonmanipulable moment wherein the horizons of the interpreter's world and that of the text's world touch, collide, and interpenetrate. The best thing the preacher can do is give in to the process, to enter into the "play," indeed, to *be played* by the interactions and disclosures of self and text. Understanding of text and self becomes the interpretive point of contact between worlds, a merger of textual and interpreter horizons, and it is from that apex that the sermon begins to emerge, that the sermon is given birth. The shaping and testing of the sermon must now take place. The preacher must strive for rhetorical clarity, focus, and effect, and the preacher must apply the key tests for any instance of theological discourse: Is it congruent with one's faith traditions? Is it fitting in this context? Is it meaningful and true in this sociocultural situation?[24] Other important tests for biblical preaching are the following: Is this sermon good news in the sense that it portrays God and God's people at work in the world for just and redemptive ends? Does it adequately portray the bad news for which this sermon is good news?

These sermon-building and sermon-testing procedures are necessary, but they all follow and flow from that merger of horizons that takes place in the interpretive moment that Gadamer describes. In that momentous event wherein understanding takes place, the preacher comes to *know* what the word is for his or her community this week. Such knowledge is convictional in that these moments have a kind of *leap-of-faith* character to them. The preacher senses strongly that the word has emerged and begs to be shaped into a sermon, but a nagging doubt clings to the process: Is this really *the* word? Is this really a *sermon*? Is this that which *most needs* to be said *this week* to *this people* in *this situation*? Sometimes the preacher never knows whether or not what he or she has is a sermon until the sermon is in the midst of delivery.

The word that emerges for the sermon through this process is both strangely familiar and radically new at the same time. That is because every sermon results from a new and unique collision of textual and interpreter horizons that has never happened before and will never happen again in precisely the same way.

What does all this have to do with *just preaching?* Everything, really, because preaching that takes justice as its starting point recognizes that preaching and its relationship to the Bible and society are a dynamic not static, a circular not linear, process. Just preaching recognizes that preaching's message is itself a collaboration of the needs, issues, and promise of our current societal situation with our faith tradition's witness. This collaboration is not a simplistic "contemporary culture raises the questions; scripture answers it." Nor is it the collaboration of a hermeneutically impossible "building of bridges" between the Bible and our time.[5]

The collaborative approach suggests a conversation and a working together toward a common end. How does this differ from traditional approaches to preaching? More shock-homiletics: Just preaching is often the experience of having a sermon in search of a text. Preachers know that this is a common experience, and they even talk about it together, but in hushed tones, fearful that one of their professors might catch wind of it and rescind their M.Div. degrees. But like the so-called sin of eisegesis, sermons in search of texts are what we're hoping for most weeks, and this is a good thing. Having a sermon idea before one reads the biblical text can open up the biblical texts in a new way, just as having a text before a sermon can open up a sermon in a new way. Neither, though, really happens in mutual exclusion of the other. Nor should our fear of "arm-wrestling" the Bible to our position scare us into a cover-up or denial of what we truly bring to the text. We don't ask the Bible to lie about what it wants to say so that it simply serves us up a sermon for this week, do we? Or, *do* we?

The Bible itself has a panoply of messages, with multiple trajectories of theology vying for attention. This isn't to say that the Bible is hopelessly contradictory, though there are more tensions therein than have often been acknowledged. Moreover, the Bible doesn't necessarily demand that we take it and use it and its "message" for our preaching. That's something that the practice of our historic faith communities—the *tradition*—decided for us. This tradition is a good one. We continue it when we insist on using the Bible as a key point of contact for preaching in every sermon. Our tradition and our traditional uses of the Bible in preaching have led to experiences that have affirmed the continuity of faith and the presence of God. Both these reasons are good ones for continuing the tradition.

Just preaching continues the tradition by taking justice as the key point of contact with scripture. We do so because we believe that the Bible discloses and helps hone our understanding of preaching's message—the good news of God's covenant-making and covenant-keeping, God's persistent desire and demand for justice, and God's empowerment of just actions for redemptive healing in the world—in indispensable ways.

Conversely, it is the lens of preaching's message that guides our use of scripture in preaching. This is to "come clean" on another important point: there is no such thing as an *unmediated* biblical message. Every use of scripture is predicated on assumptions about (1) what the Bible is and (2) how the Bible functions in application. For preachers, the mediator between biblical text and sermon is the preacher's understanding of the core message of preaching, what I have defined as the good news of God's covenant-making and covenant-keeping, God's persistent desire and demand for justice, and God's empowerment of just actions for redemptive healing in the world.[6] That core message functions for me in the study and appropriation of any individual text for preaching. But I am also open to my understanding of preaching's core message to undergo challenge and change based on my reading of any biblical text. The hermeneutical circle comes full circle here too: the process of discerning preaching's message in a metasense (one's understanding of preaching's core message) and in a specific sense this week (what expresses itself this week in the sermon) is circular. This is because preachers' ongoing contact with scripture and experience continues to shape their understanding of what preaching's message is, which in turn becomes the hermeneutical grid or lens through which they discern what aspect of scripture is preachable this week as good news. A just preacher is attentive to God's revelation wherever it may emerge, especially in the locales of (1) the scripture of one's faith tradition and (2) the concrete life situations of people in the real world struggles for and against justice today.

Taking justice as one's starting point in preaching forces us to reimagine the preaching task. That's because the ship is intentionally being turned around in the homiletic process. Rather than preaching being seen as a linear-sequential, text-to-sermon process, the just-preaching paradigm sees the text and sermon in a dynamic interaction, with the active ingredients between the two being a concrete instance of injustice and the concrete need for justice in a present-tense situation. This is why preaching on justice cannot responsibly be done by merely teaching a Bible study on the prophet Amos. Amos may, and probably will, be brought in as a conversation partner as the preacher clarifies her or his own social and political analysis, critique, and prophetic call, but just preaching's starting point is not necessarily Amos.

Just preaching's starting point is a *problem in the present.* Just preaching asks, "What is wrong?" and "What should be done about it?" Amos and the larger backdrop of one's understanding of the Bible, one's theological orientation, and one's ecclesial and social conditioning all function to help the preacher discern the problem that should be addressed in the present.[7] All these factors, including the preacher's own socioeconomic situation, gender, and ethnic background, function to focus the lens of theological and social analysis. They all collaborate in the preacher's hermeneutical imagination to help her or him discern what the problems are, how intense they are, and what ought to be done about them.

Just preaching asks, How should preaching's message and agenda be shaped by

- injustice in our time?
- the ways justice is and isn't in process today?
- scripture's perspective on justice?

A rudimentary paradigm for just preaching looks like this:

1. Identify and name a problem in one's sociocultural situation.
2. Analyze it from sociocultural, political, theological, biblical, and ecclesial perspectives. Be open to the initial assumptions (in step 1) being seriously challenged by deeper analysis.

3. Bring to the conversation key texts from faith and cultural traditions. This includes scripture, but also literature and other important texts that illumine the study of this particular issue. Analyze texts in their contexts to discern what may or may not be analogous fits to the current situation. Don't force, and even be suspicious of, premature fit. Narrow the conversation for the sake of the sermon to one key text from the faith tradition. Be open to the revelatory possibilities in the witness of the key texts from tradition, especially as they illumine the problem addressed and the possible actions toward remedy that are emerging.

4. Compassionately probe the personal issues involved with the real people who are affected by the injustices observed. Never let the study get lost in the abstract. Maintain personal and concrete connection with the real people involved. Be open to the revelatory possibilities in the mix of human experience.[8] We may "know" what the problem is and even how it ought to be addressed in preaching, but when we see it unfold in the intricate details of people's real-life struggles for justice, we come to "know" it in a new way. This "knowing" discloses (a) a necessary complicating of the issues, which prevents one from oversimplistic descriptions and prescriptions, and (b) concrete narrative examples for the sermon. The latter is not permission for mercenary strip-mining of human experience for rhetorical effect in the sermon. Yet it is a call to the careful and compassionate stewardship of people's real-life struggles for justice. The preacher is accountable here to fairly represent the truth, not to embellish, contrive, or plagiarize for personal gain or mere rhetorical effect.

5. Narrow the focus for the sermon to one issue and one set of texts that best collaborate for the sermon's focus and function.

6. Build the sermon, using the appropriate rhetorical and homiletical tools.[9]

7. Test the sermon, using the appropriate theological tools.[10]

This is to take one theological and social trajectory–justice–one that is central to the Bible itself, as a lens for viewing preaching's task, method, and message. This isn't to say that justice is scripture's only message, but it is to say that justice is one message within scripture–both First Testament and New Testament–that is central and persistent. It is also to say that though Judaism and Christianity, and all the frequently divided denominational tribes within each, continue to disagree on ever more finely sliced points of theology, this book is a witness to a unity of message and effort across widely diverse ideological and theological positions. Just preaching can bring otherwise widely divergent faith communities together on a matter of common cause and agreement, one which is at the same time of ultimate concern for God.

3

"Faith Plus Persistence Pays Off"

Luke 18:1–8

DIANA BROWN

And will not God grant justice to [God's] chosen ones who cry to [God] day and night? (Lk. 18:7)

We all know the old adage "The squeaky wheel gets the oil." *Persistence pays off.* When you start your car and the "check engine" light comes on, at first you may not pay it any attention. If the light comes on every time you start the car, you take the car in for service. Paying heed to the warning early enough may help avoid costly repairs. *Persistence pays off.* While making dinner, your three-year-old stands in your way, proclaiming that he is hungry. He asks for a cookie. You don't want him to ruin his appetite. You calmly assure him that dinner will be ready in a few minutes. He continues to plead, "Mommy, please!" You turn to him with your stern look, the one that says, "You better get out of here before you get more than a cookie." The story could have ended with your child getting the cookie. But this time *your* persistence paid off.

In our scripture lesson for today, Jesus told his disciples about their need to pray always and not to lose heart. The New International Version says, "They should always pray and not give up" (18:1). Then Jesus shared this story. A judge in a certain town neither feared God nor cared about people. In this town was a widow. This widow kept coming to the judge because someone was harassing her over a legal issue. The text refers to the harasser as an opponent or adversary.

It is interesting that Jesus uses a widow in the story. For in those days, women—and widows in particular—had very little if any voice at all. Scan the scriptures; very rarely do we find women even speaking. Widows were not valued or respected in their communities. Frequently, they were victimized and preyed on by their male creditors. Remember the widow that Elisha encountered? Her husband died and left her in debt. The creditor threatened to come and take her two sons into slavery. Consider the widow at Zarephath. In her despair she gathered sticks to make a fire to bake a cake. She was down to her last handful of flour and drop of oil when Elijah asked her to prepare him something to eat. Don't forget Ruth, who had to glean for food. Ruth would go to the field early in the morning, not a moment's rest, picking up what others left behind to sustain herself and her mother-in-law, Naomi. We all know the early church had to appoint seven to see that the widows were getting an equal share in the daily food distribution.

Widows: victims of predatory creditors. Widows: barely able to get enough food for their families. Widows: burdened down and desperate enough to give up on life. Widows: their children forced into slavery. Widows: forced to work long hours, getting very little for their labor. Widows: finding it impossible to get ahead, struggling to glean enough for one day.

Our text doesn't tell us who the widow's opponent was. But we can gather she was being oppressed. She pled to the judge: "Grant me justice against my adversary! Grant me justice against my opponent!"

Many widows have it difficult today. Insurance, Social Security, and pension plans have made life better for some. But many in today's society struggle with the same opponents and adversaries as the widows of antiquity did. Using credit to get ahead, only to go deeper into debt. High costs of food and inadequate housing. Crime-ridden neighborhoods. Working long hours or even several jobs just to make ends meet. Forced to leave the children with limited or no supervision. Afraid the streets may claim their sons or daughters. Who am I speaking about? Who are the widows of today? *They are the working poor.*

How does the life of the working poor parallel that of the widow? Like most widows, they are voiceless. Very little attention is paid to their needs. In the state of New Jersey, 184,000 women and children are living in female-headed households below the federal poverty level. Families that have a male present face many of the same issues. A working mother who has an infant and a preschooler is classified as working poor if her income is at or below the poverty level of $14,494. But here in Bergen County, with its high cost of living, that same mother would need to earn $47,563 to adequately meet her family's basic needs without assistance.[1] Many of us would be classified as the working poor! The working poor are not "widows" in the literal sense of the term, but their situation and plight are analogous to those that we read about in the Bible.

The working poor are decent, hardworking individuals. Maybe someone in this congregation can identify with this message. I'm here to tell you, God hears your cries. God sees your burden. The writer of James said to the rich, unjust employer: "*Listen!* The wages of the laborers who mowed your fields, which you kept back by fraud, cry out, and the cries of the harvesters have reached the ears of the Lord of hosts" (Jas. 5:4). Being concerned for the working poor may not seem to be such a big deal for some. But it should be, because many of the working poor look like you and me. Many of our own children are living in poverty.

I recall last winter sitting in Elijah's Promise, a soup kitchen in New Brunswick. I noticed that although I wasn't homeless, hungry, or poor the volunteers at the kitchen treated me like I belonged. They didn't assume that I wasn't poor. They didn't assume that I wasn't hungry. They fed me as they did everyone else. They were accustomed to seeing people like you and me. I listened to the conversations around me, people talking about work. One young man said to me, "I go to work every day. I even volunteer at the youth recreational center. I come here for meals and use my money for rent and transportation." Others talked about day labor and shared with one another as to where they could find it too. These are only a few of the voices of the working poor. Their voices can be heard among one another. Can those voices be heard among those who control the economy? Can their voices be heard among the economic giants that get the tax breaks? Can the unjust judge hear their voices, the judge who neither fears God nor cares about people? The widow didn't appear to have any difficulty locating the one who had the power to change her circumstance. It wasn't by chance that she stumbled on the judge. She targeted the very one she knew could make a difference. Then she went after him.

Like the widow, we must target the judge of today. Who in our society has the power and authority to affect the change that the poor need? The judges today are those who wheel and deal in government, from Washington, D.C., to Trenton; from the Oval Office to the Congress; from our governor and state legislators to the county freeholder and other local officials. Anyone who counts on our votes to get them where they want to be: these are our judges of today.

During election season our politicians visit our churches. They come in with their entourage and frequently are ushered up to the front. Do you hear James? "For if a person with gold rings and in fine clothes comes into your assembly, and if a poor person in dirty clothes also comes in, and if you take notice of the one wearing the fine clothes and say, 'Have a seat here, please,' while to the one who is poor you say, 'Stand there,' or 'Sit at my feet,' have you not made distinctions among yourselves" (Jas. 2:2–4). We even give them time in our worship services to make their political speeches and promises. Often empty promises. But sometimes their promises are empty *because we do not hold them accountable.* We act flattered to have them with us, as if they're celebrities rather than public servants installed in positions of power to work for just systems. We need to stop trying to flatter them and learn to tell them what they need to be doing to fulfill their offices. The church has the power to effect change. The church can be the voice that holds our political leaders accountable to their promises. It can be one *loud, unified,* and *persistent* voice that makes the needs of our people known. We must be like the widow whose persistent cries wore the judge down. The judge's heart may have never really changed. But faith and persistence paid off: she finally got him to do what she needed.

Jesus said that there would always be the poor among us. Does this mean we are to ignore their presence? *No!* Their presence provides a means for ministry. We are to be like the persistent widow going to the unjust judge. "Grant us justice against the opponent!" Grant us justice against poverty. Grant us justice against unfair labor practices. Grant us justice against low wages, no benefits, and long work hours. Grant us justice. This is not a plea for election time. This is a plea until a change comes.

As we work toward a change for all poor people–black, white, Hispanic, old, and young, or for anyone living below the federal poverty level–we must be patient, as the widow was. Stand firm as the widow did. We are to press those in authority and power for improved minimum-wage laws and to maintain affirmative-action programs in education, to rethink welfare reform, not only to focus on lowering the welfare rolls but to move people from dependency to self-sufficiency.

The task may seem impossible, but nothing is impossible with God. Our Lord is full of compassion and mercy. Remember the outcome of the widow who had to deal with the debt of her husband or else her sons would have become slaves. A prophet of God, Elisha, told her to gather empty jars from her neighbors. She gathered the jars and God multiplied abundantly the little oil that she had. She had more than enough oil for her and her sons to live on. Faith and persistence pay off. During a famine the widow at Zarephath was hospitable to Elijah's request to make him a meal. Elijah, a prophet of God, told her, "'The jar of meal will not be emptied and the jug of oil will not fail until the day that the LORD sends rain on the earth.' She went and did as Elijah said, so that she as well as he and her household ate for many days" (1 Kings 17:14b–15). Faith and persistence pay off. Let's not forget about Ruth and Naomi. When Ruth and Naomi returned to Bethlehem, they had nothing. As they were greeted by others, Naomi lamented in the street: "Call me no longer Naomi, call me Mara, for the Almighty has dealt bitterly with me. I went away full, but the LORD has brought me back empty" (Ruth 1:20–21a). But Ruth got up daily and went into Boaz's fields to glean. The Lord heard Naomi's cries and through the faith and persistence of Ruth blessed them both. Faith and persistence pay off.

God used Elisha, Elijah, and Boaz to bless these widows. The widows' faith and persistence paid off in the end. Their cries were heard, and God blessed them. Do we believe that God is the same today, yesterday, and forever? Since God is the same, will not God bless the widows of today?

There is one last thing we can learn from the widow and the unjust judge. Listen, the fact that the judge neither feared God nor cared for people did not stop the widow from making her request. If that widow was able to get justice from the unjust judge, how much more will God, the just judge, grant us what we ask?

God is the just judge who can change the hearts of the unjust. God, the just judge, will provide food for the hungry. God, the just judge, will clothe the naked and provide shelter to the homeless. God, the just judge, can provide affordable housing for the working poor. God, the just judge, can provide charter schools as an alternative to inadequate schools. God, the just judge, will raise up church leaders and churches to be the voice of the people. God is calling the church to represent the just judge on earth. We must be like the widow and pursue justice. Through the faith and persistence of the church, a voice cries out for the voiceless. The working poor will be heard. Church, we must be patient, stand firm, and persevere. We are to hold our local, state, and federal government leaders accountable to the promises they make. A change will come. How do I know? It is right here in the text: "And will not God bring about justice to [God's] chosen ones who cry to [God] day and night? Will [God] delay long in helping them? I tell you, [God] will quickly grant justice to them." Then Jesus asked the question: "When the Son of Man comes, will he find faith on earth?" The answer will be yes, because as the church we will put our faith into persistent action as we cry out for the voiceless. Our faith and persistence will pay off.

"The Torah's Personal Responsibility Act"

Shabbat Hagadol, 1995

MARGARET MOERS WENIG

I preached the sermon below in 1995, as the leaders of our nation haggled over how best to "end welfare as we knew it." (The sermon itself starts on page 25.) There was a heated debate about reforming the portion of our welfare system that provides assistance to families with the lowest incomes–then known as Aid to Families with Dependent Children (AFDC). In 1996, Congress passed and the President signed the Personal Responsibility and Work Opportunity Reconciliation Act, which replaced AFDC with a new program, Temporary Assistance to Needy Families (TANF). This program was initially funded through September 2002. Congress failed to pass a new welfare bill in 2002, voting instead to extend the program so that debate could continue in 2003. By the time this book appears in print, another heated debate will have passed and Congress will have passed a new bill, refashioning welfare once again.

The 1996 reforms ended a sixty-year commitment by the federal government to guarantee assistance to any family who fell below a certain income level. Under TANF, states now receive "block grants," a fixed amount of federal money each year, to provide assistance to the neediest of families. Recipients can benefit from these funds for a maximum of five years throughout their lifetime, and twenty states have established shorter timelines. As I write this, tens of thousands of families have reached their lifetime limit; more reach it daily.

TANF allows states to establish work requirements for families receiving assistance and penalties for those who do not meet those requirements.

Most states require most or all recipients of TANF benefits to participate in work or work-preparation activities. The latter can include "workfare" assignments, such as cleaning public parks in exchange for assistance. Here in New York City, thousands of students left City University in 1996 so that they could participate in officially sanctioned work activities; a long-term college degree is not considered acceptable preparation for work under TANF.

Has TANF moved Americans from "dependency" to "self-sufficiency"? On the one hand, the Department of Health and Human Services reports that one in three adults receiving assistance are working and that the number of people receiving assistance has decreased nearly 60 percent since TANF began.[1] On the other hand, of the millions of families who no longer receive assistance, 40 percent have been unable to find work, and the average wage of those recipients who have found a job is $6.75 an hour.[2] Unskilled and undereducated recipients of TANF are often required to take any job available, all too often a low-wage job with no opportunities for training or advancement.

TANF was created and implemented in economic boom times. But our slowing economy is now creating a strain on our social-assistance programs. In 2002, requests for emergency food assistance in major cities rose by an average of 19 percent, and requests for emergency shelter also increased on average 19 percent.[3] And participation in the federal food stamp program increased from 17.9 million people in September 2001 to 20.5 million in December 2002, an increase of 2.6 million people in a little more than a year.[4]

TANF grants states wide discretion in how the federal block grants can be spent and the degree to which state funds can be allocated to supplement the block grants. States are experiencing the worst fiscal crisis in twenty years. The recession and rising unemployment decreased tax revenues while increasing demand on social services and income support. The ranks of the unemployed increased from 5.7 million people in November 2000 to 8.2 million in November 2001, the largest one-year increase since 1982. At the beginning of 2003, 8.5 million people remained out of work, with nearly 2 million unemployed for more than six months.[5] Security expenses following September 11, 2001, have added to the budget squeeze. Because most states are required to balance their budgets, significant cuts in healthcare, childcare, job training, supplemental income, and so forth have already been passed in many states and are anticipated in others.[6]

In our great nation

- sins of mothers and fathers are visited on innocent children. Some children will "make it" anyway, despite the lot they have been cast. Many will not. Is that just "survival of the fittest," or does the fate of these kids lay a claim on us?

- an illness or a layoff can devastate a hardworking family. A recession makes it harder to recover. Is that just someone's tough luck, or does their tough luck lay a claim on those of us who are luckier? And for how long?

- Some who are retarded, mentally ill, or physically disabled may never become self-supporting. Whose responsibility is it to care for those who cannot care for themselves? Ours or no one's?

- Every day of the year 2,016 children in this country are born into poverty.[7] How many of them could have been fed on even a tenth of the earnings of Enron executives?

What standard of living do we believe folks are "entitled" to enjoy? What food, clothing, housing, vacations, and entertainment can we witness some enjoying or can we enjoy ourselves while others sleep in shelters? What level of disparity between rich and poor will make us rise up and say: There's something wrong with this picture! At the very core lie fundamental religious notions of human worth, reward and punishment, sin and virtue, freedom and responsibility.

Following September 11, some Americans report a shift in priorities. I, for one, will vote for anyone who defines Homeland Security as healthcare, adequate nutrition, quality childcare, Head Start, a safe home, a good school, an affordable college education for all children, and a living wage for working adults.

The Torah's Personal Responsibility Act

For a few weeks I have struggled with what to say to you about the tension between the need to cut federal, state, and city spending and the proposed means of cutting that spending. There is much about economics I do not understand. Little I can say *with certainty* about what is wise or foolish, right or wrong in government spending.

Of one thing I am certain, however: the Torah has its own Personal Responsibility Act. The Jewish tradition's Personal Responsibility Act imposes the following responsibilities:

- It is upon us to choose life for ourselves and our children.

- It is upon parents to support their children and to teach them a trade lest they resort to stealing.[8] The community may not support a child if the parent has the means to do so.

- A person is exhorted to work at a menial task such as flaying carcasses in the marketplace rather than say, "I am a priest and a great person and that is beneath my dignity."[9]

- Rabbi Akiva teaches that we must even "treat your Sabbath as a weekday rather than be dependent upon your fellow human being."[10]

- Human beings are held accountable for their actions, and God may visit the sins of the parents upon their children.

- Jewish tradition does not condone choosing public assistance over work.

But the Torah's Personal Responsibility Act does not end there. Listen to some of its other provisions:

- Leviticus 25:35–If your neighbors become poor and cannot support themselves, you shall maintain them. They shall live with you as if they are resident aliens.

- Deuteronomy 15:7–8–If one of your neighbors is in need in any community of yours, you must not harden your heart nor close your hand against your needy neighbor. You shall open your hand to them and freely lend them enough to meet their needs.

Rabbi Hayyim Soloveitchik derives from Leviticus the responsibility of the individual and from Deuteronomy the responsibility of the community to support those who (temporarily or permanently) cannot support themselves.[11] Our responsibility is fulfilled in its highest form, teaches Maimonides, by lending money, by offering a job, or by entering a business partnership with the poor so that they can support themselves. But Torah does not permit us to abandon those who will never be able to become self-supporting.

The Torah's Personal Responsibility Act has other provisions too: clear priorities in *tzedekah* (righteousness) are to parents, other relatives, neighbors, the poor of one's own town, and the poor of the land of Israel. Does this order of priorities permit one to exhaust one's *tzedekah* on priority one or two? No. According to Rabbi Jehiel Epstein, catering to the total needs of a relative while neglecting the basic needs of other people is not permissible. Rabbi Moshe Feinstein says *an individual* may give all his *tzedekah* to a top priority recipient but *the community* may not.[12]

The Republican Personal Responsibility Act makes no allowances for those who, for physical or mental reasons, will never be able to work. Their Personal Responsibility Act punishes children whose mothers conceived them too young or while receiving AFDC or whose fathers can't be identified or found.

Are there teenage mothers receiving aid for whom there are jobs they are capable of doing? Possibly. The Talmud anticipates that any welfare system risks supporting freeloaders and enjoins us "to be good to the imposters, for without them our stinginess would lack its chief excuse."

Do we resent freeloaders? Do we want to break the yoke of poverty and dependency? Then we should be lobbying for affordable housing, quality day care, Head Start, quality public education, after-school programs, summer-recreation programs, preventive healthcare, vocational training, social services, affordable college education, and jobs that pay enough to support a family and provide health insurance.

In the past few weeks the City College of New York (CCNY), immigrant groups, AIDS services, nursing homes, United Jewish Appeal (UJA), and mental-health agencies have made desperate pleas with demonstrations, advertisements, and direct-mail campaigns to urge us to help stop the city, state, and federal governments from cutting funding to their students, clients, and patients—funding cuts that are decimating their staffs and threatening their agencies. And they all deserve support—but something is lacking in their rhetoric.

Of this I feel certain: It is not enough to lobby for funds that would save your own jobs, your own agency, even your own clients. It is not enough for CCNY to lobby only on its own behalf, for the elderly to lobby only on behalf of home care, or for families of the disabled and mentally ill to lobby on their own behalf. It is not enough for nursing-home staff to lobby only on nursing homes' behalf or for the gay community to lobby only on behalf of AIDS services. It is not enough for immigrants to lobby only on their own behalf. It is not enough for Jews to lobby only on their own behalf. It is not enough to say, as one appeal on behalf of UJA Federation said: "I am concerned with many proposals currently being considered to balance New York State's budget. I urge you to consider alternatives that will not disrupt the lives of so many elderly people, vulnerable children, and community services, especially to Jews and in the Jewish community."

If we allow the shrinking pie to pit one needy group against another, then we all eventually will starve together or eat one another alive. I am embarrassed by Jews who are up in arms about Medicaid cuts that will affect the elderly but have said not a word about cuts in AFDC that will affect poor children.

On March 24, 1995, the House of Representatives passed Newt Gingrich's "Personal Responsibility Act" that denied three to five million children the benefits they once received. Tax cuts of 1995 will, when fully implemented, total $99 billion a year, half of that benefiting the wealthiest 10 percent of households and one-fifth of it benefiting the wealthiest 1 percent.

On Yom Kippur, Isaiah warns us that it is a travesty to fast unless we have shared our bread with the hungry. On Passover it is a travesty to feast unless we have ensured that poor Jews have matzah to eat. Of this I am certain: so too would it be a travesty to stand idly by while legislation threatens to starve the poor for not helping themselves, while we celebrate the liberation of our people from four hundred years of slavery during which we did little to help ourselves. We say, "Dayenu—it would have been enough—had God only taken us out of Egypt" because we did nothing to earn it. "Dayenu—it would have been enough—had God given us the Torah" because we did nothing to earn it. "Dayenu–it would have been enough–had God given us the land of Israel" because we did nothing to earn it.

The Torah and Haggadah say God took us out of Egypt with a strong hand and an outstretched arm. If we sit down to a seder next week without stretching out our arms to write our senators, governor, state legislators, and mayor, then even the gefilte fish and matzah balls will turn to maror in our mouths.

"Not Good, Merciful"

Luke 10:25–37

KIM LATTERELL

When President George W. Bush gave his inaugural speech, he made an allusion to Luke 10: "When we see that wounded traveler on the road to Jericho, we will not pass by on the other side." He didn't have to explain; he didn't have to quote chapter and verse. Although much biblical imagery is falling fast from America's daily consciousness, the parable of the good Samaritan continues to be well known enough that he could simply brush it into his speech without citation. He assumed we knew it. And we do...or do we?

- Did you know that Jesus never actually calls the Samaritan "good"?
- Did you know that neither Luke nor Jesus calls the story a parable?
- Did you know that the lawyer isn't a lawyer in any contemporary sense, but is really a life-long, steeped-in-the-scriptures, biblical scholar and teacher—more like an equivalent to our university or seminary professor/scholar?

And did your ear catch how, when this lawyer asked two important questions, one about eternal life and the other about who one's neighbor might be, that Jesus never really answered his questions directly?

Yes, we know this story, or do we?

Some preachers—including me—might tell you this story, then order you out there to the highways and byways to be the best Samaritan that you can be. It's tempting to use this story as a morality tale, a lesson in goodness, a little ditty about being a better neighbor. I thought of including "Good Sam" bumper stickers in today's bulletin for everyone to put on their RVs.

Other preachers—well, me too—might invite you to think of yourself as the priest or Levite in this story, maybe updating it by saying "the president of our congregation, the bishop of our church." We could make you feel guilty about how bad you really are because you walk blindly by so many. We'd challenge you to open your eyes, open your car door, open your home, open your wallet, and see all the people in the ditch near you.

But what if?

What if right now, God wants you to see yourself not as the priest, the Levite, or the Samaritan? What if you are really the person in the ditch, the one who needs to be rescued?

Twenty-one of us recently went down to Juarez, Mexico, to teach our youth to be good neighbors, to be good Samaritans to our brothers and sisters across the border. We even stayed at a Pentecostal church called El Tiempo Bueno Samaritano (The Church of the Good Samaritan). We worked on a home or two. We led kid's club for eighty little children.

But…

But what if God was trying to use these little kids, these "third-world" families to reach their "first-world helpers"? What if the families were the Samaritans in the story? Why do we so quickly see ourselves as the givers of aid and not as those in need, in need of having our deadly wounds bound up and healed by others whose compassion we need for our very survival?

Just when we think we know all about this story, Jesus says, think again.

Or could it be that Jesus is the good Samaritan? The one and only "Good Sam"? After all, isn't he the one who risks entering our ditches? Isn't he the one who binds up our wounds, carries us to safety, sees that we get the care we need? Isn't he the one who covers the debts we cannot pay, no matter how great the cost? Isn't he the one who is coming back again to make all things right?

We may think we know this story, but about the time we think we do, God tweaks the angle of the narrative. Maybe the person in the ditch is Jesus. The victim of the robber's wound is always Jesus, lying there, bypassed by the most well-meaning folks who just know that God wouldn't want them to be rendered unfit for worship—made ritualistically unclean—by touching someone near death. It would be like touching one whom the law itself said was cursed and thus would bring the curse down on us.

Maybe. But if you're not duly frustrated with me at this point, do you know what I think the lesson of this story really is?

I don't think this story is about the priest, the Levite, the Samaritan, or the man in the ditch. I think, given who we are, that this story is about the lawyer. About the lawyer in you and in me. The lawyer who comes to church and wants a good, biblical sermon, a Bible study, a discussion group over the newest and hottest book in theology and mission. The lawyer who wants truth that fits on a bookmark, in a cross-stitch, or on a T-shirt.

The lawyer who wants a cross that will fit in one's pocket or an ethic that can be summed up with four little letters and strapped around a wrist. The lawyer who wants what we want, really: *Distance.*

He wants a faith that lets him keep his hands clean. He wants his days kept safe, his schedule kept predictable. He wants the okay from Jesus for a faith that stays deeply embedded in his head, safely sequestered from the streets. He wants a faith without bother, a faith without risk. He wants right answers that come without the need for right actions.

But remember what Jesus tells him twice:

- We have the right answers, we know the right way to live.
- We know what God wants of us: not mere goodness, but mercy.
- We know a neighbor when we see one.

We know need when we see it. So do something about it. Do what you know is right and merciful and you will find life. The question is less, "Who is my neighbor?" and more, "Am I a neighbor?" The first tries to limit our neighborliness to manageable proportions; after all, this thing could get out of hand. The second puts no limits on God or ourselves.

So there. We've finally got this story nailed down and wrapped up. But just when I thought I knew what it was about, something happened.

During the week we spent in Juarez I sat in a worship service on Thursday night watching the few who were there come forward and put their offerings in a little box. A peso or two at best was the most that each could share that week. We Americans were told to keep our own donations small so as not to shame our hosts, though any of us could have dropped a ten- or twenty-dollar bill and never broken a sweat. As I watched the coins fall from the hands of our friends, the story turned on me again: "So what makes you think you aren't one of the robbers?"

To fuel our lifestyles, to feed our consumption of the world's goods and services, what makes any of us think that we are anything but the robbers? The way we live leaves victims in the ditches of poverty all over the world. To fuel our wants and our newly imagined "needs," we rob, assault, wound, and abandon God's children left and right.

I thought I knew this story.

What if Jesus, the best Samaritan, has come simply to rescue them, to protect them, *from us*?

Then what?

Now what?

PART 2

Motivations for Just Preaching

It is almost cliché that preachers cajole hearers into brief spurts of action by means of guilt and coercive rhetoric. Such tactics weary listeners and fail to motivate and mobilize anyone for long. Sustained action for justice—and against injustice—derives from a perspective on life that is the result of nothing less than a transformation of the imagination and identity, a transformation for which preachers and hearers alike are dependent on God.

In a world that is deeply divided, even—sometimes especially—among people of faith, just preaching becomes a striking common ground for ecumenical and interfaith dialogue and unity. The diversity of this entire book—and this section in particular—testifies to this fact. In this section an Evangelical Lutheran, a Presbyterian, a Unitarian Universalist, and a Reformed Jew each focuses attention on different aspects of justice. Yet each operates out of the same reservoir for motivation: one's core identity, especially as that identity is given shape by God and the values of one's own religious heritage. Diversity here coalesces into a unity about who we are as stewards of God's grace, covenant, and call to just living in compassionate community. Note how each author and preacher in this section roots his or her call to action in the soil of one's identity as found in God and the understanding of God in each writer's tradition.

Preaching on matters of justice gives plenty of opportunity for preachers to name the very real bad news that exists all around us. Rather than take our hearers on temporary and spasmodic guilt trips in the form of so-called sermons, faithful and effective preaching on justice couples incisive analysis of the bad news that infects our contemporary existence with the good news of our redeeming God's relentless deconstruction of unjust powers and subsequent reconstruction of caring communities of just mutuality. Such preaching transforms both preachers and hearers to sustained lives of just and faithful action.

Enabling Grace

JAMES M. CHILDS, JR.

The preacher went on and on. He battered us with statistics. We now knew the exorbitant amount we spent on a variety of petty luxuries as compared with the relative pittance much of the world's population had at their disposal for the very essentials of life. The sharp-edged numbers revealing our tiny affluent minority's inordinately outsized share of global consumption cut deeply into the flesh of our consciences. The recitation of these statistics was calculated to convert us to the cause of justice. In the preacher's mind it seemed a good sermon in the best prophetic tradition. However, for most of us his diatribe produced only feelings of unresolved guilt. We were condemned, albeit justly, but not empowered. It was clear we were a part of the problem, but how could we possibly be a part of the solution? And when that question goes unanswered, feelings of guilt quickly turn to feelings of anger and resentment.

Trying to build love of justice on the foundation of guilt is simply bad spiritual architecture. It is somewhat like building on the sandy soil of fear. To engender the fear of punishment for harming our neighbors and thereby deter such behavior is at the heart of law as we experience it in society. By the coercion of law, justice may be enforced, but not necessarily endorsed. Respect for my neighbor's person or property for fear of the law does not necessarily mean I really care about my neighbor. Dutiful payment of taxes that fund a variety of government welfare programs does not mean I am concerned for those in need and truly want to help them. It may only mean that I fear the legal penalties of not paying my taxes.

Sometimes the appeal to fear is the threat of dire consequences other than legal penalties. For generations young people were warned against sexual adventures by raising the specter of disease, pregnancy, or public censure. There is little evidence that such warnings, however cogent, instilled a sense of respect and caring in the face of temptation rather than simply a measure of trepidation. Moreover, in the absence of more positive approaches to sexual ethics, the sexualization of the media that makes public disapproval a nonissue and the ease of safe sex and pregnancy prevention (admittedly often ignored) seem to have made the fear-based sanctions of the past something of a quaint relic. When the reasons to fear are removed, there may be nothing left on which to base conduct.

The appeal to fearful consequences is also frequently evident in the call to environmental justice. We are warned that if we do not change our consumerist, fossil-fueled ways, we will dissipate the earth's resources and alter its climate beyond recognition and even habitation. To be sure, these are real liabilities that must be spelled out in no uncertain terms. Yet by themselves, these prospects do not guarantee a sense of nature's intrinsic value or our responsibility to treat future generations justly. From the vantage point of our faith, it is God's gracious call to care for the earth and love it as God does and to love one another as we have been loved that takes us beyond necessity to commitment. In the absence of this sense of vocation, our focus might well be on the ways that new technologies and discoveries can deliver us from our fear that we must start conserving and living more frugally.

In E. L. Doctorow's novel *City of God,* we occasionally run across reminiscences and commentary attributed to Albert Einstein. One story has Einstein recounting memories of his childhood schooling at the Luitpold Gymnasium in Ulm, Germany. He describes his teacher there as one who followed what he thought of as the Germanic philosophy of education by tyranny. The instructor's demand for absolute respect and lockstep discipline, Einstein observed, had a devastating effect on his classmates. It destroyed their capacity for creativity, and curiosity was drummed out of them. For Einstein this schoolroom experience stood in stark contrast to the feelings he associated with his study of the violin and his discovery of Euclid's geometry. Both were events outside the context of the gymnasium. In each case the sheer beauty of the subject inspired him. So he devoted himself, uncoerced, to the music and to the logic of the numbers, driven simply by the joy of what he found there. Tyranny subjugated the mind. The freedom for discovery was an affirmation of the mind and thereby empowered it.[1] The rule of fear, far from affirming the students, repressed them.

When we instill either guilt or fear, we are simply pointing out moral frailty. Guilt is engendered when our moral failings are exposed to the critique of the moral law. Fear is engendered when punishments are attached to the violation of that law. The existence of a threat of penalty to strike fear in our hearts is simply a way of saying that if we don't threaten penalties, people will not do the right thing. This can be a self-fulfilling prophecy; though we may stay within the bounds of compliance, we can easily come to accept conflict and selfishness as normal. We are denigrated. We are not empowered.

Mohandas Gandhi understood that enmity means disdain for the other, which will not produce a change of heart and the will to do justice. Gandhi followed the Hindu principle of *ahimsa,* the goal of which was to change the hearts of both the people and their oppressors from hostility to peace and, by that means, to set justice in motion. Gandhi treated the British not with disdain, but with respect. He believed they had the moral capacity for change. This affirmation paid off with success. His attitude of respect enabled the British colonialists to recover and act on their sense of justice.[2]

Now to be sure, we human beings, sinners that we are, have much to feel guilty about. Moreover, given our fallen condition, we recognize that society cannot survive without the enforcement of law. The law and the penalties for breaking it help to safeguard minimal standards of justice in a world rife with cruelty and corruption.

However, Christian preaching, if it is to stimulate a commitment to justice as an integral part of the church's witness, must go beyond judgment and practical advice to proclaim God's grace and let loose its power to change people's lives. The power of God's grace expressed in the gospel of Jesus Christ sets us free from guilt and fear–free from concern for self under the burden of judgment–to be open in love for the neighbor. It is enabling grace. Furthermore, this same gospel provides us with a vision of hope for our world, within which striving for justice and the common good makes sense.[3] These two dimensions of the gospel's enabling grace are the focus of our attention in this chapter.

The Power of Gospel Freedom

Indicative and Imperative

For Pauline theology and ethics the indicative of God's affirmation, God's "yes" to us in Christ, and the imperative of obedience to the will of God coinhere.[4] Those who are "in Christ" are new creations (2 Cor. 5:17). That means that the Christian has not simply been given the possibility of a new life (a new lease on life or a chance to do better perhaps) but a genuinely new existence in which obedience to Christ is constitutive of that new life.[5]

Christians have died to the law and to sin and have been raised anew in Christ to "bear fruit for God...slaves not under the old written code but in the new life of the Spirit" (Rom. 7:4–6). We *are* children of the day, so we are enjoined to put on the "armor of light" and reject the works of darkness (Rom. 13:11–13; 1 Thess. 5:4ff.). Because of the sacrifice of Christ for us, we are *unleavened.* Therefore, Paul calls on us to clean out the old yeast of malice and evil in favor of the new "unleavened bread of sincerity and truth" (1 Cor. 5:7–8). Indeed. It is what we *are* as persons in Christ that forms the basis of Paul's admonition to Christians to shun prostitution. The sexual act makes a person one with the prostitute and that simply cannot be; those united with Christ are one spirit *with Christ* (6:16–17).

In Paul the imperative is in our hearts because our hearts are in Christ. "God's *claim* is regarded by the apostle as a constitutive part of God's *gift.* The Pauline concept of grace is *inclusive* of the Pauline concept of obedience...The Pauline imperative is not just the result of the indicative but fully integral to it."[6]

As we know from reading Paul and from our own theology and experience, the new life that is ours in Christ does not mean the end of sinning. Therefore, there is bound to be a note of judgment in the imperative. However, the force of the imperative is not in its judgment but in its appeal to the power of God's grace that has created a new reality in us and for us.

Justification and Justice

It has often been charged that theologies centered on justification by grace through faith are more likely to be deficient in their concern for justice. The stress on grace and faith, apart from works, and the fact that justification is usually understood in terms of individual salvation seem to work against the kind of activism that social justice demands. However, on closer examination it is clear that justification and justice are inseparable companions. The moral sense of the Greek word *dikaiosune* (righteousness), needs to be distinguished from its soteriological sense, but not separated. Indeed, the righteousness that Paul talks about concerns both salvation and one's moral life. Justification and justice aren't an "either/or" proposition; they're a "both/and" reality.

In the context of his discussions of justification, Paul is clear that the moral law cannot produce moral goodness or enable us to achieve right relationship with God (Rom. 3:21, 28; Gal. 3:21). To simply know the demands of the law does not provide the power to fulfill it, a point we have been at pains to make. Rather, the law is experienced as wrath and condemnation. No, justification—being made right with God or in right relationship with God—is by grace and through faith (Rom. 3:24–28; Gal. 2:16; 3:24). However, this right relationship with God at the heart of justification sets us on a course of right relationship with our neighbors as well. This we comprehend in those passages that speak of the given life being lived. In Rom. 6:13 we are to present ourselves to God as instruments of righteousness (*dikaiosynēs*). The work of Christ for our justification happened "so that the just (*dikaiōma*) requirement of the law might be fulfilled in us, who walk not according to the flesh but according to the Spirit" (8:4).[7]

Life in Christ, life under justification, enables the faithful to be for others as Christ has been for us:

God's power is the power of love, and this love is revealed and made real for [human beings] in the death and resurrection of Jesus Christ. Those who belong to [Jesus] (through faith) are thus brought under the dominion of God's power. This is their "justification," by which they are freed from the "worldly powers" which have alienated them from their Creator and are renewed for obedience to their real Lord. Just as Christ's death reveals that God's power is the power of love, so it reveals that love is to be the content of the obedience to which believers are summoned.[8]

We love as we have first been loved; that is the connection between justice and justification. Justification is of God's love, and the love that it instills in us is committed to justice. Justice is one vehicle for the concerns of love to find expression within the structures of our social and political life. "Faith active in love seeking justice" is the operative phrase.

For Helmut Thielicke an ethic lived out of life in Christ, an evangelical ethic, proceeds from the prior fact of justification and gives expression to its reality. This distinguishes evangelical ethics from philosophical ethics, which focuses on the ethical task that the moral agent must accomplish. The beginning of the Christian ethic is in the *gift* that God gives. For other ethics the beginning is the *task* we have.[9] When we think about empowering people for justice, we begin by emphasizing the gift, the gift of enabling grace.

The Freedom of the Christian

When it comes to a discussion of freedom in the gospel, one prominent item in the ecumenical catalog of Christian writings is Luther's treatise "The Freedom of a Christian."[10] Luther's well-known set of contrasting assertions sets the stage: "A Christian is a perfectly free lord of all, subject to none. A Christian is a perfectly dutiful servant of all, subject to all."[11] The freedom to which Luther refers is freedom from the demands and condemnation of the law. The life in Christ, the life of faith, bathed in the forgiveness of sin and the unqualified acceptance of God's love in Christ, is not driven by fear of penalties, but by freedom for love of neighbor. Lacking in the self-concern that has been supplanted by divine affirmation, we might say that we have left over all that energy we're not spending on self-justification to spend on our neighbors.

As the indicative and the imperative coinhere in Paul's thought, so, for Luther, faith in Christ and Christlike life go together by the power of grace: "As our heavenly Father has in Christ freely come to our aid, we also ought freely to help our neighbor through our body and its works, and each one should become as it were a Christ to the other that we may be Christs to one another and Christ may be the same in all, that is, that we may be truly Christians."[12] For those who have always suspected that Luther was "soft on good works" these words and this treatise should make clear that for Luther the demands and expectations of the Christian life of service to others in love is nothing less than the imitation of Christ. The nail he wants to drive is that this service flows from "a joyful, willing, and free mind."[13] With these comments he echoes his earlier remarks in his commentary on Galatians that if Christians act out of love, they do right, but if they act out of fear, it is not a Christian response but a manifestation of human weakness.[14]

Prophetic Voice and Gospel Promise

Despite his devotion to *ahimsa* and his respectful approach to the British, Mahandas Gandhi did confront the British with their injustice in subjugating his people. We might say that such confrontation was his prophetic voice. In the common parlance of theology and preaching we use the term *prophetic* to refer to the confrontation and condemnation of injustice. Certainly the grim truth of injustice in our world must be exposed if we are to see our way to greater justice. This truth must be spoken both to those inside the church and to the society at large. There is a clear call and need to speak the prophetic word, to voice God's judgment against the evils and injustices of our world, and to warn the faithful concerning their own complicity. However, having raised these issues, we need to turn to the grace of God among us as the power that can mobilize the people of God to work for positive change. Even when working for justice in the world at large, we finally place our hopes in God's creative and loving work.

Not long ago I was discussing with a group of pastors issues of economic justice from the perspective of a Christian ethic. The response of several was not entirely surprising. "This is all well and good," they said, "but the world in which we live doesn't know and doesn't care about this stuff. We're in a very different place." They were discouraged and frustrated. They saw themselves being dismissed by the world around them as irrelevant, relegated to the role of shamans in a ghetto of personal spirituality. Such feelings and fears, which are not new, often lead either to resignation or attack, neither of which is helpful. On the one hand, some persons in ministry accept what they consider to be the judgment of the world around them and slip away into the safety of quietism. On the other hand, those who attack shake their fists at the unjust world in a cascade of condemnations. They are determined to be prophetic. Like so many journalistic social critics without a proposal who expose our underside with acerbic eloquence, they finally become tiresome. Despite the contrast in responses, they share with their quietistic colleagues a common conviction that work for justice and the common good in this world is futile.

However, this is God's world; the whole of it is in God's plan of redemption in Christ (Rom. 8:19–21); and we are God's people called to be witnesses to that plan (1 Pet. 2:9). These promises alone should make us tenacious rather than timid, and bold rather than bitter.

It is clear that a realistic, prophetic appraisal of our troubled and conflicted world is in order. Reinhold Niebuhr, for example, has taught us that the best we can hope for most of the time is a political balance of power that provides an improved though not complete justice, certainly not one that is necessarily based on love or mutual respect. However, we are ready to work even for that and to encourage others in the Christian community to enter the fray as well, out of love for neighbor and for justice. We do so because every gain for good is a gain for our neighbors, whom we hold in Christian love. Indeed, even this sort of imperfect result points to the promise that God's kingdom will be one where justice and love are a perfect blend. And we take energy from that promise for the work of justice (more on that point later). We do have a prophetic voice inside and outside the church, but it is married to the promise of the gospel, just as the prophets of Israel condemned injustice but rested their proclamation on God's covenant love and faithfulness.

Isaiah speaks judgment against the leaders of God's people who have oppressed and exploited the poor (3:14–15). However, judgment comes in the context of a renewed promise of God's grace and favor enshrined in the glorious messianic oracle of chapter 11. So also Jeremiah decries the greed, treachery, neglect of the needy, and injustice, which fall under God's judgment (5:27–28). Yet the final judgment of God is God's faithful covenant love in the promise of a new covenant of forgiveness, election, and transformation (31:31–34). Jan Lochman has reminded us that the tablets of the law were kept *inside* the ark of the covenant. Since the ark was the visible sign of God's salvation, this physical arrangement made clear that the demands and the judgment of the law come within the context of prevenient grace.[15] Isaiah and Jeremiah fit right in.

In Matthew 19, we have the familiar account of Jesus' encounter with the rich young man. We recall how he went away grieving when Jesus said that he should sell all and give to the poor and follow him. Jesus then reflects that it is more difficult for the rich to enter the kingdom of heaven than for a camel to go through the eye of a needle (vv. 23–24). The disciples react to this dire pronouncement much as any of us would at being handed an uncompromising, prophetic judgment. They were astounded at such a hard saying. "Then who can be saved?" Jesus answers that "for mortals it is impossible, but for God all things are possible" (v. 26).

Paul wrote some stinging words to the fractious Corinthians, even calling them people of the flesh and spiritual infants (1 Cor. 3:1). Yet for all of his no-nonsense appraisal of their conduct, Paul starts his epistle by stating what will ultimately be the premise of his appeal for reform and renewal: that they have received the grace of God in Christ, that they have been enriched in every way and with every spiritual gift, and that God is faithful and will sustain them to the end (1:4–9).

Early in the Christian era, John Chrysostom railed against the selfishness of the rich and the injustices perpetrated by severe disparities in the distribution of wealth. He appealed to the rich to follow the way of Jesus by distributing their wealth to the poor. He preached justice with prophetic fervor. Consistent with his Semipelagian tendencies, his admonition to Christians and others to turn aside from their unjust greed had a somewhat moralistic edge to it, a belief that if people were confronted with their behavior, they could summon the will to change. However, Chrysostom did believe there was a need for grace in the Christian life and a power of grace operative in our lives through baptism and the Lord's supper.[16] Moreover, when his optimism intrudes on his prophetic judgment, it does so because he sees the grace of God at work:

> "For *by the grace of God* much forbearance, much virtue has been planted everywhere." Great strides have been taken. Some people have voluntarily renounced their wealth. "For did not Paul leave his tools, Peter his rod and hook, and Matthew his seat of custom? Do we not see many similar occurrences even now?"[17]

Certainly, Augustine's prophetic voice was heard loud and clear. Whether addressing those who threatened to divide the church by their heresy or speaking about the evils of the tottering Roman Empire, he was not hesitant to confront. Yet his understanding of the foundations of love and justice in the Christian life is equally clear and exquisitely expressed in his preaching:

> [God] who has called you to [God's] kingdom and glory will grant that, when you have been regenerated by [God's] grace and by the Holy Spirit, it will be written in your hearts, so that you may love what you believe and that, through love, faith may work in you and that you may become pleasing to the Lord God, the Giver of all good things, not by fearing [God's] punishments in servile fashion, but by loving justice as true [children] of God.[18]

> Certainly many observe the Law from fear, but those who keep the Law from fear of punishment would prefer that what they fear did not exist. On the contrary, those who observe the Law through love of justice rejoice even in that respect because they do not consider it hostile to them.[19]

Among theologians of our own time, Robert McAfee Brown has certainly been a strong prophetic voice on behalf of the oppressed of the world. When we look at the Bible through the eyes of the oppressed, Brown shows us, we see God's judgment on those who are guilty of injustice. He shows us this in his book *Unexpected News: Reading the Bible with Third World Eyes*. After taking us through the texts that leave us indicted for our complicity in the oppression of the poor and marginalized, he concludes with "An Epilogue for Those Who Feel Personally Assaulted." He recognizes that the preceding pages will make many a reader feel guilty and possibly resentful. He makes no effort to take the edge off that guilt. Instead, Brown simply says that he too stands with his readers under the same sentence of guilt. He further suggests that the gospel's promise of liberation for the poor is a promise for our liberation from those idolatries of wealth and power and national pride that lead us into injustices. His is a call to repentance and change. However, the final words go to Jesus from Mark 1:15: "The time is fulfilled, and the kingdom of God has come near; repent, and believe in the good news."[20]

When all is said and done, the focus is on what God is doing and on our invitation to participate. The good news is that God's reign is breaking in in Christ, and it is brimming with divine grace. It is God's reign, and God will bring it in. Brown himself recognizes this implicitly in his discussion of Isaiah 61:1–2 and Jesus' use of it in Luke 4:18–19 to signal the meaning of his person and work. He sees quite correctly that this is a promise of reversal in the fullness of God's reign, when those under oppression will find liberty. It is a promise from God, sealed in cross and resurrection, a basis for hope.[21] The power of this gracious promise energizes our efforts to anticipate this divine future by addressing our own complicity and seeking the changes that serve all people. The scope of this promise brings us to our next main point.

The Hope of Gospel Promise

I have been arguing that it is God's grace in Christ that enables us to commit ourselves to seeking justice and serving the common good. Preaching that motivates people to change and turn to the welfare of neighbors, society, and world is preaching that holds up God's affirmation of our worth and capability and God's promise to be with us in our efforts. Shaming and instilling fear of condemnation not only do not work; they are bad theology.

However, if God's gospel promise does not itself contain a hope for the future of our world, for a world of justice, peace, integrity, and the triumph of all life, then our argument is seriously undermined. If this world is just a "vale of tears" headed for destruction, from which the children of God can hope to escape to a heavenly home apart, how does work for the welfare of our world, for peace, for justice, and for the integrity of the creation make sense?

During the nineteenth century and the early part of the twentieth century, theologians attempted to deal with this sort of otherworldliness. They tried to see Jesus' proclamation of the reign of God as a goal of history and a call for social transformation. They were convinced that the biblical message went beyond a promise for individual salvation to a promise for the whole of the world. On the European continent this was known as liberal theology and associated with such names as Albrecht Ritschl and Adolf von Harnack. In the United States at the beginning of the last century it was spoken of as the "social gospel" movement and most often associated with the leadership of Walter Rauschenbusch. However, the optimism about progress that pervaded these movements proved unwarranted in the face of subsequent world events, such as the Holocaust. Moreover, the critique of neo-orthodox theologians such as Karl Barth in Europe and Reinhold Niebuhr here in America exposed the fact that the liberal outlook had understated the depth of human sin and the utter necessity of divine grace. To oversimplify a bit, the attempt to translate the gospel into a moralistic call to build the kingdom of God on earth could not stand the test of human experience or theological scrutiny.

However, the liberal and social-gospel movements did see clearly that the promise of God's coming reign is a promise for the whole world, even if the movements were off the mark in other respects. More recent theology and biblical scholarship have lifted up the fact that the Bible's view of God's dominion is a promise for the whole person and the whole world. The contemporary correction is in the equally clear biblical message that it is God's kingdom and that God will be the one to bring it to fullness. Belief in human progress is supplanted by faith in God's promise. We who live in the time between its revelation in the Christ event and its fulfillment in the eschaton, a time in which sin still persists and evil abounds, are called to preach the good news of that promised future. We do so not only by proclaiming the Christ as Savior but also by pursuing those values that Christ revealed as an integral part of his saving work, values of justice and peace and life and health that will prevail in the future of God's dominion.

As I suggested earlier, God's promise for the triumph of healing and wholeness, peace and reconciliation, the justice of total equality in a new heaven and a new earth, gives us the energy of hope. In hope, we anticipate these values in our work for justice and the common good. Once again, it is the grace of promise that fuels and gives direction to the engine of commitment. Nonetheless, it is not easy to proclaim and pursue justice, peace, and the common good in a world where evil designs so frequently seem to go unthwarted and inequities appear to increase rather than decrease. We need to be en*couraged.*

In all the synoptic gospels (Mt. 17:1–8; Mk. 9:2–8; Lk. 9:28–36) we find the account of Jesus' transfiguration. He was preparing to go to Jerusalem and enter into the events of his passion and crucifixion. He had told his disciples of the fate that awaited him. They went up to a mountain to pray, and while they were there he was transfigured. He shone with glory, and the Father's voice from heaven proclaimed him the Chosen, the beloved Son.

Given all the rejection, treachery, and suffering that lay before him, this glimpse of glory on the Mount of Transfiguration must have been very important to Jesus. It must have given him courage and resolve to go forward on his fateful journey.

We too need glimpses of glory to sustain us along the way and renew our courage. Of course, we have seen that glory in the bright light of Easter morning. We rejoice in that revelation. Yet God is gracious, and the power of that grace gives us further glimpses of the glory that will one day cover all things.

In our urbanized world the evils that arise out of poverty, unemployment, and racism take the lives of young men and women, destroy families, breed crime, and leave helpless children in poverty. For as long as most of us can remember, we have talked of such things, have lamented, have wrung our hands, have backed this program or that program or this candidate or that candidate, but we are still talking of it, and it seems that progress never gets beyond terminating failed initiatives. However, in the midst of all our desultory reflections, we are presented with examples of Christian congregations in some of the most challenging settings who reach out to organize and renew the communities to which they minister. They muster the expertise to do it, and their faith carries them through. People for whom there was little hope now see new beginnings, and we all see a glimpse of glory.[22]

Our advocates in Congress for the needs of the underserved bang on the doors of a chamber that seems only to care about giving people their money back. Why bother? That is the temptation. Yet in the midst of frustration, Christian people throughout the land were making paper chains so that their representatives see how much they care about launching a modern jubilee to forgive the debt of countries under the thumb of unrelieved poverty. It was a movement laughed at when it first began. It is laughed at no more. In fact, Congress has responded, and the initiative continues to ensure that our government will continue to respond. So we have a glimpse of glory, a shaft of light coursing through the cracks in our worldly cynicism. It is a beam of energy to restart our hearts and a reminder of our eucharistic hope for the heavenly banquet when all will have a place at the table.

So many people are virtually discarded, an unwanted burden in their infancy, in their homelessness, with their prison record, in their old age. Their numbers are staggering. We have a strong desire to look the other way, because to look directly at the reality is simply too painful. Yet in the midst of our uneasy denial, we discover the myriad of Christian social ministries that are placing children in foster homes and permanent homes, providing places and sustenance for the homeless with services of rehabilitation, offering programs to help ex-offenders reenter society with dignity, and caring for the frail elderly. It is a glimpse of glory, the glory of God embodied in the grace-filled lives of thousands of caring people, the promise in the psalmist's elated cry that God has come to life and that God is one who puts desolate people into families.

We can see multiple examples of how the glory of God's love and the hope of its promise are manifest among us in our broken world. For some, I suppose, such examples are a drop in the bucket and not very significant. However, for those who have embraced the promise of God in Christ with the arms of faith and hope, these moments of justice and compassion are the source of renewed strength and conviction, a blessing added to the promise.

In a troubled world it is natural to seek security and minimize our risks. The call to serve our neighbors and seek justice, peace, and the common good involves risk, however. It opens us to the needs of the world and the demands on our love and our resources that follow. It calls on us to have the trust of faith, faith that God's promise is sure and that life will flourish where God's will is done. Faith active in love seeking justice is really quite beyond us. However, once again, as Paul told the Corinthian Christians, God is faithful, God has claimed us, God will sustain us. Amazing grace is also enabling grace.

7

"The Politics of Compassion"[1]

WILLIAM SLOANE COFFIN

One of the great church people in this hemisphere is Archbishop Helder Camara of Recife, Brazil. I once heard him say, with a broad smile and in a heavy accent: "Right hand, left hand—both belong to ze same body but ze heart is a little to ze left."

I tell you this story because I too believe that "ze heart is a little to ze left." You don't have to give socialist answers, but you do have to press socialist questions. These are the ones that point toward greater social justice.

In religious faith, simplicity comes in at least two distinct forms. One lies on the near side of complexity. Those of us who embrace this kind of simple faith dislike, in fact are frightened by, complexity. We hold certainty dearer than truth. We prefer obedience to discernment. Too many of us bear out Charles Darwin's contention that ignorance more frequently begets confidence than does knowledge. And apparently such religious folk were as abundant in Jesus' time as they clearly are in ours. Also in Jesus' time as in ours, conventional religious wisdom stressed correct belief and right behavior.

Then there is the religious simplicity that lies on the far side of complexity. That's where, I believe, we must look for Jesus and his message. I believe that when all is said and done, when every subtle thing has been dissected and analyzed every which way, Jesus' message remains incredibly simple, unbelievably beautiful, and as easy to translate into action as for a camel to pass through the eye of a needle.

Nowhere is this simple message more clearly stated than in the parable of the good Samaritan. I hardly need remind you that the two men who passed by on the other side, the priest and the Levite, were considered the most religious persons in the Israelite community, dedicated as they were to the preservation of the faith through full-time religious service. But the third man–the one who showed mercy, who had compassion, who proved to be a neighbor to the bleeding man on the side of the road–this Samaritan was only part-Jew and believed only part of the Jewish scripture. To Jews, Samaritans were heretics; Samaria was a dangerous place. Yet it was the heretic, the enemy, the man of the wrong faith who did the right thing while the two men of the right faith flunked.

The same simple, subversive message comes through in Jesus' other well-known parable. Of course we tend to identify with the older brother of the prodigal son because, like him, we want the irresponsible kid to get what he deserves. But the prodigal love of the father insists that the son get not what he deserves but what he needs–forgiveness, a fresh start–which is exactly what–thank God–God gives all of us. We can't be relieved of the consequences of our sin, but we can be relieved of the consequences of being sinners; for there is more mercy in God than sin in us. Wrong behavior is not the last word.

The culture of his time prevented Saint Paul from seeing many things, but the simplicity, beauty, and difficulty of Jesus' message was not one of them. He ends 1 Corinthians 13 with this: "And now faith, hope, and love abide, these three; and the greatest of these is *love*." And he begins the next chapter this way: "Pursue love"–or "Make love your aim."

Make love your aim, not biblical inerrancy or purity or obedience to holiness codes. Make love your aim, for "if I speak with the tongues...of angels"–musicians, poets, preachers, you are being addressed–"and if I...understand all mysteries and all knowledge"–professors, your turn–"and if I give away all my possessions"–radicals, take note–"and if I hand over my body"–the very stuff of heroism–"but do not have love, I gain nothing." I doubt if in any other scriptures of the world there is a more radical statement of ethics: If we fail in love, we fail in all things else.

So Socrates was mistaken: it's not the unexamined life that is not worth living; it's the uncommitted life. There is no smaller package in the world than that of a person all wrapped up in himself or herself. Love is our business; if we can't love, we're out of business. And all this Christians learn primarily through the words and deeds of that "love divine all loves excelling, joy of heaven to earth come down."

In short, love is the core value of Christian life. And the better to understand what we're saying, let's briefly review four major ethical stages in history. Most people shudder when they hear "an eye for an eye" and "a tooth for a tooth." But far from commanding revenge, the law insists that a person must never take more than *one* eye for an eye, never more than *one* tooth for a tooth. Found in the book of Exodus, this law became necessary to guard against the normal way people had of doing business, namely, unlimited retaliation: "Kill my cat and I'll kill yours, your dog, your mule, and you too."

The father/mother of unlimited retaliation is, of course, the notion that might makes right, an uncivilized concept if ever there was one and one that to this day governs the actions of many so-called civilized nations. So limited retaliation is certainly an improvement over unlimited retaliation: "Get even, but no more." Limited retaliation is what most people have in mind when they speak of criminal justice: "You did the crime, you do the time." Limited retaliation is also the justification most frequently used for capital punishment, the most premeditated form of killing in the world.

Unlimited retaliation, limited retaliation. A third stage might be called limited love. In Leviticus 19:18 it is written: "You shall not take vengeance or bear a grudge against any of your people, but you shall love your neighbor as yourself."

Again, a step forward. Limited love is better than limited retaliation, and limited love can be very moving–a mother's love for her child, children's love for their parents. But when the neighbor to be loved has been limited to one of one's own people, then limited love, historically, has supported such things as white supremacy, religious bigotry, the Nazi notion of *Herrenvolk,* and "America for Americans" (which never included Native Americans). Actually, limited love is often more self-serving than generous, as Jesus himself recognized when he said, "If you love those who love you, what reward do you have? Do not even the tax collectors do the same? And if you greet only your brothers and sisters, what more are you doing than others? Do not even the Gentiles do the same?" (Mt. 5:46–47).

Jesus, of course, was pressing for a fourth state, unlimited love, the love that is of God, the love you give when you make a gift of yourself, no preconditions, no strings attached. And the neighbor to be loved according to the parable of the good Samaritan is the nearest person in need regardless of race, religion, or nationality, and we can safely add gender or sexual orientation.

Such was the love that Saint Paul extolled; such was the love of God when at Christmas God gave the world that God so loved, not what it deserved but what it needed, God's only begotten son "so that everyone who believes in him may not perish but may have eternal life" (Jn. 3:16).

In order to live for all of us, to strive for the unified advance of the human species, we have to recognize that just as there are two kinds of simplicity–one on the near, the other on the far side of complexity–so there are two kinds of love: one on this side of justice, the other on the far side.

Said the prophet Amos: "Let justice"–not charity–"roll down like waters" (Am. 5:24), and for good reason: whereas charity alleviates the effects of poverty, justice seeks to eliminate the causes of it. Charity is a matter of personal attribute; justice is a matter of public policy.

To picture justice as central, not ancillary, to the gospel often demands a recasting of a childhood faith. Many of us were brought up to believe that what counts is a personal relationship with God, inner peace, kindness to others, and a home in heaven when all our years have passed. And many of us never get over the religion of our childhood that we either loved or hated. Either way the results are disastrous.

It is also true that many pastors deliberately perpetuate a childish version of the faith, particularly if they are ministers of mainline middle-class churches, for, not surprisingly, they find it easier to talk to their congregations about charity than about justice. Charity, after all, threatens not at all the status quo that may be profitable to a goodly number of their parishioners. Justice, on the other hand, leads directly to political controversy.

So there is a real temptation to think that an issue is less spiritual for being more political, to believe that religion is above politics, that the sanctuary is too sacred a place for the grit and grime of political battle. But if you believe that religion is above politics, you are, in actuality, in favor of the status quo—a very political position. And were God the god of the status quo, then the church would have no prophetic role, serving the state mainly as a kind of ambulance service.

In the 1990s, both the Million Man March and the Promise Keepers let the political order off the hook. Theirs was a purely spiritual message that just happened to parallel the antigovernment message of the Republicans.

By contrast, Martin Luther King, Jr., led the 1963 March on Washington and later the Poor People's March to confront the government, to put the government on notice.

The Christian right talks a lot about "traditional values" and "family values." Almost always these values relate to personal rather than social morality, for the Christian right has trouble not only seeing love as the core value of personal life but seeing love as the core value of our communal life—the love that lies on the far side of justice. Without question, family responsibility, hard work, compassion, kindness, religious piety—all these individual virtues are of enduring importance. But again, personal morality doesn't threaten the status quo. Furthermore, public good doesn't automatically follow from private virtue. A person's moral character, sterling though it may be, is insufficient to serve the cause of justice, which is to challenge the status quo, to try to make what's legal more moral, to speak truth to power, and to take personal or concerned actions against evil, whether in personal or systemic form.

It is no accident that the welfare reform bill is called the Personal Responsibility Act. Most talk of responsibility these days is directed at the most powerless people in our society. If you believe, as do so many members of the Christian right, that the ills of society stem largely from the carelessness and moral failures of America's poor; if you separate economic issues from cultural concerns; if you can't see that economic coercion is violence in slow motion, that it is the economy that consigns millions to the status of the unwanted, unused, discarded; then you find little need to talk of homelessness, poverty, hunger, or inadequate medical care, for these are created by illegitimacy, laziness, and drugs, and are abetted by welfare dependency and sexual deviation. To the Christian right, the American underclass is far more a moral phenomenon than an economic one.

In this fashion the theological individualism of the religious right serves its political and economic conservatism; the victim is blamed for a situation that is largely systemic. What the religious right persists in ignoring is that although self-help is important, self-help alone will not solve the problems of the poor. And to blame the poor for their oppression and to affirm the affluent in their complacency, to oppose sexual permissiveness and say not a word about the permissiveness of consumerism—which insists that it is right to buy, wrong to defer almost any gratification—these positions are anything but biblical.

Clearly, the love that lies on the far side of justice demands a communal sense of responsibility for and a sense of complicity in the very evils we abhor.

Rabbi Abraham Joshua Heschel, a mentor to so many of my generation, constantly contended that in a free society "some are guilty, but all are responsible."

This is why poverty is a communal failure. It is hardly the fault of those Americans willing, even desperate, to work that there are simply more unskilled workers than unskilled jobs and nowhere near the money necessary for training people to land jobs that would lift them out of poverty. Or consider these two facts: (1) a child of affluent parents is six times more likely to have an undergraduate degree than a child of poor parents; and (2) the odds are three to one that a pregnant teenager is poor, which suggests that poverty traps girls in pregnancy more than pregnancy traps girls in poverty.

Without question, education is the best way out of dead-end jobs and welfare dependency. Lack of it, then, is another communal failure. A recent study in the state of Washington showed that 36 percent of those on welfare had learning disabilities that never had been remedied. Crime is a communal failure. We're not tough on crime, only on criminals. Were we tough on crime, we'd put the money to fight it up front, in prevention rather than in punishment. We'd be building healthier communities, not more and more prisons. "Some are guilty, but all are responsible." We stress the guilty in order to exonerate the responsible.

In short, it is not enough to be a good Samaritan, not when from north Philadelphia to east Oakland, whole communities lie bleeding in the ditch. What the poor need today is not piecemeal charity but wholesale justice.

And that's what is so lacking today. "The comfortable are in control," as John Kenneth Galbraith wrote a short while ago, and largely because, as one pundit put it, "We have the best Congress money can buy." Until we

Americans get serious about reforming campaign financing, our politicians will increasingly serve as lapdogs of the rich.

When I was a boy in public school, I was told that there are rich people and poor people—no connection. When I came to New York, I was told that this was the most exciting city in the world, but "we do have problems"—a lot of poor people. When I read the Bible, I find that the poor are never the problem. It's always the rich who are a problem to the poor, as Oscar Romero, the martyred monsignor of El Salvador, recognized so movingly. Never did he call the poor of his country *los pobres.* He called them *los enpobrecidos,* those *made* poor. Surely we should also be calling America's poor "the impoverished," especially when we see our Congress reversing the priorities of Mary's Magnificat, filling the rich with good things and sending away the poor empty. Why, the way we are cutting taxes for the wealthy and social programs for the poor, you'd think the greedy were needy and the needy were greedy!

Jesus was certainly something more than a prophet but surely nothing less. And that means, once again, that the love that is the core value of our individual lives should also be the core value of our life together. Love has a corporate character as well as a personal one. So just as the simplicity we should embrace lies on the far side of complexity, so the love we should embrace lies on the far side of justice, never on the near side. This understanding is crucial today, when, as I said, it is no longer an individual who lies bleeding in the ditch but whole communities in city after city across the land.

We Americans have so much, and we're asking so little of ourselves. What we are downsizing more than anything else are the demands of biblical justice.

Let Christians remember how Jesus was concerned most for those that society counted least and put last. Let us all remember what Gandhi and King never forgot—that for its implementation compassion frequently demands confrontation. I said at the outset that conventional religious wisdom in Jesus' time stressed correct belief and right behavior. Conventional religious wisdom in America does the same today.

To many American evangelists, faith is a goody that they got and others didn't, an extraordinary degree of certainty that most can't achieve. This kind of faith is dangerous, for it can be and often is worn as a merit badge or used as a club to clobber others.

In contrast, Saint Paul sees faith as confidence in the face of *not* knowing. "For we walk by faith, not by sight" (2 Cor. 5:7). Saint Paul's faith is a thankful response to grace, to the outpouring of God's love, that persistently seeks to get everything right in this world, including us. Such a faith is never exclusive, always inclusive and deeply ethical, never moralistic.

Jesus subverted the conventional religious wisdom of his time. I think we have to do the same. The answer to bad evangelism is not no evangelism, but good evangelism; and good evangelism is not proselytizing, but witnessing, bearing witness to "the light [that] shines in the darkness, and [that] the darkness did not overcome" (Jn. 1:5); bearing witness to the love that burns in every heart, deny it or suppress it as we will; and bearing witness to our version of the truth just as the other side witnesses to its version of the truth—let's face it, truth in its pure essence eludes us all.

And that's where I think a Christian should stand, one whose heart is "a little to ze left."

"Sitting Down to Eat or Standing Up to Life"

LEWIS H. KAMRASS

Patience is a virtue. So said that venerable American sage Ben Franklin. Long before they knew about stress, blood pressure, and the many other indicators of our fast-paced lives, he knew it then. We must remember the virtue of patience in our hectic world. For increasingly, we are not patient; and often, we are impatient about the most insignificant things. We lose our good nature with an incompetent clerk in a store, or a slow server in a restaurant, or the misnomer of fast food. Most of us have become impatient on the road, as evidenced by the names we hurl at another driver, or the frustrating sound of horns blaring, or, even worse, road rage flaring. We are impatient about how long the connection time takes with Internet providers when it means our messages take three minutes instead of one to communicate and deliver. In this speed-addicted generation, patience truly is a virtue.

And yet sometimes we find ourselves far too patient when it comes to the most significant things. Why is it that we are so frustrated and impatient with insignificant things, yet are far too willing to be patient with the wrong that persists in those things that matter most? What does it say of us as a society when basic injustices exist, poverty amid affluence, intolerance within a sea of diversity, isolationism in a world where America is the only major power, children who do not receive healthcare or housing in history's most affluent society, the exponential rise in spending for luxury items but not in charitable giving? How appalling is our willingness to be patient with all the wrong things! With all due respect to the wisdom of Ben Franklin,

I would like to suggest that only sometimes is patience a virtue. For sometimes, it is also a sin.

We were too patient with the American government's response during the Holocaust. We were too patient with ethnic violence and bloodshed in distant lands, and certainly in this last decade, when genocide reared its ugly head again in Africa and in Europe. We were too patient with the immoral core of Communism. We are too patient with our government in addressing real poverty and basic human needs. We are too patient in our gleaming suburbs when our cities decay and crumble. Such patience is a real sin.

There is a well-known story of Nikita Khrushchev, late premier of the former Soviet Union. In the middle of a speech denouncing the corruption and terror of his predecessor, Khrushchev was interrupted by a voice in the audience: "And where were *you* during this time?" Khrushchev angrily demanded to know, "Who said that?" When no one from the audience dared to respond, Khrushchev quietly replied, "*That's* where I was."

There is another story, one from our own tradition. We are all too familiar with the tale of Joseph, the young dreamer of dreams who annoyed his older brothers to no end. Sheltered and favored by his father, he was sent out on the road to find his brothers. When they saw him coming, they conspired to kill him, taking off his coveted striped coat and placing him into a pit. And then we read one curious phrase in that story. Immediately after acting on the plan of fratricide, in earshot of Joseph's anguished pleas for rescue and mercy, the Torah says of the brothers, "*Va-yeshvu le-echol lechem* (Then they sat down to eat)" (Gen. 37:25).

They sat down to a meal? How could it be? Their brother cried out to them for his life, and they sat down to eat? The ancient rabbis (Exodus Rabbah 41:7) tell us that on six different occasions in the Bible the act of sitting down results in some disastrous event. Although the results differ, the act of sitting down in a fragile moment is a portent of some sin to come. These few words of Torah, "*Va-yeshvu le-echol, lechem,* (then they sat down to eat)" are both a penetrating instruction and an abiding challenge to us. For sitting down to eat means turning away from the urgency of the moment, to the small details of our private lives. Sitting down to eat in the face of injustice or danger means we become too patient with life's significant issues. Sitting down to eat means we are anesthetized to the pain of others. Sitting down to eat is a commentary on lives that are deaf to the cries of our brothers and sisters who are in the pit. *And this is not the Jewish way.* Sitting down to eat in the face of evil, injustice, or danger is the sin of indifference. And let me say on this Yom Kippur, we are all sinners. Our sin is that we are too patient. "*Va-yeshvu le-echol lechem.*" We sit down to eat, turning away from others.

As we sit here today, AIDS is devastating not only some people, but an entire continent. In less than a generation since it was first diagnosed,

AIDS has killed nineteen million people in the world. In many African nations, it is expected to wipe out half of the teenagers. In seven sub-Saharan African countries, more than a fifth of the population ages fifteen to forty-nine is HIV positive. This plague is not only affecting the victims but entire societies. More than thirteen million children have been orphaned by AIDS. Economic and agricultural resources in these countries are in decline. Already fragile medical delivery systems are strained. Education is in shambles.[1] But that pit is far from our lunch table. We hear little about it, and when we do, we turn our ears away from the cries and our eyes away from the grim photos and depressing images. We have our own issues at home, we say. "*Va-yeshvu le-echol lechem.*" We sit down to eat and we turn away.

Closer to home, we hear the news of Columbine and other high schools plagued by the horror of violence and guns. We watch in shock when a gun-carrying man invades a Jewish day-care program. Children in the United States are more than ten times as likely to be victims of violence than children in the other twenty-five developed nations combined.[2] In 1998, guns killed ten thousand Americans, while that same year only nineteen Japanese died of gun casualties. And the weapons that kill are no longer handguns, but a new generation of assault weapons and machine guns. Do we want our nation to be characterized by such violent statistics as these? Pervasive violence bombards our youth in their own living rooms. Combining television and movies, studies find that the typical American child will observe forty thousand dramatizations of killing by the time he or she reaches age eighteen.[3] Is this the food for their souls with which we want to raise a generation? We reason that we have little power in the face of Hollywood and gun lobbies. So our youth go to school each day, play gory video games, and watch movies that glamorize violence. Like our patriarch Joseph, they are placed into a pit. And while their well-being is jeopardized, *Va-yeshvu le-echol lechem,* we sit down to eat, and we turn away.

Far too many children in this affluent nation dwell in poverty. We see images on the news of the families who live in cars and under bridges. We hear the laments of people who are working full-time in low-wage jobs, who cannot afford healthcare for their children, or who cannot pay the rent at the beginning of each month. Ensuring our own children's high-quality education, we turn a deaf ear to other children who live only miles away, but light years apart. Affluence and opportunity abound for those of us who dwell outside the pit, and yet the pit is nearby, filled with voices crying for rescue and mercy. *Va-yeshvu le-echol lechem.* We sit down to eat, and we turn away.

Of course we have reasons for our well-intentioned indifference. We are paralyzed by our finitude in face of the infinite proportion of the problems. The momentum of the status quo is strong. Besides, we are busy. With our jobs, our families, and our neighborhood concerns, we have little left for other problems, especially those on the other side of the globe or those who seem hopelessly encased in systems and institutions. We ask ourselves, what difference could one person make?

But we are never just one person. The power of an idea *and* a group is limitless. We have seen it in every age. And every cause needs an army of foot soldiers, supporters, and leaders, all working together to transform ideas, enthusiasm, and passion into progress. That is how problems are addressed, injustices corrected, and devastation eased. Yes, we have our own complicated lives that consume our energies and our commitments. We cannot solve all the problems of others. But can we turn away? Can we allow ourselves the luxury of patience and indifference?

Our ancient rabbis teach us that Sodom and Gomorrah were destroyed not because their inhabitants were all evil, but because they turned the other way and permitted evil. Their sin was to sit and eat bread while all around them others suffered and perpetuated suffering. Each year the Day of Atonement asks us difficult questions: Do we have a passionate issue in our lives that transcends self, family, and immediate circle of friends? What are we going to do about the stirring in our souls that occurs whenever we truly look, and don't turn away, from the images and cries of suffering in our world? Have we been too patient for too long? What cries can we no longer allow ourselves indifferently to sit and eat through?

As Jews, an indifference that is acceptable to others must be *un*acceptable to us. For we Jews have been chosen to be different in life. To be a Jew means not to accept the world as it is, for we are meant to dream of what it might be. God's presence in our lives gives us the strength to be different, not indifferent. As Jews we refuse to accept what others find acceptable, never content with the status quo. For we have the voice of God echoing in our ears, as did Abraham, Isaac, Jacob, and Joseph, urging us to reach higher. And that is why one finds Jews at the forefront of nearly every movement for social change. It is why we are activists. It is what it means to be a light unto the nations. We must live by a different standard, one that is often more rigorous, yet always schooled in justice. And most of all, it means rejecting the seduction of the prevailing indifference and apathy that surround us. Refusing to heed the call of the false gods of other cultures, we listen for the cry from the pit that recalls us to our covenant of brotherhood, a covenant rooted in a God who is faithful to that covenant and who empowers us to our own fulfillment of it with one another.

This is our history and our calling: to live for *tikun olam,* for repairing the world's brokenness. And it begins by examining closely our place at the world's table. It begins by rejecting the temptation to sit and eat bread while others cry out from the pit. It begins by choosing to go beyond our personal and pressing needs to the needs of the world community with whom we are linked. It begins by resolving in our hearts that we are connected to the devastation in distant Africa, to oppressed peoples throughout the world, to the horrors of a dilapidated city, to the inadequate school in another neighborhood, to *some* cry to which we will *not* turn an indifferent ear.

As we reflect on our deeds of the past and our resolve for the future, let us resolve to be impatient with the world's most urgent cries. Choosing life means working for just change. It means finding something that stirs our hearts and touches our souls and then working with others in its cause.

> O God who hearkens to our pleas and to those of the world, stir us to be impatient with injustice, with plague and disease, with poverty and despair. Most of all, challenge us to be impatient with our own indifference, that we might truly hear the urgent cries of those souls whose anguish calls out to us from the pit. Guide us to rejoice in our blessing, not merely by sitting down to eat in our own insulated privacy, but by standing up for purpose, remembering it is for this that we are called to life. Then will our prayers for the world be answered, and then will our own search for meaning be fulfilled. Amen.

"Not Innocent or Perfect, Just Faithful: Dealing with Racism"

MELANIE MOREL SULLIVAN

Racism has been called "America's fault line" and our country's original sin. Some social scientists think that racism is the template for all the other "isms" or oppressions that work together to separate people from one another.

The United States Civil Rights Commission defines racism as any attitude or institutional structure that subordinates a person or group because of skin color. Another definition used by many denominations and antiracism organizations is "racism = racial prejudice + institutional/systemic power." This way of defining racism emphasizes that racism is not merely personal bigotry based on skin color, but racial prejudice combined with economic, political, and social power—power that is legitimized and institutionalized throughout society. Racism essentially isolates, exploits, and discriminates against certain people on the basis of their racial and ethnic characteristics, which reinforces the superiority of the racial and ethnic identity of the dominant group. In effect, racism says that some human beings are more precious to God than others.

In the 1960s it was relatively easy for liberal whites to feel we were on the side of the angels. The outward signs of legal racism were blatant and obvious—"Whites Only" signs; legally segregated schools, transportation facilities, and entertainment; rampant cross burnings; fire hoses turned on children; bombings and shootings where the perpetrators are found "not guilty" by all-white juries. This kind of racism—let's call it traditional or historic racism—is easy to spot and was remedied by the passage of Voting

Rights and Civil Rights legislation, but only *after* the nation's conscience was aroused in 1965 by the murders of *white* Civil Rights activists.

Racism today is different; it's a "new and improved" replacement for continuing the oppression of people of color and upholding white supremacy in ways that are more subtle, more indirect, and thus all the more efficient and effective. The old racism said, "Get rid of the niggers!" The new racism says, "Affirmative action is unfair, paternalistic, and a form of 'reverse racism.'" The old racism explicitly provided separate and inferior schools for children of color. The new racism moves all the middle-class and upper-middle-class white folks out and away from black people and urban tax districts. The same results—separate and inferior schools for black students—just more subtle means of implementation. The old racism made black small businesses and professionals necessary and vital, since African Americans were legally unable to use the comparable white services. The new racism destroys black small businesses by redlining neighborhoods, denying small-business loans to black business owners, and encouraging white developers to level areas deemed "urban blight." Black professionals are allowed token placements in white corporations, but their numbers are few, and the glass ceiling is low and thick. The old racism was up-front and in your face; the new racism thrives on denial and invisibility.[1]

It was easy to see who was at fault under the old regime of traditional racism with the contorted red faces of screaming whites in the streets, the wildly swinging batons of white deputies, the smug closed expressions of white elected officials blocking doorways—those were the markers of hate, fear, and prejudice that we witnessed on our black-and-white TV sets.

The "kinder, gentler" form of today's racism makes assigning blame more difficult. Neo-racism wants to put the blame for those who are oppressed on individual bad choices or personal character flaws, rather than on the interlocking socioeconomic conditions that condone, support, and profit from racism. Neo-racism, like classism, says that people on the bottom have only themselves to blame. In other words, nonwhites are the bad guys, and white society excuses itself from responsibility.

I sympathize with those who want to cling to a sense of purity and innocence. I want to be innocent too—in fact, if anyone can claim innocence, it's me and people like me. My parents were both Civil Rights activists in Louisiana during the 1960s. Our phone rang at all hours of the night, and threats to firebomb our house were commonplace. I was absolutely forbidden to say the word *nigger,* even to quote someone else. To this day the word sticks in my throat. I have never felt or expressed or participated in overt prejudice against people of color. I have marched in demonstrations and chanted at rallies. But I know for a fact that I have gained, over and over again, oftentimes without my direct knowledge and almost always without my consent, from the system and institution of racism in our country. The system is set up to benefit people of my skin color, and benefit I have.

I have come to accept–slowly, reluctantly, painfully–that I am not innocent, and I know now that none of us is.

Several of you have already commented to me that this sermon series is bothering you, making you uncomfortable, getting under your skin.[2] "You want us to be perfect," one person told me. "This stuff [ableism and classism] is natural, it's part of being human," another said. "You're making us feel guilty," a third said. My brothers and sisters, I don't want or expect us to be perfect, and I agree that fear and prejudice are, to a degree, inborn in human beings–though I'd *never* agree that biology is destiny. And guilt is a paralyzing emotion, more often keeping us "stuck" rather than motivating us to act effectively.

The good news is that we are called by God, not to be perfect or pure or innocent, but to be *faithful,* faithful to our principles and values and faithful to our covenant. Our first principle is not "the perfection and total goodness of every human person" but the "inherent worth and dignity of every human person."[3] Our sixth principle does not proclaim the goal of "world utopia" but of "world community with peace, liberty, and justice for all." Our seventh principle, the interdependent web of all existence, of which we are a part, reminds us that we cannot separate ourselves from the work that must be done. Our Universalist heritage lets us know that diminishment of the full humanity of one group of people diminishes and devalues us all. Our Universalist ancestors preached the good news of universal salvation, not because they thought *nobody* ever sinned, but because they knew *everybody* did and that God our gracious parent loves us and forgives us anyway. Even in our modern, more inclusive spirituality, we are called to this work. In the Buddhist tradition, a true *boddhisattva* will refuse nirvana until all living beings are released from suffering.

What can best reverse the effects and power of neo-racism is loving community, empowered with knowledge and understanding, united across all the categories of human difference to work toward the end of oppression and oppressive structures. Notice that the solution takes love linked with both knowledge and understanding. This is vital, and if you take nothing else away from this sermon, take this: love is not enough; good intentions are not enough. For white people to unite with people of color to undo racism we must be armed with compassion, a spirit of loving fellowship, a conviction that we are all of us children of the same loving God, *and* we must also educate ourselves and gain understanding of the experiences and lives of all people of color living in our country.

"As a white person in America, I do not have to think about racism and prejudice everyday. I can pick and choose when and where I wish to respond to racism and bigotry."[4] If you want to know what you can start doing today, right now, to start making things better, that would be it: choose to be responsible, to be aware, to notice, to think more about racism, to educate yourself about all you don't know about the lives of people of color and the system within which we all live. Let us be responsible, even if we are not necessarily the guilty parties. Let us make the choice to be in solidarity with all who are oppressed—with those who are disabled; with those discriminated against because of their skin color; with those who are poor; with gay, lesbian, and transgender people; with all those in need not just of care and concern but also of the power and the advocacy that we can give as members of the dominant social group in our society. Let us educate ourselves and use the power and influence we have been given as white, straight, temporarily able-bodied, middle-class people, to work for justice and equity. Let us ask our leaders some hard questions: Why are most of the homeless in our city black? Why is there so little affordable housing outside the projects? Who benefits from things as they are? Who doesn't? Our society was designed, not by God, but by human beings, and we have the power to make necessary changes to bring about peace, justice, and wholeness.

Let us resolve never to be silent or passive in the face of blatant injustice, but let us not fail to perceive the indirect and subtle injustices that surround us. Let us do this work because we are called by God to do this work, and when we do it we are doing the work of God. I leave you with this prayer by Icelandic Unitarian leader V. Emil Gudmundson:

> And now, may we have faith in life to do wise planting that the generations to come may reap even more abundantly than we. May we be bold in bringing to fruition the golden dreams of human kinship and justice. This we ask that the fields of promise might become fields of reality.

Amen—Ashe—Shalom—Namaste—Blessed Be!

PART 3

God's Stake in Just Preaching

Most preachers struggle with the image of the avenging God who swoops in with harsh judgment on those who prey on the weak. They love the image from a distance, in much the way that most of us like to see the movie hero/vigilante take on the bad guys and circumvent the always too slow and too blind legal system, bringing much needed quick and decisive justice.

Such struggle is not because preachers lack appreciation for the prophetic prowess of people such as Martin Luther King, Jr., Rather, preachers stand perplexed and often paralyzed at how prophetic ministry can be implemented on a week-to-week basis in churches and synagogues, where they know that every wound opened on a holy day must be bound up the next week and where they know that those whom they indict are the same ones who sign their paychecks.

And yet there is a God who bleeds because of the shape of our world. The preacher witnesses this bleeding whenever he or she reads the prophets, ancient or contemporary. Carrying forward the prophetic mantle into the present means being faithful scribes of the old prophetic traditions as well as from time to time being inspired prophets in the face of today's injustices.

The authors of this section make clear that God is not neutral regarding the affairs of this world. Rather, God takes passionate interest in the down-and-dirty business of human commerce, access to society's privileges, and basic matters of human decency and welfare. Where such matters are manipulated by the powerful for their own benefit and to the detriment of the most vulnerable, the communities of faith—and especially its preachers and prophets—are always called to speak up and act out for redrawing of the lines, in ways both large and small, for no act done or word spoken in harmony with God's vision and purposes for human community and society goes wasted.

Ancient Utterance and Contemporary Hearing

WALTER BRUEGGEMANN

The radical faith of ancient Israel in the Old Testament, perched on the lips of the prophets, continues in our own time as a particular, concrete, and urgent imperative about power, money, goods, and access.

I

These prophetic voices in ancient Israel did not appear *de novo*, but were long schooled in deep traditions about the character, will, and purpose of the God who created heaven and earth.

First, the God uttered by the prophets is already known and celebrated in Israel's deepest, oldest doxologies. This is who YHWH has been–in the purview of Israel–from the outset; it is not possible to go behind the doxologies to find a less committed God, for these cadences of praise are the deepest sounds that Israel can imagine or utter. Thus, the temple choirs, perhaps borrowing from older, pre-Israelite phrasing, sang without reservation:

> Father of orphans and protector of widows
> is God in [God's] holy habitation.
> God gives the desolate a home to live in;
> [God] leads out the prisoners to prosperity,
> but the rebellious live in a parched land. (Ps. 68:5–6)

> The LORD sets the prisoners free;
> the LORD opens the eyes of the blind.

The LORD lifts up those who are bowed down;
    the LORD loves the righteous.
The LORD watches over the strangers;
    [the LORD] upholds the orphan and the widow,
    but the way of the wicked [the LORD] brings to ruin.
                                                (Ps. 146:7c–9)

Imagine what it was like to hear these affirmations sung regularly! The doxologies do not doubt the immense power and large sovereignty of the God here praised.

That YHWH's power and sovereignty are mobilized in the direction of the marginal is astonishing. Both songs portray the God of Israel as actively, powerfully engaged. Both songs identify YHWH's particular attentiveness to those whom the world wants to make invisible. Both songs identify as a special concern widows who are without a male protector in a patriarchal society. Both songs reference orphans who are vulnerable. Both songs comment on prisons because, already in that ancient world, prison was a place for the poor, who had no adequate means of self-defense and so were at the mercy of exploitation and greed. Both songs, moreover, voice a threat to "the rebellious" (68:6), "the wicked" (146:9) who do not share these passions for a reordered society.

Second, Israel's songs of YHWH's peculiar social intentions are matched in Israel's most elemental *narrative memory,* which was regularly recited as an identifying mark of this community. Thus, in the Passover narrative, Israel remembered how its own unbearable pain became the key datum of life and faith: "The Israelites groaned under their slavery, and cried out. Out of the slavery their cry for help rose up to God" (Ex. 2:23).

Israel remembered that the pain of oppression and abuse was so intolerable that it simply required out-loud expression that could not be stifled any longer in conformity. The cry of pain was not addressed by Israel to anyone in particular but simply needed to be sounded.

Israel, however, remembered more than the fact that crying was the initiating point for Israel's narrative memory of rescue. Israel also remembered who was, unexpectedly, on the receiving end of that cry as it "rose up to God." This God was remembered as the magnet that drew the cry of social pain toward God's own life, so that the cry had a decisive impact on this God and evoked in God a new, decisive response: "God heard their groaning, and God remembered [God's] covenant with Abraham, Isaac, and Jacob. God looked upon the Israelites, and God took notice of them" (Ex. 2:24–25).

This is a remembered characterization of a God who is *reachable* by voiced pain and who responds in transformative ways to such a cry. In response to the cry, "God heard, God remembered, God saw, God noticed"; in 3:7–8, moreover, added to this series of verbs is a final one: "I have come down to deliver." This exchange of cry and response sets in motion the stunning narrative drama of chapters 3–15 whereby the slave band in Egypt is transformed into a people covenanted to YHWH; conversely, Pharaoh, emblem of rapacious power in the world, is reduced to nonpower, shown to be a hopeless bully (see 8:18 on the impotence of Pharaoh and his agents). Thus, the God celebrated in the doxologies of Israel is the one who comes to specific action in Israel's narratives.

Third, beyond the world offered in Israel's narratives that witness to an alternative God, Israel moved from narrative to commandment and assured that the same responsive concern of YHWH functions as guarantee and sanction for law. This is evident in two early laws. First, Exodus 22:21–22 has a pair of negative imperatives:

> You shall not wrong or oppress a resident alien…You shall not abuse any widow or orphan.

This is the same "widow and orphan" we have seen in the doxologies of Psalms 68 and 146. Now to these is added the "resident alien," a new category that became a third element of the socially vulnerable who must have special "entitled" protection.

But it is especially the sanction for this pair of commands that interests us.[1] After an appeal to the exodus memory in Exodus 22:21b, the primary sanction is that a protesting cry by the abused will indeed be heard by the God who has heard the slave cry and is mobilized by such a cry of pain. The threat from this God, commensurate with the threat to the rebellious in Psalm 68 and against the wicked in Psalm 146, is that the wives of the abusers will become widows and the children of the abusers will become orphans. That is, the status of the abuser population will become as wretched as those whom they abuse and the abusers themselves will be killed. It is clear in such an articulation that this God is no evenhanded sovereign, but rather is a deeply committed partisan in the struggle for neighborly relations. YHWH who speaks the command is the Great Equalizer who readily intervenes on behalf of the vulnerable to guarantee them well-being.

The second commandment in Exodus 22:25–27 is different in tone, but it exhibits the same concerns. It begins with two negative imperatives concerning treatment of the economically disadvantaged:

> You shall not deal with them [the poor] as a creditor; you shall not exact interest from them.

This commandment insists that the relationships in the community between "haves" and "have nots" is not to be determined in economic categories. Rather, in this community ordered by covenant, those who lend and those who borrow are neighbors; the neighborly fabric of the community is not to be distorted by or administered according to the conventional economic impositions of credit and debt.

The sanction here, unlike 22:24, is not threat but affirmation. The grounding of the commandment is that YHWH is compassionate and will attend to the cry of the needy and will side with the needy. It may be that action against the abuser, spelled out in verse 24, is implicit here as well, but that is left unsaid.

The same defining concern in Israel's Torah provision is voiced in the series of specific commands in Deuteronomy 24:17–22. In every case the Torah and the God who speaks through Torah are insistent that the disadvantaged and economically marginal are to be protected. That protection, moreover, is commanded, sanctioned, and legitimated by the God who is endlessly attentive to the oppression, abuse, and disadvantage that are a product of the workings of socioeconomic, political processes that are elsewhere regarded as routine and conventional.

II

So imagine that these great prophetic figures we know so well—Amos, Hosea, Isaiah, Micah, Jeremiah—are products of this sustained pedagogy in the peculiar covenantal ethics of Israel, grounded in the peculiar character of the God of Sinai.

Imagine them as little children regularly attending Passover liturgy, hearing with regularity the particular dramatic affirmation that their community of Israel exists precisely because God hears the cries of the abused and intervenes on their behalf.

Imagine them as boys (and Huldah as a girl) in liturgy regularly, where they heard sung (or themselves sang) the great doxologies that voiced the claim that the God of Israel is precisely the one who is "father" of orphans and protector of widows.

Imagine as they grew older, in their adolescent years, that they moved through liturgy and hymn to serious instruction in the commandments and noticed even there the God who responds to the cries and needs of the vulnerable and powerless.

Doxology, narrative, and *commandment* all converging to nurture younger members of the community into a particular angle of vision! They received a particular critical perspective on social reality that managed in daring rhetoric to insist that the Holy God "in his holy habitation" (Ps. 68:5) is intimately and attentively engaged with the economic, political realities of the world. Long after, when they had departed this pedagogy of doxology, narrative, and commandment, the cadences of attentiveness, the solidarity of God with the needy, the severity of God toward the abusers, and the readiness of God to take sides, all of that was profoundly defining for their prophetic voices. We do not know much about the psychology of the prophets or the ways in which they came to be summoned and authorized to prophetic vocation, even though a great deal has been written on the subject. What we do know, however, is that the prophets, for all their wild imagination and daring rhetoric, were not odd and inexplicable in Israelite society. Rather, they were products—in the extreme to be sure—of a community that operated with a different kind of social analysis and a different kind of social expectation, both grounded in the character of the God whom they had long known from doxology, narrative, and commandment.

III

The prophets were real live human beings existing in real concrete social circumstance. They were adults (or as in Jer. 1:4–10 a soon-to-be adult) capable of seeing the world in adult ways, critical and discerning, informed by deep memory from which they did not depart. The strangeness of these prophets, now remembered and given to us through a complicated editorial process, is that they did not (and I think could not) see the world in the same way as most of their contemporaries, especially the power elite. The latter had long since decided that the old traditions of doxology, narrative, and commandment were nice for "little children" but had nothing at all to do with the "real world," for the "real world" was defined apart from God and shaped by credit, debt, mortgage, interest, surplus, and profits, without any disruptive theological footnote.

In the eighth century B.C.E., during the prosperous regimes of Uzziah in Judah and Jeroboam II in Israel, the economy grew and the prosperous prospered in exaggerated form. Into that happy scene comes the disturbing utterance of Amos, who characterizes in fine hyperbole the extravagant self-indulgence of the prosperous:

> Alas for those who lie on beds of ivory,
>   and lounge on their couches,
> and eat lambs from the flock,
>   and calves from the stall;
> who sing idle songs to the sound of the harp,
>   and like David improvise on instruments of music;
> who drink wine from bowls,
>   and anoint themselves with the finest oils. (6:4–6a)

Predictably the negative recital ends in verse 6 with an adversative conjunction *but*:

> *but* are not grieved over the ruin of Joseph! (v. 6b)

"Joseph" refers to Israel, the northern kingdom. Amos speaks of its "ruin" that was not yet visible to most. He expected that those who paid attention would see and if they saw, would grieve; they would be sad about their future and perhaps take steps to "establish justice in the gate" (5:15).

But of course the prophet is not finished until he utters his climactic *therefore* in 6:7:

> *Therefore* they shall now be the first to go into exile,
>   and the revelry of the loungers shall pass away.

What a strange thing to say: "exile" and then an accusatory hyperbole about self-indulgence that he names "revelry of the loungers." Exile, displacement, loss, and termination were on no one's horizon…except for Jeremiah, the product of the doxology, narrative, and commandment. Exile (= deportation) was perhaps already known as the preferred policy of the dangerously looming Assyrian Empire. And no doubt Amos had such a reference to imperial policy in mind. In fact, however, Amos's grounding is theological: he knows in deep ways the neighborly intention of God. He can see at a glance that the luxury of verses 4–6 is an extravagance wrought at the expense of the poor; it will not go on, moreover, because YHWH wills otherwise (see 4:1–3; 8:4–6).

In the seventh century, with Israel now gone and Amos vindicated, Jeremiah–child of doxology, narrative, and commandment–read his Judean situation and noticed how the economy was organized so that the same crowd of the vulnerable are the victims of an unnoticing social arrangement:

> They have become great and rich,
>   they have grown fat and sleek.
> They know no limits in deeds of wickedness;
>   they do not judge with justice
> the cause of the orphan, to make it prosper,
>   and they do not defend the rights of the needy. (5:27d–28)

The imagery is of a hunter who traps birds. The "great and rich" have all the necessary equipment (cages, traps, nets = tax laws, mortgage arrangements, interest rates). With "no limit" on the number they can "bag," they go their way, becoming "fat and sleek" in numbing self-indulgence, undeterred by doxology, narrative, or commandment.

IV

The close discernment of the prophets and their capacity to utter what they saw and knew in clear and imaginative ways are crucial for "just preaching." In my judgment one other factor belongs alongside such an assessment of the prophets. Especially in the oracles of Hosea and Jeremiah, but also in the prayer of Amos 7:2–6, it is clear that the God to whom they bear witness is not an outsider who stands over against failed Israel and who takes glee in harsh judgment. The articulation of God's pathos–God's suffering solidarity–indicates that the failure to care for the "little ones" in Israel is not only disturbing to God but hurtful to God's own life, because of God's intense solidarity.[2]

God's pathos concerns the suffering of Israel, as in Hosea 11:8–9 and Jeremiah 31:20. From that, however, we may extrapolate that God is hurt whenever God's dearly beloved–the widow, orphan, and alien–are hurt.

It is God's capacity for solidarity in pain and grief that gives resonance and depth to the severity of prophetic judgment. The distortion of the world causes grief and dismay to this one who dearly loves the world, so that the prophetic utterance, bespeaking God's own inclination, is characteristically a mix of anger and anguish. Any prophetic utterance that lacks the anguish that qualifies the anger is less than a full voicing of this God as given us in the prophetic tradition.

V

The script of the prophet is a script for our own "just preaching." The text provides a skeleton and spine for contemporaneity in our preaching, a text that invites, generates, and authorizes imaginative linkages between what they uttered and what we may utter after them. A caveat, however, needs to be entered. There is a long tradition of so-called prophetic preaching that is filled with anger, indignation, and condemnation, so that the preacher's own juices of anger can run loose in the process.

I suggest that we need to unlearn that common notion of prophetic preaching on two counts. First, it is clear that some of the most effective "prophetic preaching" in our time by such dazzling voices as Desmond Tutu, Daniel Berrigan, and Jonathan Kozol, to name three choice cases, has the power of indignation, but comes across as utterances of hope-filled, compassionate truth-telling largely free of rage. I suggest that we have misread the prophets to think them voices of simplistic rage, for hard truth can be told quietly if it intends to evoke a response rather than simply be an imposition of rage on the listener.

Second, it is clear that most pastors (who have at best precarious tenure, who are administratively responsible for program and budget and institutional maintenance, and who worry about their pensions) are not free-floating voices who can simply emote. Thus, I suggest that "just preaching" may well be done by *scribes* who attend to prophetic *texts,* for what scribes characteristically do is to preserve, value, and interpret old scrolls.[3] To think of one's self as a scribe "trained for the kingdom" may deliver one from the excessive "righteous indignation" that is connected to conventional notions of "prophetic preaching" (Mt. 13:51–53). A scribal notion may suggest that the prophetic chance is to help the listening community discern differently through the lens of the old tradition of oracles presented in treasured scrolls (see Jer. 36:32; Neh. 8:1). Seeing differently and imaginatively through such a "scrolled" lens leaves a choice for changed attitude and policy; the work of the scribe, however, is to let the prophetic text authorize the difference.

Such scribal work, mediating the text of Amos and company,

- can present *effective social analysis,* for it is still true that "haves and have nots" are in it together, with a growing gap in our time between them because of the manipulation of taxes, interest, loans, and so forth; the church is characteristically weak and timid about social analysis, but without it there is no effective prophetic utterance

- can make visible and prominent the "widows and orphans" among us, *the vulnerable marginalized* who lack clout, who are deficient in health insurance, for whom it is not easy to focus on the education of children, and who live pitifully and meanly on $7 an hour
- can make the connection that the failure of the life of the "have nots" eventually will destroy the life of the "haves," because there are no "safe houses" outside *the common fabric* of lived humanity

Beyond the social analysis, the scribe can also lift up texts

- that witness to the terrific loss that comes on the community, what in prophetic parlance is *judgment,* but judgment communicated with more sadness than rage
- that testify to the *pathos* of God, to the pathologies of human community that contribute directly to God's own pain, a pain that reaches an extremity in the cross
- that find around the edges of failure *new beginnings,* new social possibilities that are given here and there in the midst of the deathliness as the prophets watch for and discern signs of newness

The work of the scribe in *judgment,* in *pathos,* and in *hope* is to invite the congregation to come outside the narcotic of consumerism to rediscern the world as a place where issues of life and death are at work, not because of a God angry without pain, but because life is not sustainable without intentional investment in a human future.

VI

The scribe does not read the prophetic scrolls and rearticulate prophetic oracle in a vacuum. If the scribe is the pastor of a congregation, prophetic proclamation—judgment, pathos, possibility—are made credible by a context of intentional pastoral, liturgical, and educational work.

All around the prophetic assertion are *cadences of doxology* that tell of God's wondrous abundance as the bottom truth of creation, an abundance not cheapened even by cunning tax and mortgage arrangements.

All around prophetic assertion are *many retellings of the narratives* that attest to the reality of God in the life of the world, an attestation that calls the congregation away from the narrativeless life of consumerism to the dramatic narrative of covenantal engagement that issues in health, liberation, and well-being.

All around prophetic assertion is the rich probing and teaching of *old commandments* as the nonnegotiable condition for the life of the world. Many church people do not know the commandments, either to probe deeply into "the Big Ten" or to face texts that are completely unknown in the church, commandments of neighborliness and compassion, of holiness and justice.

A sustained offer of doxologies concerning the miracles of abundance, of narratives of the give-and-take of covenantal mutuality, and of commandments as preconditions for life in the world make room for prophetic analysis and articulation. When done in context, the scribe may not need to raise her voice or exude indignation. It is enough to see differently and to imagine alternatively, for such posturing of hearers permits and evokes different action.[4] Neither a scribe nor a prophet can dictate or coerce. It is enough to line out the world differently, to resist the phony reassurance of therapeutic consumerism, and to show insistently that the first command of loving God is always followed quickly and with equal insistence by the second command, the imperative to love your neighbor (Mk. 12:28–34). Giving voice to the neighbor command in a context of satiating consumerism is a stark *either/or* that requires great courage, especially if it is linked to the characteristic prophetic agenda of tax, mortgage, and interest arrangements.[5] "Just preaching" is about voicing the either/or alongside (a) pastoral candor about the terrible ambiguity about which we all know and (b) the wondrous chance for choosing again, differently, obediently, freely, hopefully, gladly…again. When the scribe works the *either/or* in a context of doxology, narrative, and commandment, there may arise, through long seasons of listening, another prophet or two for the next age of the church. In the meantime, being a faithful scribe for the kingdom is, I do not doubt, more than enough.

"The Prophet's Sons and Daughters"[1]

Amos 7:10–17; Acts 3:17–26

PATRICK D. MILLER, JR.

I want to make one proposal: It is simply that as ministers of the gospel you are the sons and daughters of the prophets, and so are invested with and encumbered with *a prophetic ministry*. I would like to think a little bit about what that means in the light of scripture and with particular reference to two things: the conditions of a prophetic ministry and the task of a prophetic ministry.

The Conditions of a Prophetic Ministry

The stories of the prophets are fairly clear about the primary condition for the prophetic work. It is a sense of being called and of living and working under authority. Those are, of course, one and the same thing. The call is of God, and the authority of the prophet is tied to that call. He or she stands under the constraint of God and as bearer of God's word. Amos and his fellow prophets did not assume their functions in God's governance and purpose out of a desire or a disposition or a particular bent for that sort of thing. Some may have done that, but they are not the ones to whom we still listen. Quite the contrary, you will recall that most of those prophets whose words still address us objected to the very idea of a "professional prophethood."

In some cases, as for example that of Jeremiah, the call is expressed in a kind of election that belongs to his very being: "Before I formed you in the womb I knew you, and before you were born I consecrated you" (1:5). His calling is not a happenstance. It is what he was born to be and to do by the very plan and intention of God. If Reformed Christians, and I trust many others also, say with vigor and joy that we know ourselves, even before we were born, to have been elected in love, Jeremiah's call lets us know that there were and are some who discover that they were, even before they were born, elected into vocation, into a prophetic ministry.

There is nothing accidental about God's call, though it may be experienced "by accident," so to speak. I am sure it was a big surprise to Jeremiah. And Amos lets us know that he had a very good vocation as a businessman before, in his words, "the LORD took me from following the flock, and the LORD said to me, 'Go, prophesy to my people Israel'" (7:15).

Participation in the ministry is not primarily a job or a contract. It is not something we are hired or even invited to do. However it may be experienced, the ministry is something into which we are called. We come to that conviction in various ways, some of them more like an actual calling, a conscious sense of being impelled into the ministry from beyond oneself, others more like a discernment that is rooted in one's self-assessment and self-understanding, one's openness to the world and to the gospel. However that conviction may come, the ministry is created by the call of God, and the authority under which you preach and teach is inherent in that calling and in your self-understanding as one who is under God's constraint and God's demand and whose word is the word of the Lord.

The Task of the Prophetic Ministry

That calling, however, is to a task. And for the prophetic ministry that means more to a task than to an office. Amos may have been a businessman but he is now a prophet. The big deal, however, is not being a prophet, assuming a role. In fact, what Amos says to the dean of the National Cathedral at Bethel is not, "I am a prophet," but rather, "The LORD took me…and said to me, 'Go, prophesy to my people Israel.'" And Isaiah hears the words, "Whom shall I send, and who will go for us?" (6:8). And to Jeremiah comes the word of the Lord: "You shall go to all to whom I send you, and you shall speak whatever I command you" (1:7). The prophetic ministry is the service of God *under assignment*. One may indeed speak of the prophet's mantle, of the descent of the spirit, of an anointing—all ways of saying that one now belongs to this category or this group or office in God's kingdom. An identity is thereby given. But the identity is *missional*. What is most prominent is the sense of being commanded and sent and commissioned to do something.

So what is that task? If we read through the prophets, we might list a whole bunch of things. Let me suggest that underneath their many oracles and many situations are three things that belong to any prophetic ministry.

Criticism

In a prosperous, self-satisfied, and self-authenticating society, the prophets and their sons and daughters bring the power of God's word in criticism of all forms of self-interest that neglect the weak and the small and the powerless and do not set righteousness and justice as the primary criteria for deciding what to do and for whom to speak. The divine insistence on justice in the human community brooks no qualifications. Psalm 82 reminds us that gods cannot stay gods without providing justice for the weak. And the faithful prophets and their sons and daughters remind the people of God that they cannot be God's people and be indifferent to the distortions of human life and human society that wreak havoc with fairness and justice, with what it takes to make and to keep human life human.

From Amos and his prophetic sisters and brothers, we learn what we cannot ignore in our own time and our own prophetic ministry: the centrality of the *legal* and *economic* systems for the maintenance of justice. The prophetic critique carries in it a clear understanding of what it is that God seeks in the human community. The notion of justice inherent in the message of the prophets has been accurately described in this way:

> All citizens should have a share in the control of the society's basic economic good as the instrument of their status, access to rights, and freedom. The administration of order should protect and support this distribution against economic and political processes that erode it. Institutional law should be subject to interpretation and correction by the worth of persons and moral values. Wealth which prejudices the welfare and rights of others is unjust. Treatment of the least favored in the society is the fundamental criterion of the achievement of justice.[2]

In the face of a human society where such a notion of God's justice was ignored or trampled underfoot—and stronger language than that is often used—the prophets did four things:

1. They announced God's judgment on a society that could not live by righteousness and justice and trust in the Lord alone.

2. They sought repentance and a mending of the ways: "Amend your ways and your doings," preached Jeremiah in the temple (7:3).

3. They appealed to the *faith* and *conscience* of their people in simple but clear ways, calling on them to hate evil and love good, to render in their courts judgments that are true and make for peace.

4. They confronted the people in power, whether by intention or by outcome, and called for them to change direction or face God's judgment.

In such a prophetic ministry, it does not matter where your pulpit is or who is your audience. Where God's righteousness and justice are not in practice, there the sons and daughters of the prophets name the sin and call for another way of doing things. That may be in the pulpit on a Sunday morning. It may be in conversation with officers of the church. It may be in the classroom. It may be in letters to the newspaper, addresses to civic clubs, or on the streets–wherever. The niceties and distinctions that we sometimes worry over between civil religion and ecclesiastical context, between church and state, between preaching and meddling, were not and are not of consequence for the prophetic ministry. It is not something that operates here and there, a couple of days a week. It goes on constantly in public and in private, in preaching and pastoral care. To Ezekiel, God said, "I have made you a sentinel for the house of Israel; whenever you hear a word from my mouth, you shall give them warning from me" (3:17). That is a *pastoral* task, to be *God's sentry* in the midst of your people, alerting them, together and individually, when the word of God is not present in the life of the community and when God's justice is not the order of the day.

Imagination

The second aspect of a prophetic ministry is this: In whatever the situation, the sons and daughters of the prophets are charged with imagining a different way, with envisioning and announcing the new possibility of God's way in the world, what Walter Brueggemann calls an alternative community and what scripture means when it talks about a covenant people and the kingdom of God, a community of people in time and space who live by the rule of God and by God's ways, where the care of the weakest is the criterion of a just society, where one's ultimate trust is not in the gods of productivity or in Wall Street or even in an Alan Greenspan, all of them weak reeds, but in the Lord of all the worlds that are, the creator of the universe, from whom comes every good and perfect gift.

Such a community is found here and there in congregation after congregation. The prophetic task is to be the bearer of God's word to effect and mobilize that community of faithful obedience. If the scriptures are the plumbline by which the prophets' sons and daughters measure the faithfulness of the contemporary church and call it to account, they are also the impetus for imagining a truly peaceable kingdom, for envisioning a city of righteousness, whose builder and maker is God, where old people can sit in safety in the parks and children play along the streets, where nations come together to study peace and not to build new armaments and missile shields, where nations pour their resources into economic production for the common good and the enhancement of life for all. The prophet's sons and daughters dare to proclaim what is impossible in a world that lives by the pragmatic and reasonable because they *know* the answer to the question: "Is anything too difficult for God?" and are willing to hang their hats on that conviction, maybe even give their lives for it.

Announcement

Where they find themselves in the midst of a defeated, undone, and despairing community, the sons and daughters of the prophets dare to announce the good news of God's power and God's presence. There is a difference between cheap grace and the power of the gospel. I cannot tell you what it is. You have to find it out in the midst of your people, whoever and wherever they are. When you do, then, like the prophets of Israel and like John the Baptist's gnarled finger in Matthias Grünewald's great painting of the crucifixion at Isenheim, you will find yourself pointing always to the one in whose ministry you are about to enter, whose presence sustains in every circumstance, whose help is truly sufficient for every pain.

What then about possible outcomes for such a prophetic ministry? I can think of a couple. One is burnout. That clearly happened to the prophets; read your Bible. Elijah took off and left town in utter discouragement and fear. And Jeremiah complained all the time and was ready to give it all up. As best I can tell, however, burnout was not allowed for the prophets, and it may not be allowed for their sons and daughters. Elijah heard a voice saying: "What are you doing here?" and was sent back with an even more radical task in confronting the royal powers. Jeremiah was told, "If you are having difficulty with a congregation like this one, what are you going to do with the hornets' nest that is just in front of you? You think the Boston Marathon was hard, what are you going to do when I put you in the Kentucky Derby—on foot?"

But there is no demitting the task, no words, "Lord, I didn't bargain for this when I answered your call" that will get you out of the prophetic ministry. I wish I could give you an easier word than that, but it would not be what the Bible says.

But maybe, just maybe, there can be other outcomes: What about a congregation renewed and committed to God's way, to the proclamation of the good news in every nook and cranny of our society and our world? What about the kingdom coming to life in the midst of a people pledged to God's way of righteousness and mercy and trust? What about students who hear your words and find their consciences forever disturbed? I don't know. Is anything too difficult for God?

And what about fringe benefits for the prophets' sons and daughters? Well, I *can* tell you about that. There aren't any. You will have to find the goodies elsewhere. I wish I could tell you that I thought Amos felt satisfied at the end of the day or that Isaiah went home to play catch with little Shear-jashub with a sense of a job well done. He probably went home worried about what he was going to have to do the next day that would make his people even more resistant to the divine word.

No, there are no fringe benefits to the prophetic ministry—except one: the promise of God's companioning presence along the way. And you should realize the reason for such a promise is that you are going to need it. But when you do, you will have it. The promise of *Immanuel* is specifically a word to the prophets: "I am with you." In the fiery trials, in the heat of the battle, in the lassitude of indifference, in the face of resistance to the word of the Lord, in the times when it all falls apart and your very well-being and maybe even that of your family is threatened, "I am with you." If you think that means everything will work out all right, I'm not sure. I just know that the grace of the Lord Jesus Christ and the love of God and the fellowship of the Holy Spirit will indeed be with you. That grace and love will have to be sufficient. I believe it will.

"Two Fingers under the Door"

Isaiah 9:1–6; Luke 2:1–14; Titus 2:11–14

MARY CATHERINE HILKERT

> A cold coming we had of it,
> Just the worst time of year
> For a journey, and such a long journey:
> The ways deep and the weather sharp,
> The very dead of winter.[1]

I suspect that all of us can identify with T. S. Eliot's "Journey of the Magi" in one way or another as we gather to celebrate the feast of joy and light surrounded by darkness.

> It is indeed a season of light and a time of joy
> as we re-gather as families and communities,
> as we feast and sing,
> as we see the world through the eyes of our children,
> and bestow gifts on one another.[2]

But it is also the dead of winter, not only because El Niño and La Niña have deserted us, but because we miss those who have gathered with us in the past. We remember those among us who dwell in the shadow of death even now. We know that this season of light is a season of real darkness for those who struggle with depression and loneliness. We know that family and community and church gatherings are also places and times of stress and sometimes of pain or unreconciled places.

Still, we come together longing to believe that "the people who walked in darkness have seen a great light; those who lived in a land of deep darkness—on them light has shined" (Isa. 9:2).

It sounds so beautiful—like a victory that was already achieved—until you realize that Isaiah spoke these words as a promise and encouragement to hold fast and to hope when Israel was facing one more foreign invasion; Assyria was at their door. Israel was facing military defeat and exile when Isaiah called for unyielding trust in a God who is "Immanuel," God-with-us. Isaiah announced what God would do in the future as if it had already happened. God's promise is that sure.

He told them—he tells us—that we can "step out on the promise." No matter what, God will be our light and salvation. A people of faith can live on memory and hope, as our Jewish brothers and sisters do during the festival of Hanukkah. When we Christians hear the Isaiah reading in our Christmas liturgy, our memories and hope center on the life, death, and resurrection of Jesus.

The reading from Titus proclaims boldly that the grace of God has appeared in Jesus Christ. Or as a friend wrote to me recently, "Christmas is so simple: What we long for is already here."

The liturgy reminds us that Christmas is not only about celebrating what God has done in the *past,* even what God has done in Jesus Christ.

Rather, the mystery of the incarnation continues in the power of the Spirit: "Today is born a Savior." Not two thousand years ago. Not "someday God will come on our behalf." Today—here and now—God offers light in midst of all our darkness.

As the Dominican mystic Meister Eckhart asked more than seven centuries ago:

> What good is it to me
> if this eternal birth of the divine Son
> takes place unceasingly
> but does not take place within myself?
> What good is it to me
> for the Creator to give birth to His Son
> if I do not also give birth to him
> in my time
> *and my culture?*[3]

This mystic is asking if we are ready to participate in God's birthing, if we are ready to be bearers of light in the darkness. And he is reminding us not to miss the coming of God because we were expecting something more dramatic. The gospel tells us where to look for signs of God's favor: not in a "god-hero" with political power or military might. Instead, the light comes into the darkness through a vulnerable child, through a poor family who clings to God's promises. We are to look for signs of God in places as basic as an animal's feeding place.

God's light is available all around us, but we might miss it if we dismiss the word of the shepherds of our day—whoever it is we consider outcast or unclean.

The vision the angels announce isn't the dramatic coming of God we were expecting. It seems more like the one that a single mother, writer Anne Lamott, described in her book *Operating Instructions.* She loved her son, Sam, but she lamented that, "he came without operating instructions!"[4] One time, when he was about two, he accidentally locked himself in a bedroom. When she realized what had happened, she tried to explain to him how he could get out. But he didn't understand, and she could sense how frightened he was. She called for help, but while she and Sam waited for help to arrive she said that all she could do was to get down on the floor and slide her hand under the door. Only two fingers would fit, but somehow that was enough for him to hang onto.

Reflecting on the incident, she commented that that was her experience of God as well. Most of the time we find ourselves clinging to two fingers under a door. But that's enough to see us through, to sustain our hope.

Christmas and the mystery of incarnation are about God in the ordinary, God taking on human flesh and all our struggles, God empowering us to sustain each other even when all we can offer is two fingers under the door:

- a phone call
- a promise of prayer
- an apology
- an effort at reconciliation
- a card or a cup of coffee
- a visit to the sick or homebound
- helping to develop a ministry to those in jail
- going out of the way to help someone stranded on the road
- taking time with a child

Christmas proclaims that "what we long for is already here," in ordinary persons' holding two fingers under the door to one another. We wanted a God who would take away the darkness; instead we got a God who promised to enter into our darkness and to be with us there so that it would not overcome us.

We wanted a sign of God's fidelity; God asked us to be that sign for one another, sometimes in large system-changing ways, yes, but sometimes in seemingly small ways, yet ways nonetheless that hold back the darkness from overcoming us.

We wanted a promise we could live on; God gave us a simple meal to sustain us on our journey and a mission: to give birth to his Son in our time and in our worlds of influence.

Like a baby in a feeding trough, like two fingers under a door, like a solitary light in the dead of winter—Emmanuel.

"Hang Up and Drive"

James 2:1–17

ROGER LOVETTE

The bumper sticker said: "Hang Up and Drive!" This is a not-so-subtle suggestion to put your cell phone down and keep your mind on the road. But there is a larger lesson here for the church. Sometimes we shouldn't talk at all. In fact, our speech puts others and ourselves at risk. The church's real job is to move on down the road.

The disciple James would have understood this sentiment. In the early days of the new church, he wrote his words to little clusters of scattered Christians. Those little outposts were surrounded by a pagan culture that made them wonder if the Jesus way was the right way. Like modern Christians, they talked a lot. But also like us, often they never got beyond the talking stage.

The church in every age has faced a crisis: What is our basic mission? James wrote those early believers to encourage them to move beyond words to actions.

Ask people today what best describes Jesus, and you hear a lot about compassion and caring, how he reached out in love, especially to the poor and disenfranchised. Ask these same people what best describes today's church, and the answers are quite different.

We only have to attend a board meeting of the average church and listen to their concerns. First on the agenda is a reading of the minutes and making corrections in the document. Next come the reports. The finance committee notes that outgo exceeded income for the second month. After much discussion all agree that something has to be done. Someone gives a detailed analysis of the bake sale. The time of the morning worship service is discussed. Finally, we get down to new business. "We have a letter from

Mrs. Jemison," the chair says as she puts her glasses down her nose. "It seems that someone stole a package Mrs. Jemison had left for a high school graduate in the fellowship hall. Something must be done about these outsiders who use our building in the evening. She wants us to ask them to find another place to meet."

A lot of time is spent that evening discussing why the paint on the outside of the sanctuary is peeling off after only two years. Someone raises the question about the wisdom of allowing the Korean church next door to use the overflow parking lot. On and on it goes. At 10:00 that evening the meeting adjourns and the people go their separate ways, feeling good that the work of the church continues.

Clearly this was church work, but was this the work of the church? Was there any moment in that long meeting when the church moved beyond talk? At what point did they leave maintenance issues and move on to the kind of matters to which Jesus gave his whole life? Is there a good reason for the gospels' omission of Jesus' committee meeting minutes?

James asked his fellow believers four questions in the second chapter of his letter. It was his way of helping his fellow believers rearrange the priorities of their faith:

1. What do acts of favoritism have to do with following the Lord Jesus (2:1–2)? He asks, Do you treat those well dressed with gold rings the same as those with little of the world's goods? Are you guilty of the sin of partiality, or can all find equality in the church?

2. Is your word for neighbor a big word or a little word (2:8–9)? James wondered if their word for *neighbor* was big enough to take in those in need. Jesus had already defined neighbor in the good Samaritan story. Would people for whom life had not been easy find a welcome place in the church?

3. Can you have judgment and mercy (2:12–13)? James said that for the Christian, mercy always triumphs over judgment. The good neighbor does not judge. Mercy builds connection between believers and a hurting world.

4. Can we have genuine faith without works (2:14–17)? James phrased this last question, which is also the theme of his whole letter, this way: "If a brother or sister is naked and lacks daily food, and one of you says to them, 'Go in peace; keep warm and eat your fill,' and yet you do not supply their bodily needs, what is the good of that?"

I think that James's response can be seen in an organization called Interfaith Hospitality Network. It has been a force that has helped the church to move beyond business as usual. Interfaith Hospitality Network reaches out to homeless families who have nowhere to turn, families who double up and triple up with friends or family, who stay in unsafe crowded shelters, or who call their car "home."

Three years ago our church was invited to participate in this program, which was just beginning in Birmingham. We were asked to be one of twelve congregations that would house homeless families for one week. We had shelters in our city for women and for men. Some shelters took women and children. No organization in our community was meeting the needs of homeless families. To participate, we would need to provide lodging for them in our church building four weeks a year. We would also provide supper and breakfast while they were with us.

When the idea was first proposed, the project did not seem practical for us. Our church is small. We had few rooms that could be used for such a worthy endeavor. Most of our people were already overworked and overcommitted. We had a history of starting tasks and not finding enough volunteers to finish them. I loved the idea of helping the homeless, but I was not sure we could tackle this program.

Our laity were not as dubious as their pastor. "Let's try this," they said. Reluctantly I agreed. It would take about fifty volunteers to run the program for a week. Someone would have to turn Christian education rooms into bedrooms. Someone would have to set up the cots and other furniture. We were asked to provide sheets, towels, soap, and two meals each day. At least two volunteers would have to stay each night at the church in case there was a need.

Our laity made a believer out of me. The church came through. Our little Baptist church joined hands with a Unitarian congregation down the street for our first assignment. If that isn't miracle enough, those that stayed and worked say this program has changed their lives.

A week after we finished our first venture with homeless families, the church threw a luncheon for the volunteers. Around those tables we told sad and funny stories, stories of how some of the guests had tried to play matchmaker with some of our members. We learned that our new friends did not like to eat on paper plates. They wanted real plates and real knives and forks. This request sounded kind of picky to a few of us until we realized that it really is the seemingly small things that make the difference between feeling truly welcomed and feeling merely tolerated.

One conservative man stood after our luncheon and said: "I have to confess that I have learned something this week. I've lived a long time and I thought I knew just about everything I'd ever learn. But these folks taught me something. Most of them are just like us. They have just had some bad breaks. I'm not going to be as judgmental as I have before." One woman said, "If I ever had any doubts about this program, it's seeing the little children that changed me. Why, they are as smart as any kids I have ever met. I just wonder what chance they'll have. Maybe we've helped some."

Since that time more than thirty families have come through our doors. We have no trouble now recruiting volunteers. Our members look forward to these quarterly visits by our guests.

James told his friends that without action their faith would have a hollow ring. Interfaith Hospitality Network has taught us many lessons. Probably the most far-reaching of those lessons has been a recommitment to the real work of the church. As James stressed to the small clusters of scattered Christians in his time, we are in the people-welcoming business. Like the God who welcomed us, we are to show no favoritism between different kinds of folks as we open our doors. We are to continually learn that the word *neighbor* is a whole lot bigger than those who live close to us. James also reminds us that we have to suspend our judgments about homeless folk and just show mercy, as Jesus would have. But maybe, most of all, we are to reaffirm that without the hard work of reaching out and helping others, there is no real faith.

On the Sunday morning we began our participation in the Interfaith Hospitality Network, we moved a cot into the altar area of the sanctuary. Beside that well-made bed was a little table and a lamp. On the communion table we placed towels, soap, canned goods, a loaf of bread, and a stack of magazines. That morning, during our prayer time, we asked God to use the things we had brought to help those that would come through our program. We asked that somehow the hands and hearts of our efforts would help in the name of Jesus. Little did we know that as we began this work those cots and towels and food would bring us closer to the vision of a welcoming church that James had for the church in his time.

The bumper sticker may be right after all.

PART 4

Is It Just America? Poverty and Homelessness in the Homeland

Rarely is the problem that one sees the real problem. Leaves extend from branches. The branches lead back to a trunk. The trunk is anchored by roots that wind their ways deeply and intricately through soil and around rock. The same holds for solutions: rarely does the treatment of a leaf do much good if the branch to which it is attached is severed from the trunk. And if the branch remains intact, not much can be done if the roots are diseased. The leaf may feel better for a couple of days, but it's still doomed if surgery at the roots isn't undertaken.

This is why work for justice must transcend traditional understandings and forms of "benevolence" and "charity." As Matthew Fox stresses, true compassion is not pity, is not sentiment, and does not condescend. Rather, true compassion is *making justice* and doing the works of mercy. It is not private and egocentric, but public, and works toward the systemic remedy of societal ills.

Typically, religious groups that have wanted to respond to the needs of the poor have engaged in acts of "limited accompaniment." These activities take the form of walking alongside those in need and meeting their immediate needs, that is, soup kitchens, toys for tots, and overnight shelters. These ministries are important and must continue and both extend and deepen their reach. But while faith communities must continue substantive ministries of accompaniment, they must go beyond these too, expanding limited notions of accompaniment to include "advocacy." Advocacy cannot be an excuse to leave the frontlines, by any means. But it must be done as a means of changing the systems that are in place that cause the sicknesses at the front lines. Advocacy traces the frontline illnesses from leaf to branch to trunk to root and then works toward systemic correction for long-term change and results.

Just preaching aims to expose societal ills and empower people for ministries of both accompaniment and advocacy. As Rabbi Kroloff says in his sermon "*Tikun Olam*: Mending the World," "If we believe that God upholds the cause of the orphan, the widow, and the stranger, we are expected to do the same. Make no mistake about it: we show our love for the Eternal by modeling our moral behavior after God's." Preachers of justice model their "oral behavior" after God's concern for the cause of the orphan, the widow, and the stranger. Such "just orality" leads, performatively, to a "just morality," which works to renew and rebuild society from root to leaf.

Poverty and Homelessness in the United States

KAREN OLSON

A while back, I pulled a 1976 edition of *Webster's New World Dictionary* off the shelf and looked up the word *homeless*. It wasn't in there. *Home* was, of course—the place where a person or family lives; one's dwelling place. But there wasn't yet a word for the growing number of people who had nowhere to live—people who were becoming harder and harder to ignore.

We began using the word *homeless* in the late 1970s to describe the men and women who called park benches, doorways, subway grates, and back alleys "home." In many of our major cities it was impossible to walk a single block without seeing someone who was homeless—a woman pushing everything she owned along the street in a shopping cart; a man huddled in a doorway, holding a paper cup in his outstretched hand, beckoning to us, asking us to care. If we walked fast enough and avoided their eyes, we could get past them, but could we get past the problem? Perhaps we could deny that these were people who had names—and who once had homes of their own. Perhaps we could deny that they were somebody's mother, brother, or child. If we walked fast enough and avoided their eyes, maybe they would become just a part of the cityscape, and we could deny our common humanity.

Homelessness was newly visible, spreading far beyond the skid rows where it had formerly been contained. We carry these earliest images of the homeless with us today. All too often the image is a stereotype: a dirty face behind a cardboard sign: "Homeless. Please help. God bless."

But people we refer to as "the homeless" have become a very diverse group. In fact, the word *homeless* describes a situation more than it does a population. The only thing that all the homeless have in common is the fact that they do not have a home.

Look beyond the stereotype. That young mother we pass on the sidewalk, with a two-year-old in a stroller and a five-year-old by her side, is homeless—and so are her children. One out of every four homeless persons is a child.[1]

Families with children are the fastest-growing segment of the homeless population. They make up more than 40 percent of those who are homeless in major cities and more than 50 percent in rural areas.[2] Among industrialized nations, the United States is unique in that women and children compose such a large portion of those who are homeless.[3]

Homelessness can tear families apart. Mothers with young children may be accepted into one shelter, while their husbands and teenage sons must seek shelter elsewhere. Parents who want to keep their children out of shelters often leave them with relatives and friends. If families are homeless for long, they run the risk of losing their children to a scrutinizing foster-care and social-service system.

Why, in our affluent country, are children experiencing the turmoil of homelessness? Why do parents have to make the agonizing choice to separate from their children in order to retain custody of them? And as people of faith—as leaders of faith—what is our obligation to those who are homeless? What is our responsibility?

The Root Cause of Homelessness

There are as many paths to homelessness as there are people who have trod them. For one person or family the immediate cause may be the loss of a job. For another it may be an addiction to drugs. For another it could be domestic violence, a separation, or a divorce. For yet another a chronic illness or serious accident could be the triggering event.

Whatever the *immediate* cause, the *root* cause of any individual's or family's homelessness is the gap between income and the cost of housing. In other words, few people would be homeless if enough housing that they could afford were available or if their wages were enough to afford the housing that is available. Because the number of low-income housing units has decreased and the number of people earning poverty-level wages has increased, more and more people are competing for fewer and fewer apartments and houses. In this brutal game of musical chairs, the losers end up homeless.

So homelessness is not the problem. Homelessness is only a symptom. Poverty is the problem. People in poverty are living on the edge—just one paycheck, just one illness or injury, just one small crisis away from losing their home.

Affordable Housing

A home promises us rest, security, health, and family. A home promises shelter from the weather and from life's burdens. But for millions of people who are homeless or inadequately housed, the promise of home seems like a distant hope.

With the affordable housing supply shrinking, millions of households are left with few choices. This dramatic decrease has a variety of causes. Thousands of units of housing were lost in the 1970s and '80s because landlords chose to abandon buildings instead of paying the mortgage, the taxes, or the rising costs of maintenance. Many more were lost when owners converted units of housing for a higher-income market. Whole sections of cities were "gentrified" to make way for luxury condominiums and expensive rental housing for young professionals.

These changes would have hurt low-income families less if the lost units had been replaced by new affordable units. Most were not. Tax and financing incentives for private investors to build new low-cost housing disappeared. Local regulations steered resources toward middle-income, owner-occupied housing rather than affordable rentals. At the same time, the federal government dramatically reduced its commitment to creating and maintaining low-cost housing. Almost all federal production resources have been cut. Governments also destroyed housing in an effort to improve "slum" areas in the cities, and they failed to replace all the units.

This combination of factors has led to fierce competition for the affordable housing that remains, driving rents up and pushing apartments out of the affordable range. In this competition, three households out of five will lose.[4] Some will be forced into housing that is substandard or that they can't afford. Others will become homeless.

As the housing crisis of the 1970s and '80s accelerated, the first to lose out were the most vulnerable—those with substance-abuse problems or severe mental illness. But they were only the vanguard of the "new homeless" to come. Next came those who were out of work with education and job skills too inadequate to find new jobs; then those who had a job but were not paid a living wage sufficient to pay for rising rents; then single mothers and their children; and then two-parent families.

Many who are homeless live in shelters, parks, cars, campgrounds, and abandoned buildings. They are easy to identify as homeless. But others who appear to be housed are at the very edge of homelessness. Many double up or triple up with family or friends in temporary and unstable arrangements until they are forced to move on. Many more are facing eviction with nowhere to go, or have stopped paying the utility bills in the hope that they can continue paying the rent. They are facing homelessness too, though not as visibly.

Many families are forced to spend an exorbitant amount to stay housed. One in seven households has "critical housing needs," which means that the family must pay more than half its income for housing or live in severely substandard housing or both.[5]

Consider a mother of two children who became a guest of the Interfaith Hospitality Network. I'll call her Maria. Maria was working forty hours a week at two part-time jobs—as a clerk in a discount store and as an aide in a nursing home. She made $7 an hour and spent more than half of what she earned to pay the rent on a cramped apartment in a four-story walkup located in a rough section of town. To make sure that she would be able to pay the rent, she had to skimp on food, never bought new clothes, and cut back on heat. To earn enough to truly afford the apartment, she would have had to more than double her work hours.[6]

Medical bills made Maria and her children homeless. Neither of Maria's employers provided health insurance for part-time workers, and Maria couldn't afford insurance premiums on her own. When her daughter fell ill, Maria took her to a hospital emergency room, where tests revealed that she had juvenile-onset diabetes. There was no spare money in Maria's budget to pay for treatment and medication, so she began juggling her bills. One month she wouldn't pay the electricity bill, the next month the phone bill, and so on. The unpaid balances and late charges began piling up. One month, threatened by a collection agency, she paid an overdue bill instead of the rent. Two months later, she and her children were on the street. Maria looked for another, cheaper apartment, but she couldn't find anything in a neighborhood that she would want her children to come home to after school alone.

Housing that is affordable to families like Maria's is often unsafe and unhealthy, and it is often in unsafe and unhealthy neighborhoods. Inadequate heat, lead-based paint, poor plumbing, and exposure to pollutants, molds, and allergens put children's health at risk. The neighborhood schools are often inadequate, because public schools are funded by community taxes, and in poor neighborhoods the tax base is simply not there.

The federal government has reduced its funding commitments to low-income housing by 51 percent since 1976.[7] Yet the government's commitment to *wealthy* households remains strong. The largest federal housing subsidy is the mortgage interest deduction, which benefits higher-income households the most. The value of this subsidy is $65 billion, nearly double the whole federal budget for housing assistance.[8]

Adequate Income

The decrease in low-income housing would not be so devastating if families could afford the housing that exists, but they can't, because rising rents have not been matched by rising incomes. Working doesn't guarantee decent housing. Eighty percent of the households with worst-case housing needs are working households.[9]

What is an adequate income? Is it an income above the federal poverty line? Nearly 33 million U.S. citizens are living below the poverty line, but being above the line does not mean being out of poverty. The poverty line is a forty-year-old standard of household income based on a severely limited food budget. It does not take into account today's housing, childcare, or healthcare costs.[10] Millions of households that are technically above the poverty line face the same nearly impossible decisions that the "officially poor" face.

Consider one family that became guests of IHN, "Cheryl Hopkins" and her two children. The poverty line for a family of three with two children is $14,269 per year, and the Hopkins family was not making enough to be above the line. They were not making enough despite the fact that Cheryl was working full-time as a cashier at a major retail clothing chain and had been working full-time all year.

Cheryl's job paid only the federal minimum wage, stagnant at $5.15 per hour since 1997. Thirty-five years ago, Cheryl would have been able to keep her family above the poverty line on the minimum wage—then only $2.90 per hour. Increases in the minimum wage have not kept pace with the rising cost of living. Today Cheryl would have to earn more than $7 per hour simply to reach the inadequate poverty line.

Cheryl's workday was extended by the bus ride she had to take from her apartment in the city to the mall in the suburbs where she works. In cities across the country, as in Cheryl's, affordable housing and low-wage work are increasingly far apart. Cheryl and other workers like her have to spend more time and money getting to and from their jobs.

Cheryl's kids were at home alone after school for several hours, and she worried about them. Unlike many mothers in better circumstances, Cheryl couldn't send her children to a quality daycare center. In every state but one, childcare fees cost more than tuition in a public college.[11]

Cheryl was constantly juggling the bills, forced to make agonizing decisions that affected the quality of life for the entire family. Should she risk postponing the rent so she could repair the car and get to work? Should she take her son to the doctor or just give him his sister's medicine? These families live under constant stress, always in the shadow of the one misfortune that will prove to be too much and put them on the street— homeless—as it did Cheryl and her children.

Cheryl's story is not unusual. Almost half of poor households have at least one full-time worker in the family.[12] And most minimum-wage workers are women.[13]

It is not surprising that Cheryl was working in retail, because she and others like her cannot find better-paying manufacturing work. A steep decline in domestic manufacturing jobs over the past several decades has meant a decline in unionized labor and an increase in low-paying service jobs that have failed to replace the wages lost with the losses in manufacturing jobs. For every dollar the average goods-producing worker makes, the average service worker makes 88 cents, a difference of thousands of dollars per year.[14] Many of the job categories that are growing most rapidly pay only poverty-level wages—wait staff, cashiers, childcare workers, teacher's aides, retail salespeople, janitorial staff, guards, home health aides, and nurse's aides.[15]

Cheryl was fortunate to have a full-time job of any kind. Many new jobs are temporary jobs, part-time jobs, jobs with no security and little or no benefits apart from a paycheck. Today, almost one out of every four workers is employed in nonstandard work arrangements—part-time work, temporary help, on call, independent contracting, and contract firms—which typically offer lower wages, fewer benefits, and less security.[16]

A Call to Justice

The United States is the wealthiest nation in the world. No one should have to call a subway grate, a park bench, or a shelter "home." No child should go to school hungry. No parent should have to work forty, fifty, or sixty hours a week and still have to decide between paying the rent or buying winter coats for the children.

Our nation is blessed with incredible resources. When we decide that something is important, we put our hearts and minds to it and we get it done. We develop vaccines for the most intractable diseases. We build networks of computers to share information instantly across vast distances. We send satellites to photograph distant stars. We accomplish the seemingly impossible. We can make great strides against poverty and homelessness. It is not a matter of means. It is a matter of will.

Instead, we are becoming increasingly polarized, with the rich and the poor growing farther apart. The richest 1 percent of us owns more than 38 percent of the wealth—*more than the poorest 90 percent of us combined.*[17] And income trends have only exacerbated this growing gap in wealth.

Poverty and affluence stand side by side in the United States. Walk downtown in one of our cities and you will see the contrasts face-to-face. A woman sits on a crate near a subway grate, hoping to stay warm. Behind her in a jeweler's window is a lavish display—enough wealth to house and feed her and forty others in her situation for a lifetime. Down the block is a towering condominium complex where one-bedroom units sell for hundreds of thousands of dollars. On the street below, a homeless man carries his makeshift cardboard "home" folded under one arm, on his way to a warm spot in the alcove of the neighborhood church.

Who will speak out against this growing divide? Who will act to amend these disparities? Will our government, with its unparalleled influence, choose to end poverty? Will our corporations, with their unparalleled wealth, choose to end poverty? Will our communities, with their unparalleled social connections, choose to end poverty? *Unfortunately, I believe the answer is no.*

Will our congregations, with their faith and their commitment to a God who calls us to action, choose to end poverty? Will our congregations hold our government accountable, hold our corporations accountable, and hold our communities accountable to end poverty? *I believe the answer can be yes,* but only when each pastor, each priest, each rabbi, each imam—every member of the clergy—proclaims the call of God to "defend the poor and fatherless; do justice to the afflicted and needy" (Ps. 82:3, NKJV).

People of faith provide shelter for those who are homeless, and we must continue to do so, *but we must also speak up and act* for safe and affordable housing to shelter everyone. We serve at soup kitchens and we stock food pantries, *but we must also speak up and act* for adequate incomes, so that all workers can afford warm and nutritious meals for their families. We tutor children who are "at risk," *but we must also speak up and act* for quality education and childcare, so that no child has to live with those risks.

God calls us "to share your bread with the hungry, and bring the homeless poor into your house" (Isa. 58:7). But God also commands us to "speak up and judge fairly; defend the rights of the poor" (Prov. 31:9, NIV). Will we listen? Will we act? Will we heed God's call?

15

"*Tikun Olam:* Mending the World"

CHARLES A. KROLOFF

Whether you are Jewish or Christian, your religion delivers a clear and unmistakable message about poverty, hunger, and homelessness. That message is the same whether you turn to the Hebrew Bible or the New Testament. Both religions teach: Faith is not enough! Unless we translate our religious beliefs into deeds, they are hollow. They don't ring true!

"Love your neighbor as yourself" is the clarion call of Leviticus; a call echoed by Jesus in the gospels. And John, in the Christian tradition, echoed the Hebrew prophets: "How does God's love abide in anyone who has the world's goods and sees a brother or sister in need and yet refuses help? Little children, let us love, not in word or speech, but in truth and action" (1 Jn. 3:17–18).

How do we experience the presence of God in our lives? Prayer is one answer. Love is another. Healing the sick, feeding the hungry, housing the homeless, securing justice for the oppressed—all these actions bring us closer to God. If we are going to wipe out homelessness, all religious groups must work closely together with one another and with the public sector. No group can do it alone. If churches, synagogues, and mosques are to make an impact, interfaith efforts are a must. Americans of all faiths are very much alike when it comes to helping the needy.

Jews know what it means to be homeless. By the end of the Holocaust, six million Jews had been exterminated and millions more uprooted from their homes. Throughout our history, we have been forced to flee for our lives.

Any Homeless Person Might Be Elijah or Jesus

According to a Jewish tradition recited every year at the Passover Seder, Elijah the prophet was himself homeless. Before he died, he announced that he would return once every generation disguised as a poor, oppressed person, arriving at the doors of Jewish homes. How Elijah was treated would determine whether humanity had improved enough to expect the coming of the messianic age. Through this tradition, the rabbis taught us an essential lesson: any poor or homeless person might be Elijah.

Christians have a comparable tradition. A saintly Irish Christian brother put it simply and clearly: "You've got to take care of the poor. You never know which one of them might be him."

I remember the first night that I spent as a volunteer at the Interfaith Hospitality Network in Westfield, New Jersey. It was one of the most profoundly spiritual moments of my life. Most people who help out at shelters or transitional housing feel a strong sense of God's presence. I certainly did. These are "transformative experiences." Afterward, we are never the same.

> Relationships with poor people are converting. My experience is that middle-class churches that open their hearts to the poor benefit at a deep spiritual level as much as the poor benefit from the bricks and mortar.

> When our compassion for a specific individual or family causes us to ask why they have become homeless, we can begin to change the system that oppresses them while we work for their individual empowerment. Charity must always be coupled with justice if we want permanent solutions.[1]

How We Show Our Love for God

If we believe that God upholds the cause of the orphan, the widow, and the stranger, we are expected to do the same. Make no mistake about it: we show our love for the Eternal by modeling our moral behavior after God's. Christians, Jews, and Moslems alike believe that every human being was created in the image of God. This does not mean that we "look like God." Instead, it refers to our moral conduct, which is supposed to resemble God's justice and compassion.

Isaiah taught that caring for the poor is an indispensable requirement for a life of piety:

> Look, you fast only to quarrel...
> Such fasting as you do today
>   will not make your voice heard on high.
> Is such the fast that I choose?...

Is it not to share your bread with the hungry,
    and bring the homeless poor into your house? (58:4–7)

The Ethics of the Fathers teaches that all our possessions belong to God: "Give unto God of what is God's, seeing that you and what you have are God's" (*Avot* 3.8). This is illustrated in a story told about Rava, a fourth-century teacher. A poor man appeared before Rava, who asked what he usually ate. The poor man replied, "Fatted chicken and old wine." Rava asked, "But don't you feel that you are a burden on the community?" The man replied, "Do I eat what is theirs? I eat what is God's."

The message is clear; our resources belong to God. If we do not give to the poor, we are questioning God's authority and flirting with idolatry. And right now, the problem in our world is not that there are not enough resources for everyone who exists. God has given us the resources to support quite a large population on this planet. Not a limitless number, to be sure, but many billions. Now the challenge is ours—to allocate our resources wisely and avoid obscene disparities between rich and poor. There are communities where children die of hunger while a few miles away a family is trying to figure out whether to take its Rolls Royce or its Jaguar for an outing. Something is badly askew when such enormous social distortions prevail.

We Are God's Partners

Some people blame God for poverty. They argue that if God is all powerful and merciful, then the Almighty should have created a world where there are no homeless people. Others argue that the presence of homeless people demonstrates that there is no supreme power, for if there were, God would certainly care enough to alleviate their plight. In other words, either God is not compassionate, is not all powerful, or does not exist. According to this reasoning, since the world is in such bad shape, God can be compassionate or omnipotent, but not both. Or perhaps God simply does not exist.

These arguments ignore two central ideas in liberal Jewish and liberal Christian thought: One, that God created a world which is imperfect. Two, that we are partners with God in improving the world. In Hebrew, we use a compelling phrase to describe the purpose of that partnership: *tikun olam,* which means "mending the world." God seems to have left a lot of important tasks for us to do. That is our purpose on earth—to help finish the job God began.

Not Choice, But Obligation

There is no word in Hebrew for "charity." The term that comes closest is *tzedaka,* which literally means righteousness or justice. This demonstrates that helping others is not a matter of choice. Rather, it is an obligation. The Talmud teaches that everyone is required to provide for the less fortunate— even someone dependent on charity has to provide for those suffering more than himself or herself.

In the gospel according to Saint Mark, Christians learn about a poor widow who contributed two copper coins. Jesus told his disciples that the poor widow put in more than all those who contributed of their abundance, because she put in everything she had. During a visit to a Manhattan drop-in facility, I met a homeless man on his way to visit a homeless friend who had been hospitalized. He was carrying soda and a bagel, all the refreshments his strained resources would permit. He understood that even he was obligated to give.

We Must Be Advocates

One of our obligations to homeless people is to be their advocates. Alex de Tocqueville once said: "The habit of inattention must be considered the greatest defect of the democratic character." Our representatives rarely receive more than three visits or ten letters about any subject. When the numbers exceed that amount, they sit up and take notice. Personal visits are the most potent. Letters are next; telephone calls are third best. There are 535 senators and representatives in the United States Congress. It would take only 53,500 citizens from this vast nation to average one hundred communications to each federal legislator—that is 1,070 per state, an easily reachable number. Many churches, synagogues, and mosques have that many adult members alone. What an overwhelming impact we could have.

Just how much do we care and how much are we willing to sacrifice? Most of us feel generous toward our fellow human beings. And yet, how often do we sacrifice? Review the past year of your life. How often did you go out of your way to help the needy?

If I Am Only for Myself

The Hebrew sage Hillel summed up our responsibility well:

If I am not for myself,
Who will be for me?
But if I am only for myself,
What am I?
And if not now, when?[2]

It is easy to become discouraged when the problem is so enormous. When I start to feel that way, I remember the story of Rabbi Israel Salanter, who was once walking in the rain. He felt his feet getting wet because his soles needed repairing. He stepped into a cobbler's shop to have them mended, but noticed that the cobbler's candle was down to one-eighth of an inch. Knowing that the cobbler needed the light of the candle to walk home, Rabbi Salanter volunteered to come back another day. But the cobbler insisted on doing the work and said, "My father taught me that as long as there is a little candlelight left, there is still time to mend."

While there is light remaining for us, let us resolve not to put off to another day what we need strong and compassionate advocates to do today, who insist that there is still time for *tikun olam,* for mending our world.

"Bring Forth Justice"

Isaiah 42:1–9; Matthew 3:13–17

BRIAN BYRNE

What do we do with a story like the one in Exodus, where Moses fled the oppressive power of Pharaoh with thousands of people in tow? God promised Moses deliverance, yet as they reached the Red Sea it seemed their escape route was closed and certain death would follow. But God would have the victory. The sea parted, the Israelites passed through, and when Pharaoh's army followed, the sea closed in on them.

Did it really happen that way? Many have a problem accepting the historicity of this story. For me the problem is greater than history; it's a problem of the present: If God could be said to deliver the Israelites in such dramatic fashion, why doesn't God deliver the millions of children who starve to death each day around the world? Why doesn't God rain down manna from heaven today for all those trapped in a wilderness of poverty and hunger?

We see a rather dramatic shift in the way God's power is imagined as Israel's faith transitions to the time of Isaiah:

> Here is my servant, whom I uphold,
>> my chosen, in whom my soul delights;
> I have put my spirit upon him;
>> he will bring forth justice to the nations.
> He will not cry or lift up his voice,
>> or make it heard in the street;
> a bruised reed he will not break,
>> and a dimly burning wick he will not quench;
>> he will faithfully bring forth justice.

He will not grow faint or be crushed
    until he has established justice in the earth. (Isa. 42:1–4)

Isaiah claims that God is going to empower God's own servant(s) to do the work of bringing forth and establishing justice. That is a major shift in imagination: instead of the people sitting back and waiting for a display of God's power to deliver them, God promises to empower the people to embody that power to change the world.

It is the promise of Incarnation—the word made flesh. It is no wonder Christians love the prophet Isaiah with all of his allusions to this empowered, but suffering servant. Jesus is for us the surprise imagined by Isaiah, not at all what we might have expected.

Even John the Baptist, who like Isaiah looked forward to the Messiah as someone who would deliver the faithful masses, didn't recognize Jesus as fitting the bill. After baptizing Jesus and bowing out, John watched from prison, shaking his head as Jesus failed to live up to John's prophetic expectations. Finally, he sent a messenger with a note to Jesus: "Are you the one who was to come or should we expect another?" Jesus responded, "Go and tell John what you have seen and heard: the blind receive their sight, the lame walk, the lepers are cleansed, the deaf hear, the dead are raised, and the poor have the good news brought to them. And blessed is anyone who takes no offense at me" (Lk. 7:22–23). Blessed are those who can accept the way my power manifests itself in the world.

When Jesus the servant appeared on the scene, it was not the kind of power that people expected, but it was Isaiah's picture: "He will not break a bruised reed or quench a smoldering wick until he brings justice to victory" (Mt. 12:20). Jesus made his way through the countryside encountering one person at a time. People came to him—some seeking to be made whole, others seeking wisdom—and walked away, sometimes healed, sometimes just confused. For some, Jesus seemed to demand too much. Others' lives were transformed, and they joined Jesus' entourage. There must be a quicker, more efficient way to get this done. What kind of God and what kind of power are these?

On September 11 we saw power where we couldn't have imagined it before. Had the thought ever crossed your mind that terrorists could hijack planes and turn them into bombs? Now it seems so simple, yet it had never occurred to me that it was a possibility. The world we live in is full of possibility, for both good and evil. Tremendous power is hidden behind the thin veil of moral and immoral imaginations. Who could have imagined a century ago that the atom could be split and that, when it was, it could unleash such tremendous power? We have seen the destructive power of that discovery, but have only scratched the surface as to its potential benefits. As people of faith, we have to ask the question of whether the power we bring to any situation is the power to heal or to destroy.

In the mid-1980s, the Interfaith Hospitality Network (IHN) did not exist. No one had thought to bring churches and synagogues together to provide hospitality to homeless families in this way. We just finished our week with IHN, and the families have moved on to their next host congregation. How many of you could have imagined that this would work five years ago? The first reaction of nearly everyone I tell about this ministry is the same. It sounds like a good idea, but will it really work? But it does. It works because people of faith, using imaginations trained by God's version of power, recognize that it puts the biblical principles of hospitality and justice into a practical format. The word *hospitality* might evoke images of tea parties and bland conversation, but there is much more to it. Henri Nouwen writes:

> If there is any concept worth restoring to its original depth and evocative potential, it is the concept of hospitality. It is one of the richest biblical terms that can deepen and broaden our insight into our relationships to our fellow human beings. Old and New Testament stories not only show how serious our obligation is to welcome the stranger in our home, but they also tell us that guests are carrying precious gifts with them, which they are eager to reveal to a receptive host.[1]

This is one of the keys to what this program is all about—the possibility of transformation for both the guests and the hosts. One woman who has been involved as a volunteer told me that for many years she had wanted to work with homeless families, particularly children, but found it easy to find excuses not to go to the downtown shelters. She and her family were visiting East Congregational United Church of Christ as we were just getting started with IHN. After I mentioned the program in my sermon she commented, "I nearly jumped out of the pew when I heard you say that you were bringing homeless families to me." She called the opportunity to minister to homeless families in her own church "miraculous—a gift from God." She interviewed for a job recently and told her prospective employer that she needed four weeks off a year so she could continue her work when IHN guests came to her church. She concluded, "IHN has absolutely changed my life and the life of my family."

There is a remarkable story in Acts 3. Peter and John are going to the temple when they encounter a lame beggar at the gate. They don't have anything to give him. Peter says, "I have no money to give you, but I can give you something else. Get up and walk!" The lame man got up and walked. Loren Mead in his book *Transforming Congregations for the Future* writes of this incident:

> The kingdom appeared when Peter acted in its power. I think the task of the local congregation is to help ordinary people become

engaged in that mystery, people willing to make the leap from the known to the unknown as Peter did; people who act on the basis of the new society, who claim the power of that kingdom, who then act for peace and justice and love and healing. The congregation's task is to call that faith forth in us and send us to act with no positive assurance that anything at all will happen. In all the complexities of history, in all the encounters with organizational realities, in all the theological debates and philosophical analyses, I think we have lost sight of that simple focus of faith. I have no idea if congregations will grow or decline if they act on that focus, and frankly I don't give a damn. But I know they will lose their soul if they don't. That part is simple.[2]

For me, that is the power behind the work we do with IHN—ordinary people who have made the leap from the known to the unknown, acting for peace and justice and love and healing. It is a beginning, though, and not the end. It is my hope that IHN, and any other ministry like it, will be a springboard for broader, systemic change. When people's imaginations become transformed for God's sake, we will see the continuing fulfillment of Isaiah's prophecy:

> Here is my servant, whom I uphold,
>   my chosen, in whom my soul delights;
> I have put my spirit upon him;
>   he will bring forth justice to the nations...
>   he will faithfully bring forth justice.
> He will not grow faint or be crushed
>   until he has established justice in the earth. (42:1–4)

God is going to empower God's own servants to bring forth justice. Instead of sitting back and waiting for the display of God's power to deliver the people in far-flung corners of the earth, God empowers us this day to embody that power to do nothing less than change the world that is within our reach.

17

"Emancipation from Poverty"

Luke 4:16–21

JAMES FORBES

When Jesus stood up to read that day in the synagogue, it is clear that he made a bold declaration. He was not just reading from Isaiah 61, the passage that says, "The Spirit of the Lord is upon me, because he has anointed me to bring good news to the poor." He actually gave a *declaration* of emancipation from poverty, because when he finished reading he said, "Today this scripture has been fulfilled in your hearing." After Abraham Lincoln's Emancipation Proclamation it was no longer legal for anybody to own slaves. That was over, even though there was a great battle—the Civil War—to determine whether there was power to back up the proclamation.

In the case of Jesus, I believe it should be clear that Jesus was not simply talking about emancipation from oppression, but initiating emancipation from poverty. According to his proclamation it would no longer be acceptable for any culture or any economic system to live as if poverty was just going to be a normal part of the economic system—to live as if some were just going to have to do without and that would be okay. Some systems may assume that economic prosperity is impossible unless a certain percentage of people are allowed to slip through the net of subsistence necessities. But Jesus' proclamation was that in the sight of God, no culture, no government, no economic system can factor in the perpetual necessity of impoverishing any people, since all people are the children of God.

What do you hear the gospel saying? I want to approach today's sermon with that spirit. How do you read the gospel of Jesus Christ with regards to the poor? Oh, I know that he said on one occasion when people were worried about whether they should waste ointment on him, "The poor you will have with you always." But was that a description of the nature of human experience, that we will always fall beneath the level of our aspiration? Or was Jesus saying, "Don't worry; as long as you don't have more than 6 percent unemployment, that's fine"? How do you read the gospel today? Does your gospel indicate that God is the one who does not even allow a sparrow to fall without a providential eye? That God is the one who declares concerning every person: "They are all mine"? If this is the God of our gospel, and if we live in a land where poverty increases and folks keep falling into the deep abyss of economic deprivation, then *the year of release will require some revolutionary changes.*

It is not right to have a permanent underclass. It is not right to have a group of people who have no hope of ever escaping from the clutches of the gnawing hands of abject poverty. That's how I read Deuteronomy and Leviticus and those texts that talk about Jubilee and the year of release. This is especially crucial for those of us in liberal or progressive churches. We quote Luke 4:16–21 so much that it is like the Magna Carta of our faith. But words lose meaning with too frequent use. I got tired of quoting, "The Spirit of the Lord is upon me." We got tired of quoting the text, so I wrote a song out of those words to give them some new life and maybe revive a fresh commitment:

> The Spirit of the Lord has anointed me,
> the Spirit of the Jubilee.
> God has sent good news to the poor
> and ordered the captives free.
> The eyes of the blind must be opened,
> we must bind up each broken heart.
> Hands that oppress must learn how to heal;
> right now is the time to start.

I thought if I were to sing about it, that might help to awaken us to the challenge of these words in our time. But singing may also lull us into complacency and contentment. So I am seizing the occasion of the birthday celebration of Martin Luther King, Jr., to arouse our consciousness and stir up a sense of urgency about Jesus' promise of good news to the poor.

I remember the day when Dr. King was assassinated. I was driving across the Marshall Street Bridge on the way to the Medical College of Virginia, where I was a chaplaincy intern. I remember that when I heard the news and drove across that Marshall Street Bridge, my tears nearly blinded me and I feared for my safe arrival on the other side, so deeply touched was I. When I arrived in the parking lot, I sat there with my hands on my steering wheel, and I said, "Martin, you shall not have died in vain." It was a commitment that I made to do what I could to see that the ministry for which he had died would not languish because others did not rise up to carry on the agenda.

So here we are today. I suspect that I am not the only one who said, "I'm going to do something about the unfinished agenda." And what is the unfinished agenda? It is not the agenda of *"I have a dream…*One day black boys and girls and white boys and girls will hold hands together." I believe that we have gotten stuck on "the dream" for the last twenty years without taking time to remember what Dr. King really died for. It wasn't simply that black folks, white folks, Asians, and Latinos could be together. Of course, that was a *part* of the agenda. But we have to remember that Dr. King was not a one-issue person. Dr. King was a systems thinker. You remember how he used to talk about the inescapable web of mutuality? How that *if there is injustice anywhere, justice is denied everywhere*? He did not believe that you could effectively deal with the mandate of Christ by just dealing with the race issue. My friend in North Carolina Carlisle Marney was right when he said to me, "Jim, you're going to discover that when we get through working on the race issue, that's just intramural sports in comparison to the class issue." How right he was!

We have enjoyed talking about the dream. We like the sound of Dr. King's voice, but it's time that we heard a hard truth: We got so stuck on the dream of racial integration that it helped us avoid the more radical demand for emancipation from poverty. So brothers and sisters, I believe that this year we have a responsibility not to allow ourselves to play reductionism with the King corpus. It involves class, and maybe if there's any congregation anywhere that is willing and ready to take up this class issue, maybe it's the Riverside Church. In fact, let me pause here and list the things that we are already doing in order to remind you that I am not here to suggest that we have been entirely remiss as a congregation. I want to list some of the things that we are already doing. But I want to list them in order to go on and say, "Well, what now, my love?"

The Riverside Church has always been involved in benevolent works. We give grants to community groups that empower disadvantaged people. We take up offerings at Christmas and Easter. At a level that most people are not aware of, in our regular church programming we're involved in attempting to bridge the poverty gaps in people's lives. The Black Christian Caucus attempts to provide scholarships to enable our students to prepare for the new agenda of a society where race and class will no longer hamper the capacity for people to fulfill their destinies. Our prison ministry awards grants to inmates and former inmates and families of inmates, and our children prepare gifts for mothers who are inmates to offer something to their children. Our social-service ministry is extensive. We have a food pantry. We had a homeless shelter, and we are in the process of discovering what our next move is going to be in that regard. We have a clothing drive. We even sell what is not used and plow it back into our social-service ministries. We have small emergency grants. We don't want anyone who is part of our family to be put out of a house without some resource to tide them over until they can find a way to make it through the crisis. Maranatha has given grants and has urged the church to be sensitive to efforts to stop the discrimination against lesbians and gays. We have decided as a council to invest a portion of our endowment and portfolio in South Africa and in neighborhood minority enterprises. We have been involved in working against environmental racism. And we continue to engage in voter registration. The list could go on and on.

We have been involved. But I find myself wondering: is it time to hear Jesus all over again? "Today this scripture has been fulfilled in your hearing." Is there a Christian congregation that is prepared to hear Dr. King with respect to class action, to hear that simply helping one or two poor people here and there will not be enough? To hear that helping our own neighborhood is not enough? To hear that there is a *system of impoverishment* and that that system is structurally designed so that all our little benevolent works will not really change anything long term until the systems themselves are changed? Our good deeds may bring momentary amelioration to a few, but until the system has been confronted, the system that perpetuates the evil notion that poverty is acceptable, the kingdom of God cannot and will not be advanced.

That's why I find myself lamenting the death of Dr. King, because it's a long way from 1963 when "I have a dream" was spoken on that mall in Washington.

You see, there was 1968. What are you going to do about now? That's what I want to know. I want to know what we are going to do about now. I know some of you young people don't know what that means. In 1968, Dr. King was getting ready to bring a Poor People's Campaign to Washington, D.C. He had decided that there needed to be a coalition of poor people from all over the nation—black and white, immigrants legal and illegal. He was coming to Washington with the Hispanic caucuses of the various denominations, with our Asian brothers and sisters, Korean and Japanese and Chinese and assorted others. He was going to bring them to Washington, and I just wish I knew what he was going to say. I think he had already given us some indications. I wish I could have been there. Would he have used that occasion to lift up the proclamation of emancipation from poverty? I do not know. But I do know that Dr. King believed that America could never be faithful to the Constitution, the Declaration of Independence, and the Bill of Rights until there was economic justice, *until poverty was declared un-American.*

Now I want to say something about why we have not taken on this mission. The mission I'm talking about is class action for the emancipation of the poor from their plight. Why haven't we done it? Why have we been content to talk about racial get-togethers and so forth? Why have we not moved further? I think we have not moved further because it will be impossible to respond to that mandate without radical transformation in our personal lifestyles. I don't think we can respond to the emancipation from poverty mandate apart from looking at the level of our consumption. I don't think we can respond without acknowledging what Walter Brueggemann calls the "great disproportion." Some of us hoard resources and throw into our trash what could easily sustain the lives of others. Also—and the reason I'm speaking softly now is because I think what I'm saying will be considered incendiary—we are a part of a capitalist system that in its ideology implies that the perpetual impoverishment of some is acceptable for the sake of the affluence of others. We have been nourished in this ideology that requires the obsolescence of some of God's own children. Most of us have become beneficiaries of this very system. I have. I always lower my voice when I talk about this, because it sounds like I'm betraying my family. You know my name is Forbes, a capitalist tool. As a Christian, I believe that it is my responsibility to tell the truth, even about the system from which I draw my temporal well-being.

It does not matter what the economic system is—socialism, communism, capitalism—if that economic system agrees, consents, theologizes, and theorizes about the acceptability of the permanent state of the impoverishment of some of God's children, then that aspect of the system that condones such an atrocity is an enemy to God. What happens when the system that I derive my well-being from becomes an enemy to the God whose love and mercy and justice I pray for? What happens then? I've got trouble. That's why I sing about the emancipation from poverty:

> The Spirit of the Lord has anointed me,
> the Spirit of the Jubilee…

There comes a time when people have to decide whether their mechanisms of avoidance must be given up so that they can respond to the mandate of the Christ. I think the time has come. Let me tell you why. For two thousand years the mandate has been given. And the Lord Jesus went about doing what he could. He went about feeding the hungry. He went about identifying with them so he could experience their condition. He said, "Foxes have holes, and birds of the air have nests; but the Son of Man has nowhere to lay his head" (Mt. 8:20). He went around healing those who had no coverage. He went around giving hope to people who were despised and rejected. After having done what he could in his limited time, he transmitted it to his disciples.

Oh, I tell you, you cannot read the Bible and cut out every section that has to do with responding to the poor and the oppressed. You wouldn't have much Bible left. Jesus made it very clear, not only on that occasion when he stood up in the synagogue (Lk. 4:16ff.), but when he said, "Blessed are you who are poor, for yours is the kingdom of God" (6:20). Furthermore, he made it clear that Abraham's bosom was reserved for those who had compassion and care. The Dives and Lazarus story is about a rich man who kept everything to himself and ended up in hell (16:23). Jesus made it very clear in Matthew 25 what we ought to be doing about the poor. The Bible makes it clear that Jesus left a legacy that says there will be no one among you who is excluded from the ranks of those for whom we care. Jesus made the agenda clear. So for how many years in this millennium are we going to sleep and sing our way along before we declare as national policy that poverty is as obnoxious and abominable as slavery? Because poverty is slavery, just in another way. And those who profit from any slavery are impoverished themselves. There needs to be a national proclamation of emancipation from poverty that becomes a policy of our nation.

One more word from King. It's amazing how people talk about Dr. King. He was a civil-rights leader. He was a champion for the poor. He was a man committed to peace. He fought against the Vietnam War. He opened up accommodations. He made it possible for education and voter registration and all of that. A secular society keeps on talking about King, but very rarely do they want to acknowledge that King was basically a preacher to the nation. I think that at this celebration we've got to hear King the preacher. Robert Michael Franklin was right in his book *Liberating Visions* when he said he had found out what King's favorite sermon was. You ought to pay attention to a preacher's favorite sermon. Once you know what King's favorite sermon was, you get some sense of how it may be possible that we as a congregation may spark the possibility of a serious consideration of a proclamation of emancipation from poverty. His favorite sermon was "The Dimensions of the Complete Life." He said there that just as in the book of Revelation the heavenly city had three dimensions, so to be full and enriched you need three areas of development. Not to be developed in those three ways means personal impoverishment.

The first dimension has to do with the length of your life and how you cared for your own self. Everybody needs to do this. We have to care for ourselves. It's not possible to love others adequately unless we have an appropriate sense of love for ourselves.

The second dimension has to do with breadth. The breadth of life is your capacity, out of self-affirmation, to care for others. To be committed to community. To be engaged in strengthening others beyond yourself. Which is King's way of saying that for anybody who is not yet willing to be a part of the commonwealth, not yet willing to be a part of the beloved community, not yet willing to invest in others who are less fortunate than they are, that there is an impoverishment in terms of the breadth of their lives.

The third dimension has to do with height. King believed that the God who made us did not abandon us. King was not a deist who believed in a God who put the world together and then said, "You all work it out the best you can. I don't care." No, King believed in a God who sits high and looks low. He believed in a God to whom it matters a lot what we do for the least of these our brothers and sisters. And he believed that until we had that vertical relationship, we were not going to be able to have the breadth nor really the length of life that we seek.

I believe that the reason we have not accomplished the emancipation from poverty that Jesus declared is because we have not eradicated the impoverishment that exists within these three dimensions of ourselves. Either we don't like ourselves well enough, or we've never matured to the place where we are able to show concern for others. Or we have not made that connection with the divine presence and power. It's not just folks who are hungry who need liberation. God's word of emancipation is first of all for the likes of us. Yes, *this is it, this is it.* I'm convinced that until we ourselves have been touched by the power of God and until God has made us aware that "I am the God of Abraham and Sarah and Isaac and Jacob and the rich and the poor, and I have given enough in this world for your life to be fulfilled"—until I can feel good about myself, until I can feel "Hallelujah, praise God," about the uniqueness of my being, I probably won't respond to the declaration for emancipation. Until we are hands-on involved in a liberation struggle, we won't have the sense of victory that they knew in those days. And I believe that unless we as a congregation make up *our* minds that we're going to find a way to help announce, in the name of God and in the spirit of King, the emancipation from poverty, we fall beneath our calling.

So this afternoon, immediately after the service here, I want you to come and help us do something. I'd like for us to sit with one another to think and discuss what we can do. What we can do as individuals and as a congregation to narrow the gap between the "haves" and the "have nots," thus moving in the direction of changing the spirit of this nation in regards to entitlement. How can we be informed? Shall we have a job-development program here? Shall we partner with corporate America to say we will help train folks if you will promise to give them the jobs? Shall we have a watchdog committee that speaks to municipal and state and federal governments about the minimal conditions under which welfare reform can be positive? Will we partner with our brothers and sisters who are poor to understand their lives and let them understand the impoverishment of our lives and how together we can be the people that God would have us be? Can we decide that whatever we're going to do, we will not do it alone, but that we will call for our sister and brother churches from around the nation to join with us in the celebration of Jesus' mandate and Jesus' proclamation of emancipation from poverty? Will we finish the agenda and bring it to completion? Jesus gave the model when he said, "The Spirit of the Lord is upon me, because he has anointed me to bring good news to the poor." So I keep praying: "Holy Spirit, Holy Spirit. Fall upon us afresh. We are Riversiders. We are old-time, long-time liberals. We are progressives from way back. We have handled many missions before. Pour out your

Spirit upon this congregation, this preacher, these preachers, these choristers, these members, from corporate America, insurance companies, educators, public servants, and politicians. Pour out your Spirit upon us and catch us up into your Spirit of urgency. For you have heard the cries of your people. And now you have come down to recruit agents of liberation. May we find ourselves saying in response, 'If you need somebody, Lord, here am I, send me.'"

PART 5

Children, Poverty, and the Just Word

Those who pay the highest price for poverty and homelessness are those who are least to blame, yet who have arguably the most to lose: the children. Nationwide, between 900,000 and 1.4 million children in America are homeless for some time in a given year.[1] The long-term effects on those children have not been fully calculated. The short-term have: serious developmental and health problems.

It doesn't take a very active imagination to identify the children who are caught in the snare of impoverishment and homelessness, and their often abandoned and abused mothers, as today's equivalent of what the Bible describes as "the widow, the orphan, and the stranger in the land." The Torah, the prophets, the Psalms, the gospels, and the New Testament epistles all voice God's concern that these people are special treasures in the human community.

Just preaching gives voice to those who have no voice. Just preaching gives voice to the voiceless because just preachers believe in *stewarding* the passions of a God who doesn't differentiate among human beings based on categories of status that humans contrive and perpetuate. Just preachers are on their guard against being bought and used as pawns by this world's powerful, who control systems that are at once self-serving and other-destroying. Just preaching is society's conscience and memory: it can neither be bought nor sell out since just preaching's idea of gain and success are based on a notion of faithfulness to what God wants most. Just preaching provides a prophetic and moral backbone of support for the widow, orphan, and stranger that is forged out of memory's hot oven of remembered personal vulnerability and deliverance by a God who refuses to look the other way in the face of need. Just preaching persists in speaking on behalf of the vulnerable child, because it listens to a God whose ear is attuned to the cries of despairing children.

18

Times of Trouble

The Assault of Poverty on America's Children

MARIAN WRIGHT EDELMAN

The Cries of Our Nation's Poor Children

Thousands of years ago, a psalmist cried out, "Why, O LORD, do you stand far off? Why do you hide yourself in times of trouble?" (Ps. 10:1) That very same cry of despair and abandonment may well be on the lips of more than twelve million poor children today, children who face terrible troubles without enough help from communities, congregations, and our nation.

That cry might well have been on the lips of Tony, one of the children who attends Martha's Table, a private program in Washington, D.C., that serves poor and homeless children. Martha's Table survives on donations and dedicated volunteers. In addition to the 2,500 sandwiches the volunteers prepare and distribute every day, they run an after-school program that includes recreation, tutoring, and food.

Given the grimness and joylessness of childhood for so many poor children, Martha's Table tries hard to celebrate the birthdays of children attending the after-school program. As their birthdays approach, the children are asked what kind of special gift they would like.

Tony desperately wanted a bike for his twelfth birthday, he confided to the staff. He had never had one before. Tony was in luck. Several used bikes had been fixed up and donated to the center. The after-school staff promised Tony his bike.

On his birthday, however, Tony quietly approached the after-school supervisor. "I want to change my birthday order," he said. "Instead of a bike, I want a bag of groceries for my mom." Then he added quietly, "And it has to be things that don't need to be cooked, because we live in the shelter and we can't use the stove."

With her heart breaking, the supervisor took Tony into the kitchen and packed two big bags full of food. She even found a day-old lemon meringue pie that had been donated by a local restaurant and put the "birthday pie" on the top of one of the bags. Then she offered to drive Tony back to the shelter because the bags were too heavy for him to carry alone.

Tony picked up one bag, and the supervisor picked up the other, and together they headed out to her car. As they walked across the parking lot to her car, the bag the supervisor was carrying broke. Broken glass and spilled food were everywhere, and on top of the pile was the birthday pie, now ruined and inedible.

The supervisor began to cry.

Tony, however, just shrugged his shoulders. He looked at the mound of ruined food–garbage now–and said, "That's my life."

Twelve-year-old boys shouldn't have to make the choice between the bicycle they have always wanted and the food they need to survive. And their lives and future should not seem to be a mound of ruined groceries, of garbage.

Of all poverty's cruel effects on children–hunger, poor health, homelessness, school difficulties, and more–perhaps the cruelest is its capacity to make children feel as if they are garbage rather than a beloved child of God, made in God's very image.

As you know too well, Tony is not alone in his circumstances. Tony is just one of the twelve million children who are living in poverty in America today. One out of every six children in our nation is poor, and one in five preschool children–years when brain development is most rapid–is poor.

Poor children don't fit our stereotypes: most live outside central cities. Most poor families have one or more workers in the family. In fact, almost three out of four of poor children in 2001 lived in families where someone worked. Earnings, not welfare, make up most of a poor family's income. Most families that receive TANF (Temporary Assistance for Needy Families), which we commonly call welfare, have just one or two children.

A family of four is considered poor if its income is below $18,104. The federal poverty level for a family of three is just $14,128. In 2001, more than four million families with children had total earnings below $18,104, despite the fact that the head of the family worked. More than five million children lived in extreme poverty–earnings at half the poverty level or lower. The poverty line is so low that millions more families earn above this official poverty level but still have trouble affording food and rent and utilities and childcare.

Tony is just one of those twelve million poor children. He is just one of the millions of children who are hungry or at risk of hunger each year. Tony is just one of the one million homeless children who need us to reach out with compassion and speak out for justice on their behalf.

The Threats Stalking Poor Children

Countless threats stalk poor children, as they did the psalmist:

Their eyes stealthily watch for the helpless;
 they lurk in secret like a lion in its covert;
they lurk that they may seize the poor;
 they seize the poor and drag them off in their net.
They stoop, they crouch,
 and the helpless fall by their might.
They think in their heart, "God has forgotten,
 [God] has hidden [God's] face, [God] will never see it."
 (Ps. 10:8b–11)

Poor children are constantly surrounded by many threats that cause them to fall behind. The "lions" that poor children face every day include hunger and poor nutrition; unaffordable or substandard housing and homelessness; preventable and untreated health problems; a lack of affordable, good-quality childcare; failing schools; and violence in their homes and neighborhoods. Far too often, poor children are stressed and stretched beyond their human capacity by so many chronic assaults from so many directions that they helplessly "fall by their might."

Hunger and Poor Nutrition

One mother, who slid from a middle-income world into poverty after the death of her husband and after her children's medical problems, recalled, "There were times when money ran short and we had no food. There were times when my son would say, 'Mom, I know you just fed me, but I'm still hungry.' That hurt me more than any knife or sword could, because there was no food in the cupboard to feed him."

Hunger stalks poor children, and even near-poor children, every day. One in three poor households experience "food insecurity," as do one in four of the near-poor households. The children have too little to eat or are not certain that they will be able to eat, because the family lacks enough money. Just imagine not knowing if you will be able to eat at the next mealtime or if you will be able to eat enough to ease your hunger. Hunger's nagging and relentless ache makes concentrating in school difficult. It stunts the growth of children's bodies and drains their energy.

If your congregation runs or supports a food pantry or soup kitchen, you may know firsthand that requests for emergency food have risen. More than half the people requesting food are children or their parents. Despite an economic downturn, the number of children receiving help from food stamps has dropped over the past decade, in large part because families who have left welfare for work or eligible working families who have never been on welfare do not know what's available or cannot spend hours filling out application forms in food-stamp offices, and because thousands of *legal* immigrants lost eligibility in 1996.

Unaffordable or Substandard Housing and Homelessness

John Perkins was born in a shelter that his mother recalled as drug-infested and dangerous, all because of bureaucratic bungling. His mother, Susan, was hardly a stereotypical candidate for homelessness. At twenty-five, she was a receptionist at a trading corporation and was attending trade school. When the company suffered heavy losses, she was fired. Pregnant with John, she quickly slipped down the slope into homelessness as all the helping hands that should have been there refused to reach out to her.

Susan went first to the unemployment office to collect her benefits. They refused to give the unemployment benefits to her unless she dropped her trade-school classes and concentrated solely on finding work. Susan was trying hard to find work, and she didn't want to drop out of school, because she believed that a college degree would make her more employable. Susan then went to the welfare office. Caseworkers there told her that she was ineligible to apply because she was technically eligible for unemployment benefits even though she wasn't collecting a penny of it. They sent her home without informing her of her right to appeal the unemployment office's decision.

Susan found a few temporary jobs that kept her from getting evicted right away, but she had to go to soup kitchens for meals. Four months later, she was evicted. Homelessness is tough for anyone, but particularly for a pregnant woman. Every twenty-eight days, according to San Francisco's shelter-system rules, she had to move from one shelter to another, dragging her belongings with her.

Susan continued to look for work, but she was caught in the predicament of people who are homeless—she needed a job to secure a permanent address and phone number, but without a permanent address and phone number, she couldn't land a job. Her job search always began and ended the same way: She would stand in a phone booth with the classified section of the newspaper in hand and countless quarters in her pockets and make her calls. No one called back.

When John was born, the job search had to be put on hold. Childcare suddenly became another bridge Susan would have to cross in the rocky path out of unemployment and homelessness. For almost two years, whenever job opportunities arose, subsidized childcare spaces did not.

Many families are caught in the net of homelessness or substandard housing. Nearly three out of four poor families with children cannot afford their rent or mortgage or utility payments based on federal housing affordability guidelines that state they should spend no more than 30 percent of income on housing. They are forced to spend too much of their limited income on housing and have to skimp on food or other necessities. Many are pushed into homelessness. Inability to afford housing and utilities is one reason poor families move frequently from home to home and from school to school, as parents are forced to seek cheaper housing, double up temporarily with friends and family, or try to stay ahead of eviction notices and bill collectors. Children who move and change schools tend to have lower math and reading scores and are significantly less likely to finish school on time.

The worst housing-affordability problems result in homelessness. Children who become homeless are exposed to the communicable diseases and chaos found in shelters and suffer increased infant mortality, chronic diarrhea, asthma, delayed immunizations, family separation, missed school, and other damage. And no data can even begin to measure the damaged self-esteem and emotional toll on a child who has no place to call home.

Health Problems

When Bobby, a preschooler in Boston, scratched a mosquito bite on his leg, the area became infected. His parents took him to a doctor, who prescribed an antibiotic. Bobby's father earned very low wages at a job that did not provide health insurance, however, so the family could not immediately afford to buy the prescription. As a result of the family's poverty, the infection grew dangerously out of control, and Bobby was hospitalized for three days in order to receive intravenous antibiotics. Each of those hospital days cost about $800, doctors estimated.

Just a few beds away from Bobby lay a little girl, also from a poor family. The doctors had cured her of the illness that first brought her to the hospital. Now, however, they could not discharge her because her family lived in unsafe housing with toxic levels of lead and other health hazards. And so the little girl lay in the large, steel hospital bed, where she was becoming increasingly withdrawn as the separation from her family grew longer and longer. The hospital staff did not know when her parents would be able to secure safe housing or if the hospital would have to discharge her into foster care rather than returning the toddler to her loving but poor parents.

Poor children are at an increased risk of stunted growth, anemia, and lead poisoning. A baby who is born poor is less likely to survive to its first birthday than a baby born to an unwed mother, to a high school dropout, or to a mother who smoked during pregnancy.

Lack of Childcare

Because so many poor children live in families with a working parent, they face the double bind of needing childcare so the parent can work, but earning an income that is too little to pay for good-quality childcare. Or like Susan, they cannot even accept a job because they cannot find or afford childcare. Childcare costs an average of between $4,000 and $6,000 a year, with some infant care costing as much as $10,000 a year—for each child.

This is far more than the average poor family with children can afford to pay. Although the Childcare and Development Block Grant offers the prospect of help for poor families to pay for childcare, only 12 percent of eligible families are receiving such help.

As a result, many low-income children wind up in low-quality, even unsafe care that offers them few opportunities for learning. When children are in unstable childcare, the sudden absence of care can force parents into untenable choices: staying home to care for their child and possibly losing their job, or going to their job and leaving their child alone or in another unsafe arrangement. No parent should have to make such a choice.

School Difficulties

A social worker reflecting back on his childhood growing up in poverty recalled, "It was hard to focus on school when you were worrying about survival—things like how to get home from school safely and how we were going to eat that night. In high school, I was a D student. I grew up in the projects, sharing my bedroom with two older sisters, with plenty of crime and poverty around us. I had to start working when I was ten. My whole life focus was not on learning; it was on staying alive. I had two or three odd jobs, from cutting grass to working in a janitorial service. That money was not to save for a bicycle but to help pay for rent and food."

Poor children's troubles include repeated years of schooling, lower test scores, and less education. Poverty puts children at a greater risk of falling behind in school than does living in a single-parent home or being born to teenage parents, according to data from the United States Department of Education. And because of where they are compelled to live, poor children usually attend the poorest schools, which have fewer financial and material resources *and* difficulty hiring and keeping the most skilled teachers and administrators. The disparities between schools attended by poor children and those attended by higher income children are indeed what author Jonathan Kozol has called "savage inequalities."

Do Justice

After crying out in despair and abandonment, and feeling terror at the deadly threats on every side, the psalmist in trust declares to God:

But you do see! Indeed you note trouble and grief,
    that you may take it into your hands;
the helpless commit themselves to you;
    you have been the helper of the orphan...
O Lord, you will hear the desire of the meek;
    you will strengthen their heart, you will incline your ear
to do justice for the orphan and the oppressed,
    so that those from earth may strike terror no more.
    (Ps. 10:14, 17–18)

God *does* see the trouble and grief of poor children. We who would be God's faithful partners must likewise be the helpers of poor children and do justice for the children and families oppressed by poverty so that the terrors of hunger, homelessness, lack of childcare and healthcare, poor schools, and violence will strike them no more.

How can we help poor children and do justice for them?

1. Help others to see them as God does and to understand and respond to their plight. To be sure, education programs, congregational forums, newsletter articles, and other opportunities can be effective ways to increase congregation members' awareness of the problems confronting poor children, the causes, the solutions, and what they as congregation members can do. But also the pulpit or bimah is an exceptionally powerful place from which to proclaim God's concern for children living in poverty and to remind congregation members of the enduring faith mandate to seek justice and care for those who are poor, those who are powerless, those who are young and most vulnerable.

2. God is the "helper of the poor," and we are likewise to help children in poverty in immediate, hands-on ways. Most congregations already have programs in place to help people in need. Encourage congregation members to participate more fully in these programs and consider what more needs to be done with a sense of urgency. Children have only one childhood. Is there an unmet need of poor children that your congregation can meet? In your preaching and in your work with the congregation, explore ways to address the income, housing, childcare, healthcare, nutritional, and educational needs of poor children in your community, state, and nation.

3. Do justice for poor children and families oppressed by poverty. Proclaim justice, justice, justice as God's will for poor children. When congregation members shy from systemic change and turn to charity as a substitute, preach justice, justice, justice. Private charity—however important—is a supplement to, not a substitute for, public justice.

Psalm 9, which is connected to Psalm 10 in a way that leads scholars to treat them as a unit, reads:

> Rise up, O LORD! Do not let mortals prevail;
>> let the nations be judged before you.
> Put them in fear, O LORD;
>> let the nations know that they are only human. (9:19–20)

Truly, it is not only individuals but also the *nations* that will be judged by God. And justice is the measure by which God will judge our nation.

As the psalmist reminds us, the nations are only human, and we all too easily fail to embody God's justice. When that happens, people of faith must call for justice, must write letters urging justice for children, must call members of Congress urging our nation to do justice for children who are poor, must visit legislators and urge justice, must remind Congress that our nation is only human, not God, and it is God who sets the standard of justice.

Daily and pervasive child suffering and need are not the acts or choices of God. They are our moral and political choices as American citizens and leaders. We can change them with moral and political leadership and with balanced national investment priorities. We have the money. We have the know-how. We have the experience. We have the vision. And we have the responsibility. What we lack is the spiritual, civic, and political will to break through the profound moral indifference, lack of awareness, poisonous politics of self-interest and greed, narrow ideological agendas, and political hypocrisy between word and deed that leave millions of children behind. And no one is in a better position to lead the social, moral, and political transformation required than the faith community, which can proclaim God's call for justice and can inspire its millions of members to do justice for God's beloved children.

We *can* build a nation where families have the support they need to make it at work and at home; where every child enters school ready to learn and leaves on the path to a productive future; where babies are likely to be born healthy and sick children have the healthcare they need; where no child has to grow up in poverty; where all children are safe in their community and every child has a place to call home; and where all of us can proudly say, "We leave no child behind."

The Act to Leave No Child Behind is comprehensive legislation for America's children introduced by Senator Christopher Dodd of Connecticut and Representative George Miller of California. It incorporates policies and programs proven to improve the lives of children. Many of the provisions in the Act's twelve titles are drawn from legislation previously introduced by Republicans and Democrats in Congress. Representing a renewed commitment to our children, the Act will benefit every child in America. It recognizes that children do not come in pieces, but in families and communities.

The Act to Leave No Child Behind lays out a vision of how we can and must care for our children. Its provisions would provide every child:

- **A Healthy Start**: The Act would provide health coverage to all of the more than 9 million uninsured children in America, address childhood illnesses, and improve the quality of children's health care.

- **A Head Start**: The Act would increase funding for childcare and for three- and four-year-olds in Head Start so that *all* eligible children who need these benefits could participate. It would also strengthen our education system by improving teacher training and quality, increasing public school accountability, reducing class size, and modernizing school facilities.

- **A Fair Start**: The Act would help ensure that hardworking parents have the supports they need to remain employed and help lift themselves and their children out of poverty. It would also provide broad tax relief to low-income families who currently earn too little to qualify for many tax benefits.

- **A Safe Start**: The Act would help to ensure that more children are in safe, nurturing, and permanent families. It would extend supports to families before they suffer family breakdown and would help encourage permanency for children who cannot safely stay at home. The law would also strengthen youth development efforts and address other critical safety issues, such as gun violence and effective delinquency prevention programs.

Because of its comprehensive scope and ambitious but achievable vision, it will likely take five to ten years before every title in the act has passed and we are assured that no child is left behind. Religious leaders and congregation members can hasten that day by joining the Movement to Leave No Child Behind and calling persistently for justice and swift passage of all the titles of the Act to Leave No Child Behind.

If we—as people of faith and as citizens—do justice and act so that we leave no child behind, one day no child like Tony will be abandoned to poverty and made to feel like garbage, and every child will know from our words and our deeds that they are a beloved child of God made in God's very image.

"God's Justice and America's Sixth Child"

Deuteronomy 15:7–11;
Mark 9:35–37; 10:13–15

WALTER BURGHARDT

A Man and a Woman

I begin with a man and a woman–a Jew and a Jewess, a man from God's people rescued from the slavery of Egypt, and a woman who lived while Jesus was alive. The man is Joshua, the successor of Moses, chosen by God to lead God's people into the promised land. Listen to the Hebrew Testament as it describes how Joshua caused the walls of Jericho to fall:

> Now Jericho was shut up inside and out because of the Israelites; no one came out and no one went in...To the people [Joshua] said, "Go forward and march around the city; have the armed men pass on before the ark of the LORD." As Joshua had commanded the people, the seven priests carrying the seven trumpets of rams' horns before the LORD went forward, blowing the trumpets, with the ark of the covenant of the LORD following them...They did this for six days. On the seventh day they rose early, at dawn, and marched around the city in the same manner seven times...As soon as the people heard the sound of the trumpets, they raised a great shout, and the wall fell down flat; so the people charged straight ahead into the city and captured it. (Josh. 6:1–20)

And I begin with a woman. She emerges from a parable on the lips of Jesus (Lk. 18:1–8). The parable has two characters, two players: a judge and a widow. The judge is a symbol of power. And this particular judge is uncommonly powerful. Not only is he a judge, he is a judge in a patriarchal society in which males command and females obey. This judge is afraid of no one, neither God nor people. The widow is a symbol of powerlessness. With her husband dead, she has no male to defend her, protect her, plead her case. Some unnamed male is taking advantage of her; she wants justice; and all she can do is appeal to a coldhearted, unfeeling male judge. Not surprisingly, the judge refuses.

What does the widow do? Retire to her home, reenter her kitchen, submit in the way women were supposed to submit? Not this widow. She keeps after the judge, keeps pounding away at him: "I want justice. I want justice. I want justice." So insistent is she that the judge finally gives in. Not because he is convinced by her arguments. Not in the slightest. What moves him is clear: "Because this widow keeps bothering me, I will grant her justice, so that she may not wear me out by continually coming" (v. 5)– literally, "lest she come and give me a black eye."

Justice Consumes Them

Now let go of Joshua and the widow; we shall return to them. For the present, focus on the single word that consumed both of them: justice. But not just any justice–*God's justice.*

You see, when a fearless prophet named Micah declared to Israel, "What does the LORD require of you but to do justice?" (6:8), he did not impose on God's people a good, earthly ethic: "Give to every man, woman, and child what each person has a strict right to demand because he or she is a human being, has rights that can be proven from philosophy or have been written into law." What, then, was the justice God wanted to "roll down like waters" (Am. 5:24)? In a single word, *fidelity.* Fidelity to what? To relationships and responsibilities that stemmed from their covenant with Yahweh. What relationships? To God, to people, to the earth.

1. Love God above all else, above every creaturely idol, above power and money and fame.

2. Love every human person as another self, another I, as if you were standing in his or her shoes, especially the paper-thin shoes of the downtrodden.

3. Touch the earth, things, all that is not God or the human person, with reverence, with respect, with awe, as a gift of God, a trace of divinity.

It is this Israelite tradition on justice that sparked the ministry of Jesus. He summed it up in the synagogue at Nazareth: "The Spirit of the Lord is upon me, because [the Lord] has anointed me to bring good news to the poor. [The Lord] has sent me to proclaim release to the captives and recovery of sight to the blind, to let the oppressed go free" (Lk. 4:18). That ministry he proclaimed pithily in a new commandment, a breathtaking command he laid on us not long before he was crucified for us: "Love one another as I have loved you" (Jn. 15:12).

The point of all this? If biblical justice is fidelity to relationships, then biblical injustice is a refusal of relationships, a refusal to love God above all else, a refusal to love my sisters and brothers as other selves, a refusal to touch the things of God with reverence and respect. In focusing today on our children, two justice issues cry agonizingly for our attention: violence and health.

Violence

We want safe communities for our children. In this "land of the free," the younger you are, the more vulnerable you are. In the richest country on earth, roughly one out of every six children is growing up poor, hungry, and ill educated. Among industrialized countries the United States ranks twelfth in the proportion of children in poverty, seventeenth in efforts to lift children out of poverty, eighteenth in the gap between rich and poor children, last in protecting our children against gun violence.[1] "According to the Center for Disease Control and Prevention, U.S. children under age 15 are 12 times more likely to die from gunfire, 16 times more likely to be murdered with a gun, 11 times more likely to commit suicide with a gun, and 9 times more likely to die in a firearm accident than children in 25 other industrialized countries combined."[2] In the capital of the United States, in one five-year period, 245 children died of gunshot wounds. Between 1979 and 1998, nearly 84,000 American children were killed by guns—*more than all our battle fatalities in Vietnam.*

If you still dream that violence to children is an occasional incident in a peaceful America, or if you think it is limited to gunfire, listen to this:

> *All American children are at risk* from the proliferation of guns which threaten all of us everywhere; from the pollution of our air, water, earth, airwaves, and Internet with smut and toxic substances; from the breakdown of family not only from out-of-wedlock births but pervasive divorce and erosion of extended family supports; from epidemic substance abuse and from domestic violence that knows no race or income limits; and from the erosion of civility evidenced by road rage, profane language, and the coarse public discourse which pervades our culture.[3]

Health

Take a striking statistic. Take, in alphabetical order, twenty-three industrialized countries: Australia, Austria, Belgium, Canada, Czech Republic, Denmark, Finland, France, Germany, Hungary, Ireland, Italy, Japan, Luxembourg, Netherlands, New Zealand, Norway, Poland, Portugal,

Spain, Sweden, Switzerland, and United Kingdom. What is striking about these countries? Each and every one of them has safety-net policies for children. Specifically, here are three: (1) universal health insurance/ healthcare, (2) paid maternal/parental leave at childbirth, and (3) family allowance/child dependency grants. America's "sixth child" would fare better if he or she lived in any one of these twenty-three countries. Why? Because the United States has none of these: no guaranteed health insurance, no income safety net, no guaranteed parental leave with pay after childbirth.[4]

Safe and healthy communities for our children? In the richest country on the face of the earth? Our healthcare would be laughable, were it not so tragic, so literally deadly. Nearly eleven million of our children are uninsured. Eleven million images of God.

Today's "Joshua" and "Widow"

Now back to Joshua and the widow. But not quite the same two people. I mean today's Joshua circling today's capitol, today's woman clamoring insistently for justice now. I mean your ceaseless cry to the politically powerful in the words you heard from the Hebrew Torah, from the book called Deuteronomy:

> If there is among you anyone in need, a member of your commu- nity in any of your towns within the land that the LORD your God is giving you, do not be hard-hearted or tight-fisted toward your needy neighbor. You should rather open your hand, willingly lend- ing enough to meet the need, whatever it may be…Give liberally and be ungrudging when you do so, for on this account the LORD your God will bless you in all your work and in all that you under- take. (Deut. 15:7–8, 10)

I ask you to remind the politically powerful how Jesus rebuked his disciples when they tried to keep children from bothering him: "Let the little children come to me; do not stop them; for it is to such as these that the kingdom of God belongs" (Mk. 10:14).

Let me become chillingly concrete. When you are raising your voices for your children, *you are not on your knees begging for charity*. Your heads held high, *you are demanding justice*. What your children have a strict right to demand. "Give me justice! Give me justice! Give me justice!" Facing the White House, I dare to declare: "Mr. President, you may not divide the pie so that everybody gets a piece beginning with the richest. No, you must look first to those who need it most. Not the children of the highly taxed, the children of the lowly poor."

How do I know this? Because this is the justice God demanded of God's kings, the supreme leaders in the land who were appointed to be God's servant leaders. Read and reflect on Psalm 72, a prayer for God's king, for God's representative on earth:

Give the king your justice, O God,
    and your righteousness to a king's son.
May he judge your people with righteousness,
    and your poor with justice…
May he defend the cause of the poor of the people,
    give deliverance to the needy,
    and crush the oppressor…
For he delivers the needy when they call,
    the poor and those who have no helper.
He has pity on the weak and the needy,
    and saves the lives of the needy.
From oppression and violence he redeems their life;
    and precious is their blood in his sight.
(Ps. 72:1–4, 12–14)

A priority for the poor, particularly for poor children, is not on America's political agenda today. And insofar as it isn't, we see how far we stray from a sense of God's justice for our land.

Unhappily, our children do not enjoy a lobby comparable to those that spend billions for guns in the home, for tobacco smoke in the lungs, for salmonella in school hamburgers, for arsenic in our drinking water, for carbon dioxide in our air.

Three weeks ago, I was gifted with a brand new knee courtesy of Medicare. Now I can walk through Washington weeping for the uninsured: the crippled kid too poor for a brace, the youngsters inhaling lead poisoning in their rundown shacks, the baby born with HIV.

And still, my friends, you are far from powerless. I see in each of you, and in millions more like you across our country, a rebirth of Joshua and of the gospel widow. In my dream I see new Joshuas gathering together, not soldiers in arms, but infants in their carriages, adolescents on their crutches, teenagers in their ragged Reeboks, all marching in terrifying thousands around your capitol seven times as Andy Young did in the 1960s, clamoring with all the passion of the widow, "Justice! Give us justice! Justice for these children of God! Don't you hear the children crying?!"

And when you can no longer walk, talk! Your voices are powerful: e-mail and airmail, phone and FedEx. Teach your little ones to scrawl one word, seven forceful letters: *j-u-s-t-i-c-e.* Send it to your servants in the Senate and House, in the very White House itself. We elected them to represent us. Let's make loud and clear what we want represented in the place where laws get made and laws get changed. They will listen, if there are enough of us—if not out of compassion, then from self-preservation.

Yours too is the power of prayer—prayer that not only rises like incense to heaven, but that can penetrate the smoke-filled cloakrooms of Congress.

Believe it! A mass of committed Christians and Jews, yes, Hindus, Muslims, and Buddhists, can topple the walls of injustice, can free our sixth child from an oppressive slavery. Not by our naked humanity, but by the power of a God for whom nothing, *absolutely nothing,* is impossible. All God asks is that we love one another to death—love as God loves us—even unto crucifixion.

To sum up, I ask you three questions, and I would appreciate your response, loud and clear:

1. Are you convinced that in our country every sixth child is suffering serious injustice?

2. Do you believe that in the power of God you and your sisters and brothers can correct, even destroy, such injustice?

3. Are you willing—are you *resolved*—like the widow in the gospel to keep crying for children's justice, to keep struggling for children's justice, and if necessary to suffer crucifixion for children's justice?

Go forth, then, and in the power of God see to it that no child is left behind!

20

"Time Suspended: Poverty Meets Grace"

PAMELA D. COUTURE

I live less than two miles from Colgate Rochester Divinity School, but under certain circumstances they can be a long two miles. Last week I was driving to school down Goodman Street with many stops and starts. First, a garbage truck was blocking most of the right lane, and cars lined up behind it had to inch their way around to proceed. Then, just before the light at the expressway, a dump truck was stopped. Carefully crawling past, we all continued. Just across the expressway, I was stopped two cars behind a little yellow school bus. The bus blocked the right lane and had its stop sign extended. So, for the third time in the span of just a few minutes and less than a mile, I pulled to a stop, not paying much attention, but ready to get on with it.

In my peripheral vision, I noticed the bus driver. Something about him intrigued me, and I began to watch. He had gotten out of the bus. He was an older man wearing a fluorescent green vest. He walked slowly, with a very slight stoop that inclined him toward the house he was approaching. He took four or five steps, till he was about halfway down the walk to the front of the house, and paused, looking intently at the house. As I followed his gaze, I saw that the door had opened, and a little girl, maybe seven years old, was standing at the door, half opening it, half pulling her coat over her shoulder. No other adults were in sight. She got her coat adjusted as the door banged shut behind her, and she walked her six or seven steps toward the driver, looking at him. As she came near, he spoke to her, and extended his hand, and he walked her at her pace to the bus.

Shortly, we were all on our way to school. But I was moved to tears. That morning, many little girls had "missed the bus." Their parents would be scolding as they hurried them to school, or they would be home alone for the day. This little girl would be in school that day because her bus driver had been willing to wait for her. Not only would she arrive safely at school, but her public day began in a moment of grace. It began with a welcoming gaze, a greeting, a tender hand, and a gentle walk down the sidewalk from a graceful, grandfatherly man.

What was it that caused me to arrive at school in tears that day? There is the obvious reason: children's flourishing is important to me. I am particularly concerned about increasing the chances for the flourishing of the 23 percent of our children in the United States who live near or in material poverty, often with substandard nutrition, food, housing, healthcare, or education. Although children's poverty is material, it is also social: children are impoverished when they lack the necessary connections with neighborhoods, schools, organizations, and adult friends. In this little glimpse of an adult-child relationship, I saw a social connection that boosted this little girl's immune system against the demoralizing effects of poverty. The moment between the bus driver and the little girl radiated hope for the future. The opportunity to happen upon an unorchestrated, unprogrammed moment in which an adult took time to wait tenderly for a child in his normal walk of life made me grateful.

Think about it: preparing children (and adults) for school is a very goal-oriented event. Getting children out of bed, fed, clothed, teeth brushed, hair combed, warmer clothes on, lunch packed, back packs correctly filled, can be a daunting way to begin the morning—in some households enough energy is exerted in this process to fill the whole day. And getting children off to school should be taken seriously. Children have a day laid out for them. Their teachers usually have prepared carefully. The conscientious teachers among us make specific lesson plans for the day, and they make themselves ready through the wholeness of their being so that they can be emotionally present that day to make personal connections with students, to respond in artful ways to move a student toward a learning goal. To such a teacher a child brings not only homework but, hopefully, curiosity and a desire to learn. A child brings hope for a world that is opening before her or him. A child brings dreams and aspirations that may have vague shapes and contours, but these vague outlines wait to be fulfilled in detail as goals and education join with desires to give the future substance. In the interaction between the plans of the teacher and the yearnings of the student, a day at school becomes a work of art.

Herein we find a paradox of teaching and learning: the art of teaching requires the teacher to know the aim of teaching so well that the teacher can artfully and intuitively know when to suspend a preestablished goal to make space for the student's present curiosity. The paradox is this: to reach our learning goals, we must also suspend our learning goals, to open time in a different kind of way. We open a moment of time that invites curiosity, creativity, imagination, and wonder. In the moments in which time is opened up for us in this way, learning becomes a gift that we receive, rather than a goal that we achieve. Within our efforts to learn, learning comes from beyond ourselves; learning becomes a mystery. When we learn in this way, we learn gratefully.

The Christian season of Lent is a highly goal-oriented time. Beginning with Ash Wednesday, Christians spend six weeks in morally serious reflection from which there is little relief. Christians are exhorted to examine their lives, to contemplate their sin, to search their relationship with God and with their neighbors in prayer, and to prepare for the passion of Christ. There is little relief from the purple overtones of Lent for these forty days. The preparation, the plans, all focus on the story that will unfold in Holy Week, the story of the horrible events that emerge from Jesus' confrontation with personal sin ensnared in the evil of so-called powers and principalities. This story of the passion of Christ will tell of worldly systems that create power and then seduce those within the system to cooperate with power, even when it means exploiting others. When we listen to the passion story and take our own desire to imitate Jesus seriously, this is a frightening lesson about the world in which we live, this lesson about the extent to which the systems of power around human beings can do them in. When we listen to the passion story and identify ourselves with the disciples, we are reminded, perhaps, of an even more terrifying truth: that we who live in faith are fully capable of betrayal and abandonment, even of those we love. Lent is focused toward a passion that unfolds a drama that reveals the worst about humankind.

When we closely examine the lives of all God's children, we are also invited to study the worst stories about humankind. Every now and then I hear an astute pastor or bishop—a pastor or bishop who is in the forefront of all the church's important social causes—say, "The initiative on children and poverty is like motherhood and apple pie. This is no contest. How can anyone be against poor children?" But caring for all God's children quickly leads us to a host of knotty social issues, to the prevalence of sexual and physical abuse in the family, to the social dependence of some communities on maintaining an economy built around prisons, to our international dependence on both legal and illegal trade in drugs and guns, to the organization of economies that creates wealth for a few and great poverty, disease, and famine for most of the world's population. Children in Syracuse, elsewhere in the United States, and in other places in the world become the beneficiaries and victims of our larger social and economic systems. Whether they are primarily beneficiaries or victims is often determined only by circumstances of birth. When as people of faith we attempt to challenge or even tinker with such systems, we risk bringing the powers and principalities down on our own heads. When we people of faith live as if we can benefit from these systems without being responsible for their effects, we are like the disciples, who happily break bread with Jesus but shortly thereafter fall asleep in the garden; we are like Judas, who betrays Jesus for his own gain; we are like Peter, who denies Jesus to save himself. We might as well say, "How could anyone have crucified that wonderful, gentle man with the long brown hair and loving gaze who hangs on the wall of most church parlors? It's probably just a story." Church tradition has it right: we can only fully receive the drama of the passion story if we have focused on our goal and prepared well in advance. It is a season of the utmost moral and psychological seriousness.

But part of the preparation for Holy Week is a festival of the church: Palm Sunday. Palm Sunday is the beginning of the end of Lent. The gospels tell the story of Jesus' riding a donkey through the eastern gate of Jerusalem, cheered by crowds and followers. A scholarly study of the symbols in the story—the donkey, the procession through the eastern gate, and the "hosannas" of the crowd—show that all of the story anticipates tragedy. These symbols associate Jesus with the prophecies of the Hebrew Scriptures, with the anticipation of the coming realm of God, the king of the Jews, and of all the tragedy that is expected to befall the good king when he meets the powers and principalities of the world. The symbols mark the presence of dread, an anticipation of violence.

Yet these symbols of dread are cradled in hopeful anticipation, in shouts of joy, in excitement, in celebration. And through the traditions of the church, we have come to associate the glee of Palm Sunday with children. Palm Sunday, with its palms and greenery, is a liturgically playful festival in which we are given permission to do things that otherwise look foolish. For example, the congregation I belonged to in Atlanta joins with other downtown congregations to parade through the city streets, singing, waving palm branches, and engaging in a happy, foolish behavior that on any other day would be considered quite bizarre. And perhaps it's even more bizarre to go around waving palm branches, in a building or outside, when you live in upstate New York and it has been snowing all week. On Palm Sunday, we have permission to play as happy children, despite the rigors of Lent.

Palm Sunday creates the kind of time that is like the time created by the grandfatherly bus driver who waits for his passenger, or the teacher who suspends her or his goals in the presence of the student's natural curiosity. In the midst of a season that is rightfully serious, the celebrations of Palm Sunday open up a different kind of time, a time of suspended goals, what philosophers call "*paratelic* time," time that stands still—suspended time. The lives of adults and, increasingly, the lives of children are crowded with goals and offer little opportunity to experience paratelic time. But frequently, children remind us of their and our need for paratelic time. Paratelic time, suspended time, Palm Sunday time—whatever you want to call it—is one of the greatest gifts we can give our children and ourselves. It keeps hope alive.

It may not be within our power to eradicate sin and evil, but it is within the power of each one of us to receive and, by God's grace, create moments of Palm Sunday time, moments that sustain hope in the face of sin and evil.

Some friends and their children and I recently gathered for an evening at a musical event that was really aimed toward adults. The band was setting up on a stage at the front of the restaurant that was table height above the main floor. As some of the children entered the room and their mother chose a table in the middle, I heard one of the boys say, "But I want to sit in front." We motioned them to the front to join our table, and the performance began, less than ten feet from the four children. The children became enthralled. First they gazed intently at the performers and then inched their chairs closer to the stage until they poked their feet onto the stage. A mother who was new to the experience began to correct them, but another mother who knows these performers and their attitudes toward children assured her, "It's okay." This mother knew that these performers welcome the attention of children at their events. Eventually, the waitress brought hamburgers and chicken fingers to the children, and the children used the front of the stage as a table, eating at the feet of the performers, still riveted on their music. As we knew they would, the performers occasionally began to talk with the children between songs. Knowing they were welcome, the children became more and more intent on the music and, of course, didn't want to go home. In the music and the relationships they were building, the children were losing themselves in the kind of suspended time that children crave.

What created that paratelic time? First, it's the passion these musicians bring to their performance, the desire to perform excellently, but it's an excellence that flows into a desire to share with others, to invite, not coerce but invite others, regardless of their age, into the joy. We too can create suspended time when we invite, not coerce others to share those things that we really enjoy.

The experience of suspended time is a key to understanding many of the theological ideas that emerge in scripture from the experience of the death and resurrection of Christ. What does it mean that Christians are to live in the world but not be of it? What does it mean that Christians are to live as if the realm or kingdom of God is already here, although it is not yet here? What does it mean that Christians are to be baptized into a death that is also a resurrection? What does it mean that Christians may enter the realm or kingdom of God by becoming like little children? Such questions can be answered by long theological arguments, but they can also be answered by glimpsing adults and children enjoying suspended time together.

In paratelic time we are drawn out of ourselves so that we forget the time. This kind of experience of time is an essential part of our religious experience—in suspended time, found on a sidewalk or in music making or in many other joyous activities, we are invited to lose ourselves in the good gifts of God. Like musicians who create hospitality in an environment in which music is performed, God invites us through suspended time into God's hospitality. Like the bus driver who creates hospitality on a sidewalk, we discover that in God's time, we are not ignored, overlooked, or rushed. In God's time, God stops for us. God walks toward us. God waits for us to adjust our coats or our lives. God extends a hand, until we are ready to put our hand in God's. On Palm Sunday, God suspends time and pauses while we get our act together, as the grandfatherly bus driver did: only then can we get where the drama of Easter will take us.

PART 6

The Voice of the Poor

As a preacher myself, I am disturbed by the implications of the authors in this section. They seem to be telling me that I and most preachers function pretty much as Job's friends did. I hear them saying that Job's friends were at their best that first week of their visit: when all they did was sit in awe and silence before Job's catastrophic predicament. After they ceased their silence and started their inane attempts to "fix" Job with a theology that they'd brought with them, a theology that had no capacity to rethink itself even in the presence of a man and a set of circumstances that completely challenged everything they thought they knew, they commenced an unjust stewardship of both Job's life and God's word. I am appalled by the insinuation that just preaching finds its true center when it allows itself to hear and discover the message out at the ragged edge where the Jobs of our world continue to ask the kinds of questions and make the kinds of statements that can be made only by people who (1) have deeply suffered and (2) have the courage to keep living in the face of the suffering and to tell the truth of their pain even to those that they have no reason to trust. Someone said it well in the movie *Malcolm X*: there is nothing more dangerous in the world than someone with nothing to lose. Those are the prophets of today. To be faithful scribes of the prophets' message for our world means attending to the places where today's prophets speak.

Just preachers know that the true center isn't where the world has set the text or target. Just preachers know that it is the world's powerful, those who think they have a lot to lose, who draw the lines around the countries, who make the decisions about class and caste. Just preachers risk crossing lines—*questioning lines*—and standing in a place where true accompaniment includes a kind of advocacy that emerges from intentional and nonmanipulative relationships with those at the edges of society, morality, theology, and what we normally think is "decent church."

21

The Word Off Center

Preaching at the Margins

FRANCISCO O. GARCÍA-TRETO

Prologue: Growing up Marginal

Growing up Protestant (actually, we called ourselves *evangélicos*, evangelicals), in Catholic Cuba forced me to face from a very early age the tensions inherent in the center/margin religious dynamic implied in the title of this essay. At the time, I did not yet have the vocabulary or the concepts of postcolonial studies[1] to help me to define the issues, but I found it strange, not to say painful at times, that I was constantly being asked to reject elements of Cuban culture because they were not compatible with being *evangélico*.[2] At the same time, I absorbed, mostly unaware, a number of customs that only later I came to recognize as originating in the practice of United States Protestantism or even of United States secular society.[3] Years later, while doing research for a book on Presbyterian missions to the Mexican Americans of the American Southwest,[4] I confirmed what I had of course by then long recognized: that I had been formed in essential ways by a mission that, wittingly or not, had shared a colonizing (or "Americanizing") agenda. That agenda placed me simultaneously on the margin of Cuban culture, even as it defined me as an object of mission, marginal to the center constituted by American Protestantism. It is from this point of view, further complicated (or enriched) by my having lived now more than four decades as an exile in this country, that I view the subject at hand.

A conception of "missionary" preaching in which the margin is addressed from the center in order to proclaim the Word, and in which the Word is conveyed by those in the center (who know it) to those on the margin (who are presumed not to know it) fits the pattern I have been

145

describing. Fernando Segovia, among others, points out that these are situations in which "the political, economic, and cultural center also functions as a religious center" and where therefore other pairs of terms derived from the center/margin idea come into play to shape discourse. These "binomials," as Segovia calls them, include the very familiar pair "believers/unbelievers-pagans" and its derivatives "godly/ungodly," "worshipers of the true God/worshipers of false gods," and "religious/idolatrous-superstitious."[5] What Segovia, who grew up as I did in Cuba, but as a Catholic, does not include in this list is the pair of terms that, in my early experience, dominated that list: "*evangélico*/catholic."

In my early milieu, the Word of God was, of course, the Bible, and specifically, the current revision of the sixteenth-century Reina/Valera translation.[6] Placing this book (perhaps with a printed bookmark indicating the verses to look up for help in a variety of spiritual quandaries), or portions of it in the hands of Roman Catholics was perceived and promoted as a duty for *evangélicos*. Catholics, presumably ignorant of the Bible and eager to receive it, would, upon reading it, see the light of truth and convert.

The word, in such a scheme, was not seen as rooted in the culture it now came to, but in fact as incompatible with central elements of it, and it came to challenge, to transform, and to enlighten it. In the case of Protestant missions to Latin America, the religious elements were regarded as particularly dangerous and to be completely given up. In other words, the Word came from the (United States Protestant) center to bring light to the (Latin American) margin, so long captive in (Roman Catholic/syncretist, Spanish/Native American/African) darkness.[7]

When I became the privileged recipient of a "central" education, first in Protestant schools in Cuba and later in college and seminary in the United States, I learned the methodology of production of "central" readings of the Bible by academically authorized readers (preachers, teachers, students, and authors of didactic texts). At first my reception of such readings and methods was naïve and uncritical (I was uncritical of critical methods!), but later all that was to change as the now well-known "paradigm shift" took place in biblical studies, particularly in the United States. Borrowing once again Segovia's terms, I can say that I have also come to see the necessity to question how "readings and interpretations"–and I would add preaching–of the Word that claim such a pedigree do in fact speak to such crucial themes as "empire and margins, oppression and justice, the world and life in the world as well as the otherworld and its inhabitants; history and 'the other,' mission and conversion, followers and outsiders, salvation, election, and holiness."[8]

The issue is further complicated by recognizing that the "margins" are physically present in every metropolitan center of the West, where they can be found most obviously in their Hispanic *barrios* and in the lives of many who claim Hispanic/Latino culture and ethnicity along with being

"American." Beyond that is a growing awareness of the fact that the complex economic and political phenomenon that we call globalization is dramatically altering the dimensions of the issues in ways that already touch all of us, an awareness that is causing urgent theological reflection.[9]

In recent theological reflection within the Hispanic/Latino community in the United States, as well as in other parts of the world church, the negotiation of the Word between center and margins has been drawn in different and much more helpful ways, some of which I want to explore in what follows. Assuming that the Word in question is not the Bible but the Word incarnate in Jesus of Nazareth, I have chosen three "readings" of the Word at the margins, all of them subversive of the traditional paradigm in which word comes from the center to the margin. I add that the choice itself is subversive for me, since it includes two Roman Catholics whose readings I now acknowledge as influential on my own. While Protestant/ Catholic ecumenicity in reading the Bible has certainly become easier in the post–Vatican Council II generation, there is, I think, something else at work in this case that has to do with the common experience of marginal location. Virgilio Elizondo, a Mexican American Catholic priest from south Texas, reads Jesus–particularly the Jesus of the synoptic gospels–as a marginal figure from a marginal Galilee who challenges and sets himself on a collision course with central Jerusalem, a pattern that shapes forever the community of his followers. Roberto S. Goizueta, a Cuban American Catholic academic, proposes that the marginal practices of popular religion– overlooked or rejected by the central religious establishment–may indeed be a context where we may find and accompany Jesus as he walks among the people, in particular the poor. Harold J. Recinos, a mainline Protestant, vividly retells the painful experience of Salvadoran exiles now living in American urban barrios as a context for a reading of a "hard-hitting" Jesus that invites and challenges the center to discover authentic community with people that United States society (and its mainline churches) defines as marginal.

Galilee on the Margin

The first of these three readings of Jesus from the margin is Virgilio Elizondo's envisioning of "Jesus the Galilean: A Borderland Reject."[10] In the first place, Jesus came from Nazareth in Galilee, an insignificant village in a despised borderland. Father Elizondo, a Mexican American with deep roots in south Texas, clearly identifies his own experience of marginalization in his homeland with that of Jesus and the ancient Galileans: "Your place of origin already marks you as acceptable or unacceptable," he says, as he speaks of people marked by geography with "certain mannerisms, gestures, speech- and thought-patterns, and an accent that will probably identify the individual for life."[11]

Not only identified as marginal because of his geographical origins, Elizondo's Jesus is marginal because of his social class: "He was a 'second-class citizen' with no formal studies. He was the son of a carpenter from Nazareth. He was a 'yokel,' an upstart—a Galilean reject."[12] It seems particularly important for Elizondo to underline these characteristics of the Galilean Jesus precisely because they mark him with the same kind of marginality and social rejection that Mexican American people have traditionally experienced in United States society. His Jesus was not brought, imported, or "proclaimed" to the margin, he was born marginal and fully shared the rejection that the center directs at the margin. In the third place, Elizondo's Jesus astounded and shocked center and margin alike, particularly by an "attitude of welcoming" that led him to share table-fellowship with those who were universally rejected—"tax collectors and public sinners."[13] He not only taught this attitude of welcoming in the parables and proclaimed it as a sign of the coming of the kingdom, he put it in practice to such an extent that he was himself deemed to be one of the public sinners (Mt. 11:19, for example). The purpose of Jesus' teaching and practice was to model and establish a new community that would negate and transcend the established order of society and certainly the distinction between who was central and who was marginal.

In Elizondo's thought, as in the thinking of many in the contemporary Hispanic/Latino churches, *mestizaje* is one of the most powerful symbols of the transcendence of those barriers by which human beings exclude and marginalize one another. The term, which had its inception in the colonial language of racial prejudice—it basically means "mixture (of races)"—has been redeemed by Latin American thinkers as a way of affirming the rich variety not only of racial but of ethnocultural roots that nourish our being and our self-understanding. Elizondo reads Jesus as a Galilean *mestizo*, regarded by the contemporary ethnic/cultural/religious purists of Jerusalem as marginal because of that. But rather than trying to conform to the exclusive standards of the center, Jesus confronts those standards, sometimes in shocking ways, and creates a community where anyone is welcomed—what is to become, from its very beginning, a scandalously mixed group—a *mestizo* church. In fact, the new community of the *mestizo* church prefigures an eschatological *mestizo* kingdom where ethnic, cultural, gender, and racial barriers are subsumed and surpassed. The marginal and despised *mestizo* acquires symbolic centrality as "the gospel in today's world: the proclamation in flesh and blood that the longed-for kingdom has in fact begun."[14]

Jesus the Galilean, finally, had to "go to Jerusalem," that is, he had to face and challenge a center that had become unresponsive, indeed hostile, to the marginal. This prophetic move sealed his fate, and he went to the cross. In so doing, Jesus reveals the constantly recurring conflict between center and margin, between oppressor and oppressed, between colonizer and colonized.

Walking with Jesus

Like many other Cubans now living in the United States, Roberto S. Goizueta defines his experience of marginality in terms of exile. To be in exile, even with the privileges of wealth and education, is not only to live in a land other than the land of one's birth and to speak and to write in a language other than one's native tongue; it is to be forever "in between," mediating between two cultures and two historical realities that remain alien—even hostile—to each other. As Goizueta puts it, "to be a mestizo/a and an exile is, thus, to live not only between Latin America and the United States, not only in between Spanish and English, but also in between gratitude and anger."[15] The ambiguous situation of exile, specifically in this case the situation of the Cuban diaspora in the United States, while fraught with all the painful features of marginal status, is also a place where important discoveries and growth take place. One of these discoveries, the hope of a freedom grounded in community, is one of the major offerings that the Hispanic margin is making to the United States center. Exiles know what it is to become double aliens, forever torn between two countries, feeling rejected by both. Goizueta points out that the way in which many of us find it possible to live in this situation is through a development of a new community where "we U.S. Hispanics know that we are not alone. We walk with each other and with Jesus," whom he describes as "a carpenter's son who also has nowhere to lay his head." Homeless in two countries, Latinos and Latinas construct a home "not…of bricks and mortar but out of our common struggle."[16]

For Goizueta, the presence of Jesus among his people is powerfully mediated in the rituals and practices of "popular religion," at times rejected or marginalized even by the central hierarchy of the church. One of the major examples he uses is that of the dramatic processions and reenactment of the events of Holy Week as they are carried out in San Antonio's San Fernando Cathedral. The actions of the faithful as they walk with Jesus along downtown San Antonio's streets from Pilate's court—erected across from the market—to the crucifixion reenactment in the main plaza in front of the cathedral are a sacramental act of accompaniment. In walking along San Antonio's Dolorosa Street, which in some sense becomes Jerusalem's *Via Dolorosa,* and accompanying the suffering Jesus, the believers make concrete and tangible their solidarity with his agony, while at the same time identifying it with theirs. Perhaps the clearest evidence of this is what happens in the Friday evening service, when, with the arduous events of the crucifixion over, the congregation turns its attention to the grieving Mary in an evening service in which members of the congregation go up one by one to the Virgen de la Soledad (Our Lady of Solitude) to share aloud their own painful experiences, all too often having to do with the violent death of children. Thus, Goizueta says, Good Friday ends in "collective grieving, shared by Jesus, Mary and the entire community," grieving that provides "an abiding sense that we are strengthened and given new life even in the midst of our common suffering, perhaps precisely because it is a suffering undertaken in common."[17]

Besides the sense of solidarity with the suffering of Jesus and Mary, for Goizueta "accompaniment" becomes also a powerful validation for what the church has called "the preferential option for the poor." Accompaniment of the crucified Jesus calls the church to "a commitment of voluntary solidarity with the poor that witnesses to and struggles against the evil of poverty."[18] A proclamation based on accompaniment has to be a proclamation based on practice—a truth also presented in the thought of Harold Recinos.

Welcome to the Barrio

Harold Recinos's work is shaped by the presence in the marginal barrios of United States cities of Hispanics—Salvadorans in particular—who have been driven here by the violence and misery unleashed on their homeland by events in which the United States was deeply involved. Their harrowing personal narratives of flight from the experienced realities of persecution, rape, torture, and death leave the reader shaken and ashamed. For Recinos, their presence in the United States barrios, as well as that of others whose marginalized status is the result of similar complexes of "economic and political injustice," constitutes an inescapable and crucial challenge to the "central," mainline churches. In order to be good news, the gospel proclaimed must result in real change: the Jesus proclaimed in and from the barrio must be both a prophetic critic of the concrete injustices that define the lives of the people and an agent of real change. Recinos's Jesus is both "a poor person who knew concrete misery and hope in God" and "a prophet who was critical of the way mainline religion backed social structures and rules that worked against creating a sense of real human solidarity," or in one phrase, "the hard-hitting Jesus who takes the form of the poor."[19] The parable of the rich man and Lazarus (Lk. 16) gives Recinos grounds to make the challenge that this Jesus poses to the mainline churches very specific, and meeting that challenge is definitive of what he appropriately calls "political holiness." Pointedly and urgently, Jesus' prophetic word comes from the margin to the center to pose specific questions to the mainline churches, for example: "What does it mean to have thirty-six million people in this country alone living at or below the official poverty standard each year?"[20]

In Recinos's daring vision, coming in contact with the Jesus of the margins will demand no less than a "reinvention" of the mainline, central churches, as they come "to embody the true meaning of the good news of Jesus by walking with the poor and social outcasts in ministry." Mainline Christians so challenged will come to understand "how food, healthcare, housing, social opportunities, and human dignity are linked to the presence of God in the world" and that "their mission is not bound by geographical, social, economic, racial, ethnic, patriotic, biological, cultural, or political borders."[21]

From the Center to the Margin and Back

I began by reflecting on my own early experience of a "missionary" or colonial legacy in the presentation of the Word. While I can say that personally I owe much to that experience that formed me, I have also come to see how it has remained problematic over the years. I have come to realize that in rejecting out of hand anything identified with Spanish Catholicism and Cuban popular religion, for example, I was leaving aside not only much that was valuable but a precious part of my own roots, and in this I particularly include my spiritual roots.

The views from the Hispanic margin I have reviewed are particularly useful, not only to Hispanics/Latinos, but to all who are concerned with the correlation of center and margin in the communication of the Word in a world where the consequences of a colonial and imperial past (including the cultural, religious, and theological consequences for a "mission church") are still on the table. All three of these views reach well beyond their particularity toward certain universally applicable principles that can help us sort out the complexities of such a situation and helpfully move beyond it.

Virgilio Elizondo's daring portrayal of Jesus as a Galilean *mestizo* and the bipolar relationship he sketches between Galilee and Jerusalem are much more than a reading of the gospel through the eyes of a Mexican American raised in south Texas. Elizondo leads us, first, to the realization that the Word is indeed incarnate and not necessarily at the center. His radical statement of the "Galilee Principle," that is, "what human beings reject, God chooses as his very own,"[22] which Elizondo calls "the essential starting point of Christian identity and mission today—and everyday, until the final coming of Christ,"[23] has two equally important corollaries, the first being that the word is already at and of the margins. Jesus came, and Jesus comes, at the rejected margin. It is presumptuous on our part to think that we are called to *take* the word to the margin. We are, rather, called to *meet* the word there. The second corollary is that *mestizaje* is a characteristic of incarnation and defines for the church "a new universal love that would not be limited by cultural or religious boundaries…the beginning of a new Christian universalism." *Mestizos* "are the ones in whom the fullness of the kingdom has already begun, the new universalism that bypasses human segregative barriers."[24] The Word is not only free to manifest itself—to become incarnate—everywhere; it also liberates us from artificially imposed categories that would restrict it, as well as us, to categories created and imposed by any given power structure.

Roberto Goizueta reminds us of the principle of the agency of the margins in popular religion. The Word is not only words (text or sermon), as it sometimes appears in the thought and discourse of the center. The Word, particularly at the margins, is also present in popular image, drama, procession, custom—in short, in the powerful esthetic mediations of popular religion. To ignore or to attempt to suppress these would not only do cultural violence to the margin but would also obstruct the powerful principle of what Goizueta calls accompaniment, that is, an affective and emotional identification with the sufferings of Jesus (and of Mary and of one another) at the cross, which is not only pastorally healing for the believer but which leads her or him into preferential service of others. "In Jesus Christ's own cry of abandonment, and his intractable hope against all hope, we hear our own cry and discover our own hope."[25]

In true Christian *praxis* therefore, the cross as an affirmation of life leads to committed accompaniment of particular poor people: "The foundation of the preferential option for the poor is the esthetic, affective praxis of friendship with poor persons."[26]

Harold Recinos, finally, makes it clear that the Hispanic *barrios*—a specific embodiment of the margin in our society—have a transformative mission and effect toward the mainline central churches that become involved with them. The prophetic invitation of the marginal Jesus, heard from there, is a message of radical inclusivity, in fact a call to mainline Christians to "the experience of entering a new world, that of the ignored people in the nation's barrio whose actuality has never been of concern in the world of mainline churches."[27]

In and from the Hispanic margin, as in other margins, the Word is that of the marginal, *mestizo* Jesus, challenging the center. The Word is the word of the cross, calling all to accompaniment, to walking with Jesus and with the poor. It is the word of Jesus' invitation to a radically inclusive community, where the divisions of race and culture, of wealth and gender, and, of course, of center and margin are finally transcended. How are we to proclaim this word? Perhaps that is a premature question. The word, like the spirit/wind that "blows where it lists," may be calling from surprisingly marginal places. Perhaps we first need to learn to listen. The center, after all, is just as good a place to listen as to speak.

"Give to Everyone Who Begs from You"

Luke 6:30

WILLIAM R. COATS

Many people come to my door for financial assistance. Their needs vary. To secure help, they usually preface their request with some biographical note. There is a medical crisis, or someone is out of work, or someone needs carfare to a recently obtained job, or a child is in need, or there has been an unfair eviction, or the car has simply given out.

While each need varies, the narrative request has a similar refrain. Each person is in need because of fate, bad luck, or some ill intent directed to them. They are, in short, victims and deserving of help because their straitened condition is basically not of their own making. Their job in this game of cat and mouse with the "helping agent" is to convince me that they are *worthy* of help. Are they? I have no idea. Is it even the point?[1]

It *is* the point for many who want to make sure that the helping agency isn't getting "ripped off." In America, if you are poor and you want help, you must prove somehow that you deserve it. The poor understand the game; if you're perceived as worthy, there's a hot meal, a warm bed, even sometimes a sympathetic ear. If you cross the line into the undeserving poor—the unworthy—you get nothing but a look of shame, a kind of "*how dare you?*"

Merit governs ordinary social life and enterprise, but should it determine how the poor are received, helped, and treated?

Because of this pervasive cultural assumption, a game surrounds and haunts the relationship between helpers and those to be helped. The helpers develop a sharp eye for frauds, for slackers, for those whose predicament is

153

self-caused, those who, in short, don't qualify. Those seeking help, in turn, seek to show their worth with all manner of stories. Lies abound—by necessity. Those who come to my door must lie in order to survive. Those entering programs of either the state or the church often lie as well. And always there is the threat that they will not be found deserving and then have to join the ranks of the disqualified—for whom there is virtually no help or hope. It is striking that those who ostensibly are the helpers force those who need help to lie in order to be judged worthy of being helped.

The Bible may not always be of help in face of "the game." The psalmist neatly divides the world into the wicked and the pious. The former can expect God's punishment, the latter God's rewards. Psalm 1 asserts: "The wicked are…like chaff that the wind drives away…the way of the wicked will perish" (vv. 4–6). Psalm 5 triumphantly cries: "You bless the righteous, O LORD" (v. 12).

Christian scripture, drawing on some later traditions, alters this division. It is no longer the wicked and the righteous; it is the poor and the rich. The poor are associated with virtue and hence the Lord's favor, while a wary eye is cast on the rich, whose pity and piety are questionable.

Recall Mary's sublime hymn:

> [God] has brought down the powerful from their thrones,
> and lifted up the lowly;
> [God] has filled the hungry with good things,
> and sent the rich away empty. (Lk. 1:52–53)

The rich have not qualified for the Lord's mercy, presumably because their gain is ill gotten or has been derived at the expense of the poor.

In Luke's moral universe the poor are pious and deserving, while the rich are not. Indeed much of the church's attention to the poor in the last decades has been based on the political assumption that the poor have been oppressed, but nonetheless carry with them both suffering and moral strength. It is from this soil that Marx romanticized the nineteenth-century working classes, who were the poor of his day. From that soil liberation theology sprang up and sided with the rural masses in the late twentieth century.

Perhaps even in our day concern for the poor is undergirded and given justification by a sense of either their oppression by larger systems beyond their control or by their moral worth. Thus, after arduous incrimination when we discover liars, con artists, drug addicts, lazy, or otherwise undeserving people, we drop them from the ranks of the worthy poor and disqualify them from "our help."

In spite of our political readings of the gospels, Jesus cannot be pigeon-holed as consorting only with the poor, but rather, with the lost, that is, with sinners. Anyone can be, and everyone ultimately is, lost and a sinner. Zaccheus was rich and lost, wealthy and a sinner.

Jesus is unnervingly ecumenical in his dealings with people. In John's gospel he befriends two adulterers: the woman at the well and the woman caught in adultery. The synoptic gospels strongly suggest that Mary Magdalene was a prostitute whom Jesus seemingly healed or set right. What seemed to qualify one for relationship with Jesus was one's sin and moral failure, not one's worth. Jesus didn't train his disciples to be like so many of our church's "ministries of compassion," whose first job is the adjudication of the worth of the potential recipient of our help.

In Jesus' moral universe the disqualified get the lion's share of his compassionate attention. How is it, then, that we who seek to aid the poor still harbor notions of the deserving or undeserving poor? What have we—we who dare to bear Christ's name in the world—become?

It may be helpful to recall that the apostle Paul, in his letters to young churches, sought to construct an imaginative vision for those churches in the wake of the crucifixion and resurrection of Jesus Christ. In this universe, one reads back from the last events of Jesus' life to establish first that all people are sinners, not just those who disobey the law or periodically stumble morally. For Paul "sin" is a realm of power in which all humans are hopelessly lost. The new life the risen Christ brings from the tomb blankets all men and women with the possibility of regeneration and transformation. Thus freed they can hardly ever again look at the world as a fixed place of the wicked who are to be punished and the good who are to be rewarded. Such a vantage point also dissolves the distinction between giver (as righteous) and receiver (as sinner).

If God has outrageously showered grace on sinners, then being a sinner does not disqualify one for help; paradoxically, it *qualifies* one. As Karl Barth said many decades ago in his sermons to the prisoners in Basel, he was no less a sinner than his hearers.

This changes our whole notion of "worth." For the only thing that makes us worthy of God's help is our sin, our failure, our need. We know who the "truly worthy poor" are when we see their need, not when we judge their morality or worth. And such a view begins when we recognize our own "unworthy" need first.

What I am suggesting could lead, of course, in the everyday world to "irresponsibility." Does one knowingly give a junkie money? Such practical questions rightfully must intrude in our dealings with those who have so little, with those whose lives are more complicated than we can imagine. But I believe our doubts and fears of being irresponsible, or of being "ripped off," must not deter the extravagant nature of our God, who wishes to continue the kind of " irresponsible mistakes" among the "unworthy" that God made with Jesus.

23

"Skeletons in God's Closet"

Matthew 1:1–25

THOMAS K. TEWELL

The conversation was almost over. I was on the telephone with the chair of a pastor-nominating committee who was asking my opinion about a candidate for the position of pastor in that congregation. We were almost finished with the conversation when he said, "Well, I guess I should ask you one final question. It's always a hard question to ask. But I think I really need to ask it. Are there any skeletons in his closet?"

"Let me tell you why I'm asking," he said, "Our church went through a bad experience some years ago. We called a pastor who had many personal problems that got in the way of ministry, and to be honest, he embarrassed our church. Now that our church enjoys a pretty good reputation and a certain amount of prestige again, we can't afford to take a chance. We feel the life of the pastor reflects positively or negatively on the church, and we surely wouldn't want somebody who will be an embarrassment."

As I thought about his question I wondered to myself, if the characters in chapter 1 of Matthew had been exposed to the scrutiny of a pastor-nominating committee, how many of them would have passed muster? Look through the Bible, not just Matthew 1, but throughout the whole Old and New Testaments, and pay attention to the people called to be ambassadors for God's kingdom in the world. You talk about a problem-filled past! You talk about mistakes! You talk about the potential to embarrass someone! All you have to do is read that first chapter of Matthew. It starts with Abraham, who was the patriarch of Israel but was also a liar. He told people that Sarah was his sister, and he didn't bother to tell them that she was also his wife. He did this to save his own life!

And Jacob had conflict with his older brother, Esau, who should have had the birthright. But Jacob cheated Esau out of the blessing that was really his. And Jacob's name, of course, was changed to Israel, and so that idea of chicanery, trickery, and cheating is right at the forefront of Israel's history. It's interesting that Abraham and Jacob could be called two of the most influential people in Israel's history. One was a liar, and the other was a cheat.

Then you look at the names of Tamar and Rahab–Rahab was a professional prostitute, and Tamar pretended to be one, once–and you wonder why they would be included in the pedigree and lineage of Jesus, the Son of God. Ruth was a Moabitess, and the book of Deuteronomy clearly states that no Moabitess should enter the household of faith of Israel. So why is Ruth in this list? And what about David and Bathsheba? They had a sordid adulterous affair and tried to cover it up. Ultimately King David had Bathsheba's husband, Uriah, killed in battle. King David was an adulterer and a murderer! Come to think of it, it would be just as well if the pastor-nominating committee skipped over that first chapter of Matthew completely, because the folks described there would never make the grade! And I scratch my head and wonder why God chose people like these.

There is a man in our church for whom I have great respect. His name is Joe Vedella. Joe is our outreach assistant, who works with our homeless ministry. Before he joined our staff, Joe was homeless himself. He admits publicly that he had problems with drugs and alcohol. He was also in prison and had lots of other difficulties in his life. Joe told me that years ago, before he knew Jesus Christ as he does now, he thought all the Bible characters were perfect. When he actually read the Bible he was amazed to learn that some of the characters he most admired were actually liars, cheats, scoundrels, and drunks. "Hey Tom," he said, "these are my kind of people." And maybe they're God's kind of people too–but why did God choose them?

Before we examine that, I am curious to know if any of you have skeletons in your closet? Our New York City Police Commissioner Bernard Kerik has a skeleton in his closet. Maybe you read about it in the newspaper or in his autobiography *The Lost Son.* In the book he says that his mother left the family when he was a very little boy. As a four-year-old he was taken to a courthouse during a custody battle. It turned out that the police commissioner's mother was a prostitute–with ten aliases. She was also an alcoholic and involved with drugs. She was involved with many men and traveled around Ohio from flophouse to flophouse. Bernard Kerik was stunned, shocked, and embarrassed a year ago to learn that his mother was found in a bed beaten to death with a blunt instrument. "My mother," he says, "was probably murdered." He can't prove it, but he feels pretty certain that she was murdered. It's a skeleton in his closet.

I raise this question about skeletons in our closets because it's Christmas time and families gather together at Christmas for holiday cheer, eggnog, Christmas dinner, and maybe a worship service. One of the reasons we have the Travelers' Christmas Eve service is because a number of you have told me that when you go to visit family during the holidays, you don't attend church. So often after the Travelers' Christmas Eve service, I am told that this service "gave me strength to go home and face my family!" Maybe that's why W. H. Auden, in his poem "For the Time Being," wrote, "Christmas is the time of year when we try unsuccessfully to love all of our relatives."

It's not easy in families, is it? We gather together during the holidays for a few days, in close quarters, and pretend there are no secrets. One family member may have an alcohol problem, but it's awkward to bring it up and talk about it, so no one does. Granddad seems to have a problem with Alzheimer's, and it should be discussed, but no one is willing to do it. Maybe someone in the family this past year was abused–physically, emotionally, or sexually–and you'd love to reach out to her or him with a little support, but you can't do it because it's a secret. It's a skeleton in the closet. You don't talk about it. Nobody does. You sit there during Christmas dinner; "How are you doing?" "Fine thank you, how are you?" but the skeletons are rattling inside.

A gay man I know and respect has had a partner for many years. He knows that his parents would never welcome his partner at the family dinner table, so he doesn't take him home for Christmas. They never get to spend this special day together. This man is dying inside because he can't be honest and reveal his whole life to his mother and father. He is being a phony and wearing a mask, and there's a huge wound inside him that hurts so badly.

So why does God choose those with skeletons in the closet? Because God knows that those of us with skeletons in our closets can be honest and realistic with ourselves and therefore can be honest and realistic with other people. Show me someone who is critical of other people, unduly critical, and I will show you someone who doesn't like himself or herself. So often–hear this carefully–we see clearly the flaws in others that we cannot or will not face in ourselves.

The truth is that every one of us has skeletons in the closet. Listen carefully: God doesn't call the qualified. God qualifies the called. God takes people who know their need and who acknowledge and recognize who they are and what they've done. And God says, "I choose you."

I believe that one of the reasons Matthew put all these questionable characters into the genealogy is because he himself was a tax collector. He cheated people out of money. I think Matthew was the most shocked person in the world when Jesus came to his tax-collection office and said, "Matthew, follow me." I think he was completely stunned and must have wondered, "Does Jesus know what I've done?" Of course he knew! But Jesus saw through Matthew to the man he could become.

And when he looks at all of us, God sees through us to who we might become. God chooses people with skeletons in their closets because God wants people who can be honest with themselves and can acknowledge who they are, so that they can be honest with other people. God chooses people with skeletons in their closets because God is more interested in having willing workers than in pure motives. As we read through the Bible, we see many people who served God with impure motives. The truth is that Jesus is more interested in what we do than in our motive for doing it.

Jesus told a story of two men, one who said he would do something, but didn't do it. The other man said he wouldn't do it, but did it. Jesus said it's the person who does the good deed who is righteous. The motive doesn't matter, because we're all imperfect. But if we do good deeds, God can use them to God's glory!

God uses people with skeletons in the closet because God needs diversity of experience. To be honest, perfect people don't relate very well in the world. Do you have anybody who sends you one of those perfect Christmas letters? You know the ones in which they tell you all the family's accomplishments of the past year? The kids all have Ph.Ds, summa cum laude, and you get more and more uncomfortable with each line you read, so you toss the letter aside. Then the next one arrives. They are really sickening, those letters. Perfect people don't relate to a world in need. But people with skeletons in the closet do.

That's why God called Joe Vedella to Fifth Avenue Presbyterian Church. Joe was homeless; he was in jail; he drank too much; he took some drugs. And now he's a follower of Jesus Christ. By the grace of God he cleaned up his act. By the grace of God he's gotten power and courage and boldness. And by the grace of God, at 5:30 in the morning Joe Vedella is outside this church ministering to the homeless people, who, our session and trustees and deacons have said, are welcome as our guests. We have ten homeless men who stay inside, but we've got about twenty-five or thirty who sleep outside the building.

Maybe you saw on the news Friday night and Saturday that for some reason the police are "sweeping our property" and trying to get rid of them—but these homeless friends are part of our ministry. They are not homeless; they're our friends. And Joe Vedella and others wake them up with hot coffee at 5:30 in the morning. Some wonderful volunteers and men from our shelter inside wake them up and sing "Love Lifted Me."

Sometimes when the homeless friends are around the building they say to Joe, "What do you know about homelessness?" Joe can say, "Hey, I've been there. I have experience. For years I ate out of the garbage can at

Rockefeller Center." And they start to listen. He is a little like E. F. Hutton: "When Joe Vedella speaks, they listen!" That's because what he says rings true.

Joe was on television Friday night, along with Margaret Shafer, our hard-working associate for outreach. They were saying, "We hope you'll pray for us, because we really believe we have a ministry to these dear people" to the NBC cameramen who came because the police had been surrounding our building. Outside on our signboard is a message that says, "This is God's House. All are welcome"—all are welcome, and we mean it. And you see, the truth is that everybody walking by has got a skeleton in his or her closet.

We all do, if we're honest. Some of us have a home, and a coat and tie, or a fancy dress or tuxedo; some of us are homeless and carry all the stuff we've got on our backs—but we all have skeletons in our closets, and God wants us all to come home to God!

I'd love for you just to hear the difference that Joe Vedella has made in a month in this ministry. Twenty-one people have taken a step forward because of Joe's efforts in God's ministry. He's gotten five of our homeless into drug-rehabilitation centers, and three others into detox centers to get off drugs and alcohol. He has helped another one to go to Peter's Place and to get a brand new life. He got a woman with a brain tumor into Lenox Hill Hospital for medical services. He got one guy a job cleaning hot dog stands during the night so he can get some money for an apartment to live in. He recommended a person for a section 8 permit from the city, and now that person is living in the same building where Joe Vedella lives. He talked with a man who was estranged from his uncle in Ohio, and since it's Christmas time, Joe said to him, "Gee, wouldn't you like to make up with your uncle?" Our church has gotten Joe a cell phone so he can use it in this phenomenal ministry, so he said to the man, "Let's get your uncle on the phone." And the man called his uncle and they reconciled over the phone. Joe found a woman from Lebanon and got her into Bellevue Psychiatric Acute Care Center and helped reunite her with her family. They live in London but have come here to be reunited with her. And he found a guy on the street from Ireland who hadn't been home for many years. Some Irish visitors passed, recognized his accent, and began to talk with him. And they ended up paying this man's way home to Ireland for Christmas. This is all in a month's work!

If Jesus were to come back today, would we make room in the church, on the steps, along the walls, in the sanctuary? You see, I think Jesus comes to us disguised as a nuisance, as a bother, as a homeless person—because Jesus knows if he came as the King of kings and Lord of lords, we would naturally say, "Oh, Jesus, welcome." But when he comes disguised as a homeless person, Jesus can really see into us and ask, "Are you the kind of people who would really make room in your hearts?

So why would Jesus, why would God, choose people with skeletons in their closets? So that we can be "exhibit A" of God's life-changing power. It was true for Abraham, for Sarah, for Tamar, for Rahab, for Jacob, for you, and for me. This Christmas when people pass our church and see the signboards: "This is God's house, All, All, All are Welcome," I hope they will know that we truly mean it. In the name of Jesus, we even welcome people with skeletons in the closet–like you and me!

"Bill and the Fig Tree"

Mark 11:13–14

JIM BURKLO

In the Community Kitchen dining room, while passing the serving line on his way for seconds, Bill took me aside. "Jim, I've been reading the Bible lately, and I found the passage where Jesus curses the fig tree. You know, it seems a bit out of character for him to do a violent thing like that. You've been to seminary, you're a minister; explain this story to me."

Bill did a lot of reading, but this was the first time I heard that he read the Bible. Bill lived in an old Pinto sedan with his dog, his banjo, his telescope, and the rest of his worldly goods. When he was an electronic engineer, he had paid a friend to mill that banjo out of solid brass. But once he hit the streets, Bill spent his days playing the banjo in the park, reading books, and watching the trees grow. Whenever I stopped to talk with him at the Community Kitchen, we would share our observations about the amazing ways of nature. He'd pull out the telescope, and people would stand in line in the parking lot to look at the moon through it in the twilight. Bill displayed a vivid awareness of the habits of birds, the qualities of plants, and the changes of seasons as reflected in the heavens and experienced by him while living in his car. Subject as he was to the weather and other elements of nature, he noticed much that I would have missed.

I first met Bill when another homeless man brought him by the agency office to set him up with a meal pass. Most people came into my office for the first time because they needed and wanted something: food, jobs, showers, soap, or just a cup of coffee and a listening ear. But Bill was different. He asked for nothing. He didn't hustle for his survival.

He was absolutely courteous and well spoken and in no hurry for anything.

He seemed not to be driven by passions or bad habits. He didn't grasp for life and depended totally on whatever means of survival landed in his lap.

One evening after dinner, I asked Bill how he was getting along. "I have no idea how I get along. It just happens!" He waved his big arms, gesturing the downpouring of daily grace from above. "If the food or the gas runs out, it just comes! I wake up in the morning and to my amazement, I am still alive. I have no idea how I make it." The blackened dead skin on his arms showed in patches under his arm hair. Three months before, I had given him a pass to our free clothes closet and handed him a towel, soap, and a shampoo bottle. He never showered, but he got a clean shirt. Three months later, the new yellow polo shirt was blackened down the chest, and his same old Levi's were stiffer with dirt.

"What do you think? Why did he dry up the fig tree?" asked Bill.

The story had always intrigued me as well, but I had not reflected on it with anyone before that conversation with Bill. I pondered the passage: "Seeing in the distance a fig tree in leaf, he went to see whether perhaps he would find anything on it. When he came to it, he found nothing but leaves, for it was not the season for figs. He said to it, 'May no one ever eat fruit from you again'" (Mk. 11:13–14).

My mind quickly went into action with Bill's, and I speculated on an aspect of the story that I'd never considered before. "I don't understand the story either. But it might be about timing. The Greek word for 'season' is *kairos,* which also means the right or appropriate time for something to happen. Jesus was on his way to Jerusalem for the last time when this incident happened. The story might have been an illustration to his disciples that now was the right time, the *kairos,* for bearing fruit, because now was the hour of his passion and death. He was telling them that now was the time for Israel to bear fruit, or never."

Bill nodded, pleased with this interpretation. "I figured it had to be something literary. What's that word in Greek, *kairos?*" I wrote it out for him on the back of a scrap of paper; he could pronounce the Greek letters because he had once studied a little Greek himself. I was pleased to have been asked the question and to have given such a clever answer.

On my way home I kept thinking about the story of the fig tree. As I did, I had to admit to myself that I still didn't understand it. It was still disturbing, still a side of the personality of Jesus that I didn't like. Why did he wither up the tree, depriving some hapless householder of its fruit in its own right time?

And then the more important question hit me: Why was Bill so interested in this story? In my glee to do interpretive gymnastics, I hadn't bothered to address the most important hermeneutical issue of all: what caused Bill to get stuck on the story of the fig tree?

Did Bill see himself as the damned fig tree—a fruitless, smudged lump of a man, one who had no season of ripeness, no hope of bearing useful fruit again, one for whom God's *kairos* had been mysteriously taken away? In my pleasure at my interpretive ability, I had missed the opportunity to reflect with Bill on our life situations and on what the fig tree story had to do with us. I had succumbed to the temptation to be in the helper-client, teacher-student relationship. I had succumbed to the temptation to settle with answers instead of living with questions. The story got no less disturbing as I spent more time with it. At home I read the different versions of it and other related passages.

In this story, every character blew it. The fig tree missed the extraordinary opportunity to offer the hungry Jesus some fruit. Think how wonderful it would have been to be able to serve a meal to the Christ! Can we, though, really blame the fig tree for something that was beyond its capacity to do? The problem here seems less the fig tree's than Jesus'.

Jesus' actions are troubling. He was having a bad day. He was himself homeless and hungry and about to find himself in big trouble in Jerusalem. He was in such a foul mood that he cursed a tree that any local person would have known was not ready to bear fruit. The curse killed it overnight.

Jesus' disciples were no better. Did they offer food or comfort to Jesus, who was clearly in a stressful, emotional state? No. They just seem amazed at the trick of nature that Jesus pulled off. They were oblivious to Jesus' real needs—those of his physical body and those that confronted them all in Jerusalem and at the temple.

And I blew it too, completely missing the opportunity to listen to Bill's story as revealed in the account of the fig tree. I got caught up in what seemed like a biblical problem, the very thing I'd learned Greek and exegesis for in seminary. And in so doing I had become the fig tree: fruitless in face of his need, I had missed Bill's *kairos,* his right time, for sharing his life.

Bill had been a Silicon Valley engineer making good money. Once he had a piano and played classical music with interesting and educated friends. Now he lived on the streets and played banjo for Bruno, his dog, up at Cuesta Park. He survived off fortuitous encounters with helpful street people, picking up the stray day-labor job or dollar for a gallon of gas or a hamburger.

Did Bill feel cursed by God? Did he see in Jesus' capricious act toward this innocent fig tree a picture of himself when God was having a bad day? And now I wanted to know: who or what cursed Bill and caused him to wither? Was it true that he would never bear fruit again? Would Jesus ever lift the curse from the fig tree? I waited for the rest of the story, trusting it would come in its own right time. We don't always get the answers we want.

Bill and I did have occasion for deeper kinds of sharing, for which I was grateful. Eventually I lost touch with him, but I never lost touch with what he taught me that day about the deeper purpose of reading scripture. I was a ministerial fig tree looking to bear fruit in season.

The Bible is no mere body of facts to master, no mere grist for the intellectual mill. It is no mere compendium of doctrines to accept, no mere listing of rules to obey. Rather, it is a window through which we can see into each other's souls, so that we can be more divinely and humanely compassionate to each other. The Bible confronts us with our real human condition, which so often we try to avoid. It artfully subverts our attempts to ignore the suffering, the poverty, and the injustice that surround us. When we read it and hear it, the Bible gets inside us and does things to us that we don't expect. And that's the nature of its true authority—its capacity to author and reauthor us and our life stories so that we become characters in the story that God is telling. And that is a story that includes some pretty odd characters sometimes, like Bill and Jesus. Like me and you.

PART 7

"Affluenza": Preaching the Just Word in Privileged Contexts

Just preaching is the theological and social prescription for the disease of "affluenza." The question is: can one dose of preached justice per week, or, as is more likely, one dose of preached justice every three months, have any effect on a disease that is epidemic in North American culture?

Preachers who take seriously the challenge of the widening economic gap and its consequent tearing in two of America's social and communal fabric know that they are up against enormous forces that will not be happy with their "meddling" in people's financial affairs. But it is hard to dispute the charge that capitalism has become the oversized tail that is wagging the dog of democracy. Capitalism without a conscience operates in a "grab-and-get" mode and uses the power of its resources to leverage the democratic system, not for the greater benefit of the greatest number of members within its constituency, but for the greater benefit of the few whose main goal is to continue to maximize profit and return. Capitalism without a conscience manipulates democracy to its own ends of acquisition.

Just preaching brings the moral resources of faith to our often complicated North American democratic and capitalistic situation. These resources provide a perspective that is shaped by scripture's vision of reality, one that does not offer itself as one possibility among all the others that are out there. As Erich Auerbach so starkly stated, the Bible has the audacity to claim that its story is *the* story of reality. The Bible is saying, "This is the way things are!"[1] Shot through all parts of the plot that scripture narrates is the Creator's desire and design for creation's life, one that is irreducibly interrelated, interconnected, and interdependent. Just preachers bring such a vision to bear on our democratic culture. Democracy itself has limited resources for moral vision, but people of faith within a democratic system can bring a moral and spiritual compass that calls into question an unfettered capitalist appetite and its potential for moral bankruptcy and social predatoriness.

One infrequent and haphazard dose of just preaching is probably not enough to stem the unrelenting cancerous growth of affluenza. That is why preachers are encouraged and empowered by the authors in this section to become more deliberate, more consistent, and more frequent dispensers of the vaccine.

Preaching a Just Word in Privileged Pulpits

Healing Affluenza

DALE P. ANDREWS

It is fairly difficult to speak justly about a disease that is as much a part of one's own poor spiritual health as it is a part of the culture to which the social diagnosis is addressed. And the struggle has not spared this writer. The tension heightens when speaking about "affluenza" from within the economic cultures of Western countries and in particular our North American society. We do live quite privileged lives. Our privileges have clearly become expectations. As expectations have the propensity to do, they either blind us to our self-indulgence or spawn a seemingly immune indifference. While poverty surely exists in the very midst of American wealth, even our poor do not often escape the affluenza virus. Consumer wealth and waste are the by-products of our lives across the social spectrum. To preach justly is even more difficult than to write from the safe distance of an essay. All the while, extreme poverty and the exploitation of the natural environment cry out for intercession from God.

Affluenza has been defined as a cultural disease of excess—an excess that seldom satiates the desire for more. The virus is identified by its symptoms: the feverish pursuit of products, possessions, and privileged passions, which might be outpaced only by a market-driven economy, ravenous consumption, an increasing anxiety over exponential debt, and the yield of excessive waste.[1] Affluenza has also been more personally identified by unmanageable stress and pervasive feelings of emptiness.[2] From our comfortable distance, the personal symptoms seem readily treatable. Take two aspirin—one for sensible time and money management, another for moral and spiritual priorities—and call the Reverend Doctor in the morning. As we all come to learn, numbing the pain does not heal the illness. The ability of the body to heal itself determines the level of invasive treatment that will become necessary. Human cultures and even our spiritual lives are no different. The symptoms of affluenza are better seen as indicators of the disease and the paragons of treatment needed.

Between personal habits and corporate practices, the commonly cited symptoms of affluenza range from spending frenzies to the ongoing depletion of natural resources. But the degree of pleasure may be quite dependent on access, readily available assets, and even the exclusion of others. Our inability to keep an earning pace equal to that of our spending results in overwhelming personal debt. "Robbing Peter to pay Paul," as the epigram goes, is fairly common practice to stave off impending loss of credit, repossession, foreclosure, or the increasingly familiar declaration of bankruptcy. For some, income is sufficient to feed the need for more. The remaining majority must either learn to live within more restrictive means or fall prey to the virus of possessions and passions. Most of us have fallen to the plague.

The worst of it all is that we do not defile only ourselves. Affluenza has devastating effects on other cultures. The rights of individual freedom and private property have become rights to privileged lives that bear no accountability. Our prosperity shuns any economic or moral taxation on behalf of those who do not simply fail to prosper, but lose access to the same means and resources of said freedom. People live in debilitating poverty. The very nature of our economic systems feeds first those who can pay the most, while paying the least possible for production and labor. Some economists may argue that our capitalist system thrives on the virtues of opportunity and fair trade. One need not be a historian or a theologian to show that neither trait escapes the vices of self-interest and exploitation. And yet the debate over capitalism remains fairly polarized.

One of the better philosophical arguments offered in defense of our economic systems points out that capitalism began in an effort to break the entrapment of mass poverty and to do so within religious ideals. In feudal societies, wealth was determined by land holdings, agricultural production, and conquest. With the advent of modernity, Western societies turned more and more to commerce and eventually industry as means of escaping poverty. The pursuit of prosperity would in time become linked to the rights of liberty.[3] Some historical and social analysts see in this pursuit the transformation of cultural power structures. A prevailing presumption held that the opportunities granted by commerce and industry would not only continue to create wealth but also cultivate some belief in the possibility of personal advancement. Therefore, perceived opportunities quite reflexively would increase productivity. Just the possibility of escaping mass poverty was a significant cultural and systemic revolution.

The revolution, however, has not escaped the claims of privilege and power. Nor has it escaped production of poverty and servitude. Historical examples such as slavery in the United States show starkly just how capitalism can flourish by capitalizing on human atrocities; many of these practices are at least traceable in principle to feudal life and imperialism. To some, wealth and power were redistributed or even diversified. Yet to many, those who held the new wealth and new power looked and felt much like the prototype. Capitalism may have offered new doors, and even many more doors, but the doormakers and the doorkeepers did not escape the vices of controlling access. Persons who traverse the landscape of capitalism seeking unrestricted admission still thrive on the consequential privilege its standard of living produces, regardless of our means to participate freely in it. The moral dilemma on either side of the doorjamb asks, "What's the price tag?" When preaching in privileged contexts, both the privileged and the not-so-privileged wrestle with the moral sensibilities at stake in the possession of wealth and power or in their acquisition.

To be certain, the advancements produced by wealth have been great. Wealth has produced marvelous discoveries and remedies for human suffering. Many of the very liberties we seek are frequently attained by wealth. But freedom from moral conflict is not one of them. We preach the virtues and blessings of free enterprise as God's gifts to us. The gifts eventually become expectations, and then metamorphose into rights. In our religious and political ideologies we equate our money-market and class systems with democracy itself. However, the reality is that capitalism and democracy are not necessarily commensurate principles and may even be in significant tension with each other.

Cornel West has been fairly vocal in his cultural analysis of capitalism. He points out that the goal of capitalism is the continual maximization of profit.[4] Citing James Cone, West acknowledges human sin in the drive to monopolize the market arenas through class exploitation, which is typically aided by willful and systemic racism and sexism. Our cultural sanctioning of capitalist strategies reflects deep conflicts in moral reasoning and human values. Such conflicts often place capitalism at odds with democracy. West even considers our "capitalist civilization" to be antidemocratic. Our market systems are geared to produce or sustain unrestrained affluence. Exploitation of domestic and international classes of laborers, as well as their societal and natural environments, has become routine for producing capital. These very means suppress sufficient flourishing for others in the service of our own prosperity and privilege.[5]

Just preaching must wrestle continuously with these conflicts. We wrestle with our hunger for prosperity. Our daily appetite increases as we normalize privilege. Yesterday's privilege becomes today's expectation. These are the breeding grounds of affluenza. The disease flourishes because our treatment is often limited to individual remedies or inoculations. These prescriptions are necessary to the pursuit of healing, but they are not enough. Any viable remedy will include parallel treatment of social systems and cultures.

To pose the point in the form of a question, "Is affluenza treated most effectively by curbing the consumer's ravenous appetite for products, credit, and global resources?" Certainly, the answer would have to embrace an explicit "yes, but also…" Consumers have actually become products of the market system. Still, we also produce and drive it. Therefore, the more difficult questions to ask are: "Where and how do we break the cycle?" and "Can our economic system create opportunities for prospering without the systematic exploitation of others?"

A researcher in environmental studies, J. Mark Thomas, argues that "every economic system is simultaneously a system of distribution of rewards and punishments, and the relation between persons and community."[6] He therefore concludes that the questions of economic justice and the use of human and natural resources are not answered adequately by economic reasoning. If Thomas is correct, affluenza is more than just evidence of the moral and spiritual depravity of personal human nature; it is evidence of cultural and systemic sin. Although cultures and social systems often overpower individuals, we are not excused. In essence, we feed the beast of our economic system with our overextended claims to rights of privilege and prosperity.

Just preaching will attend to the spiritual and behavioral infirmities of our social and economic systems. The just preacher will bring divine revelation to bear on personal and cultural repentance that includes systemic reform. Again, the safe distance of an essayist creates courage to make direct claims in the face of overwhelming struggles with systemic evil. Systemic evil requires intervention beyond the more fundamental redress of human depravity. Here, we are faced with the age-old challenge of "justifying the means" or redesigning them. The means of prosperity and privilege are as problematic as their consuming pursuit. Preachers and pastoral care-providers are in the business of diagnosis and prescription of divine remedy. Religious ethics and moral purpose are important tools for preaching and pastoral ministries in realizing just living. But can religious ethics or moral purpose coexist with systematic acquisition and the multiplication of wealth and power? If so, on what terms do we proceed? The endemic nature and resilience of self-interest make it extremely difficult to reform social systems and cultural abuses of power. Power does not "go quietly into the night," especially the power of our market economy. Complicating the matter are the roles of religious institutions and religious culture within social and economic systems. Our very churches, including our preaching therein, may bear some of the greatest needs of deep reform.

Churches and their institutional activities in our society adhere frequently to the prevailing social current of the dominant culture. At times they serve to stabilize other social systems or maintain harmony with them.

Peter Berger refers to this dynamic as cultural religion,[7] which concentrates social ethics in preserving or reestablishing the cultural equilibrium of its age.[8] This function has not always resulted in positive religious ethics or moral reasoning. For example, many churches in the United States helped to buttress the social system of slavery. Later, churches were duplicitous in the public policies and social mores of Jim Crow and racist violence. Today our churches frequently seem content with the legal successes of the civil rights movement. The continuing calls for racial justice in social practices and institutional life are often met with contempt; they are either dismissed as malaise or accused of manipulation. Women also struggle to overcome prevailing sexism across the social spectrums, including church ministries. A similar response to charges of class exploitation frequently claims that the poor are trapped by their own lack of enterprise. Such perceptions have become commonplace in a socioeconomic system that is built so heavily on the shoulders of consumer individualism as is our capitalistic system. The problem is compounded when churches adopt comparable individualist theologies of religious piety and morality.

We should be careful not to confuse the concern for individual thriving or individuality with individualism in religious life. Elsewhere I argue that American Protestantism struggles with the culture of individualism pervading the legacies of its revivalist traditions in personal salvation.[9] Without restating the full argument here, preemptive emphasis on personal salvation becomes the ultimate goal of our preaching and pastoral ministries. Ecclesial communities either flourish under programs of evangelism or struggle to survive. Personal salvation loses its critical reciprocity with communal goals, in particular public ministries and even reconciliation ministries. In turn, these churches attempt to develop community as countercultural colonies to secular society and even to other churches. Ironically, this very formation is itself in keeping with the dominating culture of individualism. Community then becomes more of a collective of individuals with shared values in religious piety and a faith stance in life. In fairness to these churches, neither intentions nor self-perceptions rest in the loss of community. Some argue, in fact, that they experience a much stronger sense of cohesion and shared commitments through pastoral ministries.[10] Nonetheless, community is gained ultimately by shared values of individual responsibility and response in matters of faith. Although this language of faith attempts to develop distinctive religious ethics, its moral reasoning remains in deep harmony with the prevailing culture.

How then has our cultural religion been influenced by our struggle with affluenza? What hurdles to systemic reform can just preaching expect to face in our culture of consumerism and privilege? The strongest evidence of affluenza in our churches may be the growth of megachurches and programmatic ministries. While I do not wish to vilify these churches or ministries, it is important to address the pervading market ideologies and outright consumerism at their core. Their strengths lie in the procurement of resources, both economic and human. Many are quite progressive in their sense of social obligation—more often among those churches within urban communities or racial/ethnic traditions. Market thinking and consumerism, however, often drive the construction of multiplexes that are designed to service every facet of the congregants' lives.[11] Ministry is heavily weighted to creating facilities and seminars to meet the daily demands of the members and the ideal images of family life. Admittedly, questions of stewardship cannot be treated adequately in this space. Certainly, though, stewardship must be weighed in the investment of our resources as well as in their charitable use. The actual disposition of stewardship within cultural religion is best evaluated in the evident relations between the dominant culture and religious life.

The drive to "religious consumerism" is as much a matter of institutional survival as it is a response to our culture of individualism. In the latter half of the twentieth century we witnessed an increasing displacement of churches from their historical centrality in American life. The fragmentation of communal life is a concurrent reality between family life and church life. Genuine interest in reaching out to individuals has driven our preaching and pastoral ministries into the provision of services to meet the desired activities of personal interests and recreation. Often these programs are designed to offer a religious environment for services that may be attained elsewhere, such as childcare or physical health programs. Some churches do well at creating access for those who would not be able to afford these services elsewhere. Others are more intent on creating a religious milieu for activities that are otherwise fulfilled outside the church. These programs and services are examples of how pastoral and communal care begin to pivot on the provision of commodities in the interests of the religious consumer.

Preaching and pastoral ministry in privileged contexts operate between the need to create untraditional avenues for reaching people and the mandate to transform the very culture to which churches must become appealing. Here we may gain insight into the effects of affluenza on religious life. Our drive to make churches more marketable in an increasingly competitive church environment, which takes account of programming, extracurricular activities, and preaching, is a significant symptom of the affluenza virus. We create a sort of materialism in religious services that competes for potential consumer converts. This sense of materialism is also evident in forms of prosperity preaching. We focus on God's meeting our "needs" and God's desire to bless us. Of course, identifying our real needs and blessings is a highly problematic enterprise, complicated by our self-interest; in fact, the affluenza virus directly cripples the identification process. Consumer-oriented preaching and pastoral ministry disrupts and retards communal development. Of particular concern is the imbalance created by the pursuit of commodities and services, an imbalance centered in a serious form of self-interest that loses sight of the exploitation of others or the consequences on anyone else of our consumption. The lost vista of our interrelatedness with and interdependence on others turns the virtues of individual thriving into the vices of individualistic cannibalism. Expansion of services in a culture of consumption contributes to the isolation of persons. Cultural religion, therefore, struggles to stem the degenerating tide of our lost innocence—our lost interrelatedness.

In one of the more stark examples of affluenza in religious life that I have encountered, Robert Bellah and his research team characterize our cultural religion as "religious commodification." The market pressures on cultural religion prove astounding in what has been called the prosperity gospel. In one instance, a North American church offered a "money-back guarantee": "Donate to the church for ninety days, then if they think they made a mistake, or do not receive a blessing, they can have their money back."[12] The affluenza gospel distorts biblical equations of giving and living. Do we give so that God will bless us? Do we care for another in case we will need care? Do we love in order to be loved? Do unto others as you would expect them to do unto you? Prosperity preaching frequently runs such risks. Our cultural religion preaches that God fulfills the process of salvation and sanctification with prosperity and privilege. The gifts of grace and blessings, even in answer to prayer, somehow become expectations— that is, if you have faith. Perhaps the most astounding claim of prosperity preaching that I have heard echoed in defense of North American prosperity is, "God will bless the faithful people of other lands according to the standards of living and economic prosperity of their respective societies." Affluenza thrives when cultural religion so easily internalizes personal prosperity and transcends the plight of others.

The Bellah group says consumerism impairs our vision of social ethics. The privatization of religion in our culture makes it particularly difficult to establish social reform. In effect, any efforts at reforming social ethics have to contend with the socioeconomic order and cultural moral reasoning.[13] Religious consumerism becomes a primary hurdle to reform. We have yet to contend successfully with how our privileged contexts produce faith perspectives. The dubious privilege of consumerism in religious life makes it difficult to discern systemic injustice from within a culture of individual expectations and responsibilities. Our churches produce an undesirable polarization or disassociation between conservative public theologies in religious piety and personal morality and the more liberal public theologies that place emphasis on religious and social inclusiveness. At each pole, personal fulfillment and meaning motivate religious interests. We struggle then with the "in-breaking" of social ethics amid this religious consumerism.

Should we look for a litmus test against which we can measure our preaching strategies? The standardization of just preaching might isolate one or two symptoms of any given social illness, but it cannot predict the mutations that will likely occur when cultures intrinsically seek to survive—even diseased cultures. Instead, we face resilient challenges in reform. Privilege may agree to reform, but it seldom relinquishes prosperity. We may agree to recycle our waste and even budget our resources, but the acquisition of profit and access to commodities continue to determine the good life.

Our visions of the good life may be illusions. Our realities of the good life cost others far more than we pay, especially when compared to the present moment of consumption. Actually, I hesitate to include this corrective of the "good life." A problem exists in any argument that appeals to reform on the same grounds as the need for reform—in this case, self-interest. Self-interest does not even spare our search for God. Whether insecurity or emptiness compels us to seek or respond to God, the answers we find typically meet some self-interest in our being. I suspect that even just preaching cannot escape the longings of self-interest. And it may be that we can determine some self-interest to be morally sound. Although we say that selfless love never requires its return, we ultimately fail to love if we no longer desire its return. Nonetheless, neither the ends of self-interest nor the means of its pursuit can fulfill the desires at its core. If the contentment of self-interest is a criterion, the good life will remain elusive.

Affluenza is self-interest unleashed in a prosperous, yet avaricious, society. Unleashed consumption and exploitation are the common symptoms of our social disease. The insult to injury comes in the backlash of self-interest: entitlement, exposed emptiness, longing for meaning, isolation, and broken relations.[14] Just preaching in privileged contexts seeks to break the fever of self-interest.

If we are to bring religious ethics to bear on self-interest, we will need greater insight into the dynamics of religion and culture. I have already discussed some ways in which cultural religion shares in the values of society. However, when religion and culture come into conflict, religious ethics still require social support.[15] One task, then, of religious institutions is to create or nurture social support. Even when religious institutions struggle to break free of domineering cultural values, they elicit social conformity in the actual effort. Perhaps it becomes the mission of churches to shape culture. Yet it is clear they cannot effectively do so until they establish newly shared values or reestablish lost values. It is equally clear that secular culture may indeed reshape religious values. I suppose that religion and culture can never be isolated completely. Even in extremely countercultural religious groups, we can observe the creation of a subculture extending religious values into shared experiences and worldviews. In the case of affluenza, religious values seek to reestablish the interrelatedness of lives and raise concern for our global environment in a culture that isolates us from one another and raises personal desires to ways of being.

The transformation of human life includes social systems. Inasmuch as affluenza germinates in self-interest, it breeds in social systems and their cultural structures of power. Just preaching insists on public space for religious ethics. Just preaching seeks to recreate public life predicated on our interrelatedness. Parker Palmer argues convincingly that we have become strangers who have lost what I consider to be a critical facet of our interrelatedness—a full awareness of our interdependence.[16] The isolation we have unwittingly procured in the pursuit of private prosperity makes us strangers within and between social worlds. The first steps of renewed life may be taken by risking unfamiliar skills, but most assuredly are risked in the presence of familiar faces. Just preaching endeavors to "reacquaint" strangers. It reestablishes religious social ethics in our interrelatedness and interdependence. That interrelatedness and its interdependence compromise neither our flourishing nor our freedom. Instead, the effort to reacquaint strangers calls forth each of us into a renewed responsibility for the stranger's flourishing and freedom.

Just preaching launches the reacquaintance of strangers into what otherwise has been called the "rehumanization" of the disenfranchised. Rehumanization is a "redemptive process that begins by dismantling internal supports for the denial of harm…[It] provides an interpersonal cost-benefit analysis of counterfeit success dreams and the strategies of entrepreneurial individualism."[17] We seek to create a public space in which strangers can meet and dismantle any agency that our prosperity plays in the dehumanization and exploitation of those whom our privilege might otherwise strive to keep in the distant servitude—out of sight, out of mind, out of reach. Affluenza is a deadly disease, eating its way all through our culture and our natural ecology. It wreaks havoc in our lives as well as on others. Just preaching seeks social reform in personal and public lives, both interrelated and interdependent.

26

"Famine in the Land"[1]

Amos 8:4–12

BARBARA BROWN TAYLOR

The time is surely coming, says the Lord GOD,
>   when I will send a famine on the land;
not a famine of bread, or a thirst for water,
>   but of hearing the words of the LORD. (Amos 8:11)

I polled a lot of people this week, and Amos is no one's idea of a good time:

Hear this, you that trample on the needy,
>   and bring to ruin the poor of the land. (8:4)

If you were channel-surfing on Sunday morning, would you stick around to hear the rest of that?

On that day, says the Lord GOD,
>   I will make the sun go down at noon,
>   and darken the earth in broad daylight.
I will turn your feasts into mourning,
>   and all your songs into lamentation;
I will bring sackcloth on all loins,
>   and baldness on every head;
I will make it like the mourning for an only son,
>   and the end of it like a bitter day. (8:9–10)

Why is Amos in such a bad mood? Because the rich have used their riches to burden those who will never work their way out of debt. Because the clever have used their cleverness to trick those who cannot think as fast. Because making a profit has become more important than anything else in the land—more important than justice, more important than Sabbath, more important than God.

With stores open twenty-four hours a day, you can buy anything you want any hour of the day or night—provided you have the money to buy it. If you do not, someone will lend it to you at 25 percent interest. Meanwhile, the cashier who works the graveyard shift has parked her two small children on a neighbor's couch. In the morning, before she goes home to sleep, she will transfer them to a day-care center, but she is not complaining. She needs the work, even if it is part-time. If she does a good job, maybe the manager will increase her hours so she qualifies for the benefits. That would take such a load off her mind—if she knew she could afford to take her kids to the doctor. What she does not know is that the manager is under strict orders to keep her hours right where they are. He may hire as many part-time cashiers as he likes, but the company cannot afford any more full-time employees.

While she punches the keys of her cash register, someone else is tapping at the keys of a computer across town. It may be nighttime on this side of the world, but it is always daytime somewhere else—someplace where banks are open and money can be moved around, even if it means the unfortunate collapse of some small government in Malaysia. That sort of thing cannot be helped. It is one of the risks you take when you sit down at the poker table of the world economy.

As the sun comes up and this gambler goes to bed, a seasoned CEO knots his tie in front of the mirror. Today is the day he meets with the financial managers of the company he has just bought. First they will go over the figures together, and then he will announce what should be obvious to everyone: he cannot afford two payrolls. He is very sorry about this downside to the merger. He is especially sorry for those who were so close to retirement, but it is his business to stay in business. All employees should prepare for the transition, which will take place in thirty days. He assures everyone of his best wishes, which he will back up with letters of reference for anyone who requests them. He wants to thank those present for their time and their attention. And now, if they will excuse him, he has another meeting to attend.

> The LORD has sworn by the pride of Jacob:
> Surely I will never forget any of their deeds. (8:7)

Amos is in a bad mood because the health of the market has become a higher good than the health of the people, and God cannot stand it anymore. It is time to expose the sickness of this system. It is time to smash the economic idol and have a proper funeral for it, with sackcloth and ashes for all the next of kin.

Most of us are used to hearing passages like this one as personal indictments, which makes them strangely easy to ignore. When the finger is jabbing you in your own chest, it is pretty easy to defend yourself. As a prophet, Amos's scope is wider than that. He is jabbing an entire nation on God's behalf. He wants to know when they all agreed things have to stay the way they are and why they think it is all right to keep profiting from an economy that is repugnant to God.

The place was Israel, and the time was twenty-seven hundred years ago, but see if parts of it do not sound familiar to you. The nation has enjoyed forty years of peace and prosperity, largely because the evil empire of Assyria has been busy with troubles of its own. Without any hot or cold wars to fight, the nation has used the lull in hostilities to grow strong. With no one watching, Israel has reclaimed lost territories and handed them over to royal friends. As the rich have gotten richer, the poor have become poorer. Some people have winter houses and summer houses, while other people have no houses at all. Some people eat veal medallions with mushroom sauce and sip Merlot, while other people make pancakes out of wheat sweepings off the floor. The worst part is the alienation between the two. They have forgotten that they are kin, and the imbalance between them has tipped the scales of justice right over.

Meanwhile, the nation's wealth and military power are being read as signs of God's favor. Religion flourishes among the prosperous, who pour money into their sacred rituals. There is a lot of talk in big houses about "thanking God for our blessings" and "welcoming the day of the Lord," when the rude fact is that a large percentage of the population is still living in hell.

This last part apparently bothers God the most. It falls under the category of taking the Lord's name in vain, so God recruits a herdsman named Amos to challenge the theology of the upper classes. Amos does not have the education to use big words. He calls the rich men robbers and the rich women cows. He mocks their religious assemblies and condemns their offerings as failed attempts at divine bribery. He ticks off the different ways God has tried to get their attention. I have tried famine, drought, blight, and locusts, God says. I have tried illness, sudden death, and political upheaval. But none of it has worked. The nation's business is to stay in business, and it has managed to do just that.

That is when God delivers the end-of-the-world scenario we heard a little while ago, about making the sun go down at noon and darkening the earth in broad daylight. Neither of those is the scariest part, however. The scariest part is God's promise that people who ignore God's word will eventually find themselves without it. One day they will wake up to discover that God has packed up all the good words and left the country with them.

They will hunt in vain for any sign of those words. When they want to say something to heal the rifts between them, they will stand there and look at each other with blank faces. When they take their children in their arms and try to remember the word for what they feel inside of them, nothing will occur to them. When they are falsely accused or charged twice what they owe, they will rack their brains for the word that means that it is not right, but they will not be able to find it.

They will not be able to find any of the words God used to bring the world into being, such as "light," "good," or "blessing." With those words subtracted from it, the world will seem no more than a shadow of itself. The only words left will be words that drag it back down toward chaos again, words such as "darkness," "evil," "curse." When that happens, God says, people will know what a famine really is:

> Not a famine of bread, or a thirst for water,
> but of hearing the words of the LORD. (8:11)

I will let you decide whether that prophecy has come true. Is anyone here hungry for the words of the Lord? Not religious rhetoric, not politics wrapped up in scripture, not this group declaring moral superiority over that group, but words that seem to come from beyond those who speak them, words that startle the ear with their clarity, their freshness, their power. Has anyone here run to and fro seeking such words and failed to find them?

They are rare, that is for sure. Most of us do not have the words to talk about what is important to us anymore. Plus, our ears have been so assaulted by the imposters of God that many of us are hard of hearing. Most of what we hear sounds like noisy gongs or clanging cymbals. And yet, every now and then, divine words do break through—clear notes emerging from a background of static. Sometimes they come straight out of the Bible. Other times they come through human speech, and not always in a church. I have heard God speak on the steps of the Lincoln Memorial and in a night shelter in Atlanta. I have heard God speak through jailbirds and heads of state.

The question is, how do you know? With so many words coming at you, how do you know which ones are God's and which ones are not? I am not sure there is only one answer to that question, but I am aware of things I listen for when I am trying to tell the difference. The first thing I listen for is arrogance. In my experience, God's subject matter is rarely surprising. God seems to stick to three or four basic themes: uncompromising love, perfect obedience, endless forgiveness, justice for all. Since any human being who speaks of such things speaks as someone who has failed to do them, enormous humility is required to pronounce these words. They almost never serve to support our own positions. They almost always yank our supports out from under us, so that we learn never to rely on our own constructs. This is not divine meanness. This is divine passion that will not allow anything to stand between us and God—not even our own beliefs about God.

So I generally do not listen to people who quote God to support their own positions. I am also wary of people who want to coerce me, since God does not do that. The choices may be as clear as life and death. The consequences may be spelled out one-two-three, but God never takes away our freedom to choose.

The last thing I listen for is fear. While I am extremely vulnerable to scare tactics, I try not to succumb to them. The words of the Lord may sometimes frighten, but fear is never their goal. Their goal is the healing of the cosmos. Their goal is abundant life.

Imagine a parent watching a two-year-old pick up a rattlesnake. What does the parent say? "Drop the snake!" What scares us is the loud voice God sometimes uses to warn us away from things that can kill us, but it is a rare prophet who does not wind up a prophecy with a vision of homecoming. Even Amos's mood improves at the end.

"I will restore the fortunes of my people Israel," God says through him. "I will plant them upon their land, and they shall never again be plucked up" (9:13–14).

I guess the best way to combat the famine of hearing the words of the Lord is to speak them ourselves—never with arrogance, never to coerce or frighten, always with the understanding that they are like nitroglycerine in our mouths—but also with the willingness to speak them and, better yet, to live them, as our way of letting God know we have heard the words of life.

It is not anything we are supposed to do all by ourselves. God does not call many of us to stand alone, like Amos, warning a whole nation about the snakes it picks up. What God does instead is to call us together, into communities like this one, where the words of the Lord can go to work on us and through us, until the sound of them becomes like a heartbeat in our ears. The thing is to let them give us life. The thing is to let them turn our lives into blessings on all other lives, so that new crops of God's sustaining word spring up on the earth.

27

"From Charity to Justice"

CLIFF LYDA

"For with the judgment you make you will be judged, and the measure you give will be the measure you get. Why do you see the speck in your neighbor's eye, but do not notice the log in your own eye?" (Mt. 7:2–3)

In recent years, I have been making a difficult but necessary spiritual journey. The journey has been that from a typical American, middle-class moral consciousness to the biblical mandate to do justice. It has not been easy. Like so many in the United States, I have enjoyed a life of privilege and power based on race, gender, and social class. Becoming conscious of that power and how it affects my response to the world has been one of the transformative events of my life.

I was born a white male in the southern United States in the early 1950s. I was firstborn. My family was economically stable, providing me with a secure environment throughout my childhood. My parents had an enduring marriage. No addiction or abuse touched my young life. My community had a good school system, giving me a quality education at no cost to me. My education continued in the public university system, augmented by generous support from my family. I was nurtured from childhood in a church where I learned the basics of faith and values with the ease of being at home. My health has always been good. I have always had enough of what I needed. I fit easily into the systems of life, whether academic, professional, or social. I have never experienced discrimination.

I am not apologizing for my life. My life is what has been given to me, and I am grateful. But it has become important–*spiritually important*–for me to recognize that I have enjoyed a great number of advantages. Without realizing it, I was given a lot of privilege.

It didn't feel like that when I was growing up, and much of the time it still doesn't. A certain innocence surrounded my thoughts about the world. I *thought* "privilege" was wealth, prestige, political, and personal influence, all of which seemed beyond my mere middle-class circumstances. But the advantages I enjoyed put me at the front of the line in most areas of life. I had no firsthand experience or appreciation for how much struggle and suffering are in the lives of many ordinary people, and I failed to see that my own level of achievement was based in large measure on what was given to me. My lack of self-awareness on this point inadvertently left me with an elitist worldview. The privilege I enjoyed in my life became a log in my eye.

The danger for me—I realize now with utter clarity—was that *an elitist worldview leads to injustice,* whether I knew it or not.

Justice is a problem for many North American Christians. Every Christian I know would agree that God wants to see justice done in this world. The problem is in how we understand justice.

In the world of *blind privilege,* justice has two elements: *procedure* and *retribution.* Justice is about the rule of law and revolves around adherence to law and the punishment of wrongdoing. It is almost always understood in individual terms. One can easily determine his or her moral standing by how well the rules have been followed. "Law-abiding citizen" is one of the highest accolades a privileged person can receive.

The evangelical tradition that birthed and nurtured me taught that Christian faith is similarly understood in individual terms. The great problem of humanity is our sinfulness, the offending of a holy God. Salvation, in part, is about the punishment of wrongdoing. Like justice, it is procedural, attained by trusting that Jesus' death for my sins absorbed an eternal punishment I deserve. It is an individual matter. Since personal sin is the great peril of life, I am most faithful to God as I pursue personal holiness. I am most valuable to the world by engaging in evangelistic witness. To share the good news of salvation from sin and eternal life after death is the great imperative for the church. Get people saved, and social ills will go away.

Eventually, this produced a strange and unnatural split in my theological understanding. I was trained to serve God in a ministry directed toward individual salvation. My response to social problems was secondary and essentially limited to charity toward individuals. I couldn't really do much to change social problems. I understood it was important to give money, advocacy, and volunteer support to ministries working to ease social ills, but I truly believed the spiritual condition of people was more important.

This was the defining characteristic of my pastoral ministry for twenty years. It is a dangerous way to understand redemption because the idea that salvation is individual and not connected to social issues reduces faith to self-centered concern about behavior and social convention. It enables the believer to benignly ignore a wide range of public pain. It can produce a self-righteousness in those who enjoy privilege, connecting morality to social advantage and prosperity. Nothing could be more contrary to the message of Jesus.

My journey toward biblical justice began several years ago during a conversation with an African American pastor. We were working together to address a transportation problem in our community, which in retrospect I obviously did not understand. This deeply spiritual man, who cared about the souls of people every bit as much as I did, lovingly pointed out that the inherent social power I had enjoyed in my life limited my experience and narrowed my vision. I needed to get out of the comfortable box that contained my life to see a wider world. He suggested I ride the bus. From the public bus system, I would see my city through a different lens.

Changing the Lens Changed Me

The lens through which I was viewing the world was one of privilege. A different view could only come through a broader view of justice. To say it differently: The privilege you enjoy—or are barred from—in life determines your view of justice, and your view of justice affects your understanding of God. Justice looks very different to someone without the inherent advantages I have enjoyed.

The Bible is full of calls for justice, but not simply in procedural and retributive terms as I had been taught. Rather, there are also demands for *distributive justice*—the demand and social assurance that all people have the necessary goods for lives of dignity. More elusively, the Bible speaks of *restorative justice*—a time when individuals and society will experience the fullness of life that God intended at creation. I had read of such things in the Torah and in the prophets but *somehow* had missed their meaning. That God calls for justice means far more than punishment for individual wrongdoing. It also means that God calls for a *just society.*

Distributive justice and restorative justice are not easily demonstrable or readily attainable. They are not self-evident in the natural life of humankind. They spring from the deep conviction that God is at work in human life, especially in the lives of those who are being oppressed. God expects justice from societies as well as from individuals. This is a sobering realization. The conviction of the deeper realms of justice changes the way you look at politics, economics, lifestyle, and relationships with others.

The change, which is far from complete in me, involves getting outside the context of our own cultural and political viewpoints. The only way to do this is to expose yourself willingly to the dilemmas of human life, especially those experienced by those outside your immediate environment.

Interfaith Hospitality Network (IHN) provides a ready context to examine the question of justice. IHN provides shelter to homeless families. It is one of the most important ministries a congregation can undertake. In partnership with other congregations, a local church gets vulnerable people off the streets and helps them rebuild their lives. By opening their buildings, by providing meals and transportation, and through conversations and other means of emotional support, church people put their hands directly on the problems of people in dire need. IHN is an authentic response to Jesus and his presence among "the least of these."

But as important as such a ministry is, it is not the answer to homelessness. The solution to homelessness isn't shelter; it is *homes*. As with so many issues in the United States, the problem is societal as well as personal.

People of privilege such as myself have to learn this. We who have been advantaged in our system typically see social problems in individual terms. If you are homeless, *you* are responsible for your condition. *You* have done something to put yourself in such a position, and *you* have to get yourself out of it. All it takes to solve the problem is ambition, hard work, and self-control.

While there is usually some truth in this assessment, it is ironic that these words of wisdom often come from people who themselves are beneficiaries of enormous social advantage and who do not realize how easy it is to judge from positions of privilege. Seldom is the log in our own eyes so conspicuous.

Inevitable societal forces are at work that result in a segment of the population becoming homeless. While personal responsibility is always an integral part of human life, there are powers that overwhelm even the most responsible of people. Factors of race, class, and economic disparity are easily ignored or minimized by people who have never been adversely affected by them. In a world of limited goods and resources, for me to have as much as I have invariably means someone else has less.

Ultimately, we deny this either because we are naïve or because we want to protect our privilege. People of faith ultimately have to recognize that a just society is not simply the sum of individual moral choices. The prophets who were given the revelation to see a truly just and peaceable kingdom call us away from an easy identification with structures that advantage some and leave behind so many more. Jesus' own preaching of the kingdom of God makes it clear that God is neither a respecter of persons nor moved by our standards of righteousness. God calls for justice from societies as well as from individuals; and if our witness is to have integrity in the twenty-first century, the church will have to stand for justice for all people, not just for those in our most favored constituencies.

I have not given up my concern for the salvation of individuals. The gospel is good news for each and for all, and apart from the grace and mercy of God no one can experience wholeness and well-being. I have simply begun to express this in social as well as individual terms. It is no surprise that eyes are opened to God's goodness when love is shared with people in need and when the struggle to bring peace and justice to everyone is entered. The log in our own eyes is blinding, and removing it is liberating to the captives, especially those of us captivated by our own privilege.

28

"Withstanding Prosperity"

Amos 6:1a, 4–7; 1 Timothy 6:11–16; Luke 16:19–31

BRYAN O'ROURKE

Several years ago, I went with another priest and two doctors to give some workshops on addiction to people on the Island of St. Lucia in the Caribbean. One day an American priest took us to see his little village and church. The houses were on stilts—about half the size of a one-car garage. There was no electricity and only one spigot of water in the middle of the village. It was what you would call "dirt poor."

The village was right next to a canal that led in from the ocean to a beautiful marina for oceangoing yachts. We next went there and viewed a gorgeous dark blue fiberglass and stainless steel sailing yacht. One of the doctors—a sailor himself—was in awe of the boat and told me that it probably cost more than $2 million. It belonged to a couple from England who kept a crew of six to run it.

I looked back across the water at the village from which we had just come, and the contrast made me both sick and angry. This gospel makes clear to me that extravagant wealth in the face of abject poverty brings hell as a reward. No two ways about it.

Last Sunday's gospel was also about money and how we use it. It ended with the words: "No slave can serve two masters…You cannot serve God and wealth" (Lk. 16:13). Then the next verse of the gospel says: "The Pharisees, who were lovers of money, heard all this, and they ridiculed [Jesus]. So [Jesus] said to them: 'You are those who justify yourselves in the sight of others; but God knows your hearts.'"

So they sneered at Jesus. What else could they do? They knew in their hearts that Jesus hit the right chord. Sure, they justified their own luxurious lifestyle, and they also justified not only their neglect of the poor but also their contempt of them.

Thomas Carlyle said: "For every 100 men who can stand adversity, there is only one who can withstand prosperity." It seems also that when people of faith get overly taken up with wealth, they slyly can convince themselves that this excess is God's blessing on them.

In the *Diary of a Country Priest,* George Bernanos has the atheistic doctor—who is generous to excess to the poor—tell the young priest: "After twenty centuries of Christianity, to be poor ought not still be a disgrace. Or else you have gone and betrayed that Christ of yours."

The sin in this gospel story, the sin that sends the rich man right to hell, is his indifference. It is his bland, comfortable indifference to the desperate and degrading need of Lazarus. From hell he calls Lazarus by name—so he knew him, in his need. But he grew indifferent to Lazarus's need, even as he lay there on his doorstep day after day. It seems that God will never tolerate our indifference to the needs of the poor.

Perhaps we would like to dicker about what constitutes excess. Well, Saint Jerome held that all abundance was for bestowing on the poor. Saint Ambrose called it an "impudent assertion" to claim that we can keep our fairly won abundance. To deny alms to the poor when we have more than we need is to steal from them. And Saint John Chrysostom believed: "Feeding the hungry is a greater work than raising the dead."

It seems to me that what Jesus requires of us here is to be disturbed or bothered by this obscene contrast between the excessive wealth for some and the great poverty for others. Even when I get overwhelmed by the number of requests for help—my mail is always full of them—I cannot turn away and be indifferent. I must accept being disturbed, lest I become indifferent.

Meister Eckhart stated: "There, where clinging to things ends, is where God begins to be." Maybe we could let go of our grip on some of that which we hang onto. And behold, here is God!

PART 8

Just Preaching Is Not Church as Usual

What if the way that we have come to "do church" works against what "church" is really all about? What if the way we have come to "do preaching" works against what "preaching" is really all about? These are questions that are not easy for preachers or denominations or historic faith communities to consider. And yet they are crucial, if we as preachers are concerned with more than mere institutional maintenance and the perks that we derive from keeping the traditional wheels rolling.

What is the "more" about which we should be concerned? If scripture is clear about anything it is clear that God's heart beats out the cadences of justice:

> [God] has told you, O mortal, what is good;
>   and what does the LORD require of you
> but to do justice, and to love kindness,
>   and to walk humbly with your God? (Mic. 6:8)

If these are the goals of God, of God's desired human relations on earth, and thus of God's ideal communities on earth, whether they be called churches or synagogues or temples, then what shapes and forms of being God's community together would lend themselves to communicating those realities? How can our forms function to convey our message? In what ways do our current forms and even vocabularies, dress, and architecture work against us in our attempts to render justice in more than mere platitudes?

The early reformers in fifteenth- and sixteenth-century Europe sought to make the Bible available in the vernacular of the people so that everyone could have direct access, or at least access free of the church's dominating control, to that word. I believe it may be time for a contemporary translation of the ways of "doing and being church" so that the just words and ways of God are freed from forms that prevent access–physically, mentally, and spiritually–by the very people who need such words and ways the most. No doubt just as the European translators suffered the charges of heresy, many being burned at the stake, anyone who raises questions about the translation of what we do and how we do it will meet similar resistance.

In many ways, the writers of this final section threw a question mark over this entire book and over all of American Christianity. They assert: Just preaching is not church as usual.

Preaching Outside the Lines

A Just Paradigm for Preaching That Empowers Just Action

BOB EKBLAD

Many a pastor, priest, and rabbi strive to preach and teach in ways that will inspire their parishioners to live lives marked by compassion and service to the poor and excluded. This prophetic task is highly complex, made especially difficult in mainstream circles by a myriad of nearly insurmountable obstacles. Before considering some of these obstacles and strategies for preaching that empowers, I will briefly present my context and understanding of the role and objectives of the preacher, followed by a dialogical sermon on John 9.

For the past twenty years I have read scripture with people on the margins of the dominant culture, who at the same time find themselves outside the institutional church. This ministry began in rural Honduras in the early 1980s, where my wife and I worked for six years with a team of Central Americans to promote sustainable agriculture and preventative health and to lead Bible studies in fields and homes with impoverished *campesinos.* We currently serve as pastors of an ecumenical ministry to immigrant migrant farm laborers from Mexico—many of whom are undocumented. I also serve as part-time chaplain of a county jail. I regularly gather with Hispanic inmates and immigrants both inside and outside the jail to talk about our lives and the scriptures. In addition, I often preach and teach in mainline Protestant churches and teach Bible courses to seminary students who are preparing for ministry.

Of all the people I read scripture with, I find mainstream, mainline, English-speaking parishioners least able to engage in open dialogue about their lives, the scriptures, and the larger world. I often witness a notable contrast between raw, honest dialogue in Spanish about faith and life with Mexican inmates and more guarded, reluctant discussion with educated, English-speaking, Caucasian Presbyterians, Methodists, Lutherans, and Roman Catholics. Those with the least experience inside the institutional church appear less inhibited when it comes to participating in theological discussion than regular churchgoers, who tend to be more passive. While there are certainly numerous factors that could explain this contrast, I regularly return in my mind to one. I see a direct link between mainstream Christians' difficulties participating in discussion about their lives and the scriptures and their lack of life-giving action on behalf of people on the margins. How might the scriptures both preached and studied finally empower mainstream Christians?

Envisioning the Preacher's Role

Clarity about the preacher's function and objectives go hand in hand with an understanding of the most appropriate means of communication. Brazilian pedagogue Paulo Freire has deeply inspired my teaching and preaching both in Honduras and in North America.[1] Freire's participatory, problem-solving model did much to empower the base community movement in Latin America. Peasants and workers who were once passive receivers of monologue-style preaching, teaching, and liturgies began to read and discuss the scriptures for themselves–becoming subjects of their own liberation process with the help of priests, pastors, and layleaders who functioned more as facilitators than as authorities.[2]

In my preaching and teaching I envision my role as that of a facilitator and midwife. As a facilitator I seek to do everything possible to set up an encounter between God and the people through assisting them to reflect on their own lives, the scriptures, and one another's experiences and viewpoints.

As midwife I assist during the birthing process, recognizing that the work is done by the Spirit in intimate communion with people in the depths of their beings. As midwife I seek to be present as appropriately as possible–getting out of the way or intervening when necessary. I set up the birthing room as it were, making sure that the interpreting process gets off to the best start with a given group and text. Trust must be established between myself and the participants, between the participants, and between the group members and the biblical text. The chosen scripture must be introduced in a way that gives people a place of entry into the foreign world of the Bible. Barriers between reader and story must be addressed through introductory remarks and questions that invite the people to ponder and discuss the biblical story.

Simultaneously, I labor to help people identify contemporary equivalents to the biblical narrative (location, characters, verbs, and other details) in their own lives and world. I strive to help people to understand the deeper meaning of the biblical stories as these stories illuminate their own lives and surrounding world. My objective is that people would find themselves inside the text as met or addressed by YHWH,[3] Jesus, one of the apostles, or whoever mediates the message or saving action in the biblical story. I see myself as one who pulls people together for a potential encounter: a life-giving meeting between individuals and God that may result in comfort, healing, a change of heart, a call. I am an unknowing midwife at best—not knowing what the encounter will birth.

My hope is that this meeting will lead others to discern God's call on their lives, when they will discover their highest vocation. People receive their vocation as they begin to follow Jesus, who turns common people into disciples and followers into recruiters of yet more disciples, who are sent into every nook and cranny of the world.

The Dialogical Sermon

For many years I have been developing a way of reading the Bible with people that is clearly different from a typical Bible study or sermon, yet similar to both. I call it a dialogical sermon, though its exact genre may be other. I seek to engage individuals in groups of two to twenty-five in a theological conversation by helping them to see themselves in the stories of struggle and liberation in the scriptures. I seek to formulate questions that draw people out about issues that directly affect them. Most often I begin with a question about people's lives and then introduce a biblical story and ask questions that help uncover the deeper truths of the text. Other times I begin with the text—which is most often the case on Sunday, when I am using the selections from the Common Lectionary.

In preparation for my dialogical sermon I seek first to determine what questions or issues the biblical text appears to be addressing. This is often the most difficult task, requiring both careful exegesis and spiritual discernment regarding the text and group participants. The questions that guide my preparatory reading include the following: What is the heart of the matter in the text? What question(s) does the biblical text appear to be addressing or in some way answering?[4] Since most texts can be read to address numerous issues, I attempt to identify the multiple levels of meaning, prioritizing the issues apparently addressed in the text.[5]

The following description of a Bible study on Jesus' encounter with the man born blind and subsequent power struggle with the Pharisees in John 9 represents an attempt to begin with text. This particular story fits the purposes of this essay in that it places three ways of embodying God side by side. The disciples, Jesus, and the Pharisees each in turn communicate through their words and actions distinct understandings of God and ways of being present to one particular marginalized person—the man born blind. While the following dialogical sermon/Bible study happened in a county jail, this sort of "encounter" can happen nearly anywhere that people can turn and face each other. After briefly presenting this jail encounter, I will present some reflections on preaching and ways of being present that empower.

Learning Together of Jesus' Liberating Pedagogy in John 9

Jail guards usher me through two thick steel doors along tan cinder-block corridors in the jail's multipurpose room on a Sunday afternoon at 3:00 p.m. The English church service has just ended, and the plastic blue chairs are in neat rows before a wood pulpit that stands like a commander before the troops. I quickly slide the pulpit against the wall beside the television and arrange the chairs in a big circle—making sure a larger, more comfortable, plastic easy chair is reserved for someone other than myself. The thick doors noisily open as guards lead red-uniformed inmates from their cells and pods into the room. I welcome seven men at the door with a handshake. Tattered, coverless books lie strewn about on the table. I collect the ones I recognize as Bibles and pass them out as the men take their seats. I spot the oldest inmate and invite him to take the most comfortable chair.

Once everyone is seated I introduce myself and invite each to introduce himself by his first name and where he is from—an empowering moment in the heart of an institution that classifies inmates as "male" or "female" and addresses them by last name or inmate number. I invite people to feel free to share their views on the biblical text we are about to read, insisting that their questions and comments are critical if we are to truly understand the text. After an opening prayer calling on God's Spirit to show us the deeper meaning of the story, I invite a volunteer to read John 9:1–2: "As he walked along, he saw a man blind from birth. His disciples asked him, 'Rabbi, who sinned, this man or his parents, that he was born blind?'"

In this story Jesus' disciples are looking at a blind man—one who has been afflicted adversely by a calamity. I invite the inmates to consider how they themselves, functioning in this case as the contemporary equivalent of the disciples, might view people like themselves who end up in jail or prison—possibly as equivalents of the blind man who is considered punished for someone's sin.

"Many people outside the jail think that people who end up in jail may be there because of the way their parents raised them," I say, looking around the circle of men in red jail fatigues and rubber sandals. "In fact," I continue, "over the seven years that I have served as chaplain here in this jail, many men and women have told me stories about their upbringing. They tell me about being neglected by their parents, severely punished, and even sexually abused. Do any of you think that you are here now in jail in part because of the way you were raised?" I ask.

The men look up, surprised. Some appear alarmed.

"No way, man," says Dominic, a white man in his late twenties looking at twenty-five years for charges of several counts of assault with a deadly weapon. "I've got no one to blame but myself." Others nod their heads in agreement.

"So there is nothing about your upbringing that might have led to some bad decisions on your part that may have eventually gotten you into trouble with the law?" I ask, probing.

"That could be homes,"[6] says Arnold, a Mexican American man in his mid-twenties who's been active in Latino gangs. "I'm not saying it's all them, but I'm sure it didn't help for me to see my old man always laying around drunk and shit, man, I didn't have no male role model. I was pretty much on my own, roaming the streets all night since I was twelve years old," he continues.

"So this may have led to you eventually getting into trouble?" I ask.

"Yeah, man, I think so. If I had had a positive male role model, someone I could look up to, things may have been different," he says.

"What about the rest of you guys?" I ask, looking around.

Nearly everyone is nodding in agreement. Some talk about being raised by single moms who were absent because of their need to put in long hours so they could support the family. Others tell how their mothers neglected them because of their addictions to drugs and alcohol and of their difficulties finding stable partners. Nearly all tell of being punished severely, but often qualify these accounts with "but I'm sure I deserved it."

"Seeing my *jefito* (dad) beating up my *jefita* (mom) all the time didn't help," recounts Juan, a heavily tattooed Mexican American man in his mid-twenties who has been in and out of juvenile detention and jail since he was fifteen. "I never learned from him how to treat a woman[7] with respect," continued Juan. "He never disciplined me. It was my mom who hit us. She would wail on me with a garden hose. I think that I've got a lot of anger and maybe take it out on other women because of this. I'm sure that has something to do with why I'm here right now."

We talk on about other external factors leading to their lives of crime: getting expelled from school, experiencing discrimination from the general public and law enforcement officers, poor treatment by landlords, low wages for stoop labor as farm workers. The men are all looking down, lamenting their upbringings, until Dominic calls everyone to attention:

"Wait a minute, man, maybe we weren't raised all that well…but one thing I know, I can't blame my old man for my predicament. I ain't no victim, man. In fact I've victimized plenty of people. I messed up, man, and I'm to blame for getting myself into trouble."

Others nod in agreement, and the conversation moves in the direction of personal responsibility. The men talk about the allure of the easy life:

drugs, alcohol, women, easy money selling dope. They talk about choosing the easier path that they knew rather than the narrow path yet unknown.

"I fell into a drug addiction—heroin," says Miguel, a Mexican American man in his late thirties. "No one ever gave me help. Now I'm waiting for a bed date [in a drug-treatment facility]. I have a little girl that CPS [Child Protective Services] took away. Hurts me a lot. I have a drug addiction. It's me that has a problem."

"Okay," I say, "so at first you all agreed that you might be in jail in part because of your parents' mistakes. Now you are focusing more on your own responsibility. You've been trying to answer the question the disciples asked Jesus: 'Who sinned that this man was born blind—this man or his parents?' Let's look closer at this question. What image of God does this question assume? What is God like according to the disciples?" I ask.

"A punisher," answers Juan. "They think of God as the one who is making the man blind and shit, either because of his own sin or his parents sin," he continues.

We discuss the disciples' image of God as retributive, celestial law-enforcement chief, which continues to reign, often unchallenged, on the streets of the United States, Latin America, and many other places. God is envisioned by most inmates and Hispanic immigrants with whom I work as a being of negative hypersovereignty. Because God is understood as in control, calamities, punishments, and other negative events are seen as being allowed to happen and thus are understood as God's will. The disciples' question is not whether the man's blindness was a punishment, but concerns the attribution of blame: is this blindness due to this man's sin or to his parents' sin?

We talk at length about the disciples' "us-them" attitude. They appear to look out from a place of comfort beside Jesus and seek Jesus' judgment on the blind "outsider." Many of the inmates have experienced this judgment from religious family members and from their churches. Most have internalized this judgment and assume it to be true.

I ask the men how many of them see their time in jail as a punishment from God. Nearly everyone naturally assumes and even believes they must accept this. After all, critiquing fate is equal to judging God himself. At this point I invite the men to look at how Jesus responds to the disciples' question and how he might in turn respond to our question. The men are ready for this turn in the conversation. I invite one of the men to read John 9:3: "Jesus answered, 'Neither this man nor his parents sinned; he was born blind so that God's works might be revealed in him.'"

"So what do you make of Jesus' answer?" I ask the group.

"It doesn't say that God made him blind," observes Juan.

"Wow, man, so it's like Jesus isn't into the blame game," says Dominic.

The discussion moves to Jesus' positive approach. Rather than worrying about guilt or innocence, questions on which the courts of law and judges that will try the men are concerned, Jesus sees the man's situation as providing the occasion for his liberating work: "He was born blind so that God's works might be revealed in him" (9:3).

Arnold wants to keep reading to see what will happen in the rest of the story—now that interest is at an all-time high.

> "We must work the works of [God] who sent me while it is day; night is coming when no one can work. As long as I am in the world, I am the light of the world." When he had said this, he spat on the ground and made mud with the saliva and spread the mud on the man's eyes, saying to him, "Go, wash in the pool of Siloam" (which means Sent). Then he went and washed and came back able to see. (9:4–7)

We talk about how Jesus is not in any way associated with blindness or with night. Jesus is light—the light of the world. He refuses to passively label or judge the blind man, but shows a proactive attitude. Jesus leads the disciples, including them in the sentence "*we* must work the works of [God] who sent me."

"So what might this story mean for you guys here in the jail?" I ask.

Since the men hesitate here to hope for anything too good for their undeserving, incarcerated selves, I actualize the text by suggesting that we read Jesus' response to the disciples as: "Neither you guys nor your parents are to blame for you being here: you are in jail so that God's works might be revealed in you."[8]

We talk about watching and waiting for God's positive work in their lives and move into a discussion on the blind man's role in the healing process.

"So what did this man have to do to get Jesus' attention?" I ask, trying to alert the men to a narrative gap, giving them another, more hidden sign that further subverts the dominant retributive system.

"He wasn't doing nothing," says Dominic. "He was just sitting there begging."

I invite the men to read verse 1 again: "As he walked along, he saw a man blind from birth." It is Jesus who took the initiative, *Jesus saw* the man, then did the rest.

"But Jesus told the man to go wash the mud off his eyes in the pool," someone notes.

"It's like us," reflects Arnold. "We're blind. God opens up our eyes. It's like God putting us in here. Jesus spits on the ground and opens our eyes, so we can open our own eyes, go to treatment, or whatever we need to do. God opens up our eyes so we can see what we can do. Otherwise we're blind, don't know what we can do. Here we think clearly 'cuz we're sober."

At this point in our dialogue hope is being restored. The men are seeing a way out of debilitating fatalism. While in some ways the meeting is over, interest is still high. We read on and look briefly at the Pharisees' reaction to the newly seeing blind man and Jesus. After all, newly seeing inmates will still have to face the judge, probation officers, their family responsibilities, employers, and other "authorities" on the outside. The rest of the story alerts them to what may still await them once they "see."

We observe that in contrast to Jesus' taking the initiative in Jesus' encounter with the blind man, the neighbors have to bring the healed man to the Pharisees–who aren't about the business of looking for "lost sheep." In contrast to Jesus' liberating image of God, the Pharisees are more concerned that Jesus has broken the law by healing on the Sabbath. They reflect an image of God as an omnipotent law-enforcer and judge more concerned with laws than people (9:13–16). The blind man shows increasing boldness before the judging Pharisees, eclipsing even Jesus as the preacher in this story (9:24–33). Finally the Pharisees, unable to tolerate this newly empowered layperson's insubordination, throw him out of the synagogue (9:34), where he had been in the first place.

"So where was this man the different times that Jesus met him?" I ask the men.

We notice together that Jesus first met the blind man outside the synagogue.[9] We read together John 9:35–38, noting that it is also outside the institutional church that Jesus once again finds him, revealing Jesus' identity to him in a respectful, dialogical way:

> Jesus heard that they had driven him out, and when he found him, he said, "Do you believe in the Son of Man?" He answered, "And who is he, sir? Tell me, so that I may believe in him." Jesus said to him, "You have seen him, and the one speaking with you is he." He said, "Lord, I believe." And he worshiped him.

"Even though the religious leaders have kicked this guy out of the church, this does not keep Jesus from meeting him there outside," I observe.

"He's better off outside the church," notes Dominic. "Who would ever want to be inside dealing with those judgmental religious dudes."

We observe together how John ends this scene with Jesus' strongest words yet in support of a relationship of equality between insiders and outsiders, between preachers and parishioners:

> Jesus said, "I came into this world for judgment so that those who do not see may see, and those who do see may become blind." Some of the Pharisees near him heard this and said to him, "Surely we are not blind, are we?" Jesus said to them, "If you were blind, you would not have sin. But now that you say, 'We see,' your sin remains." (9:39–41)

Jesus reverses the power relations in this story through a surprising judgment. Jesus freely opens the eyes of the man viewed as punished by blindness and empowers him to preach truth to insiders–those with the power. The blind man is given sight, becoming the teacher of the Pharisees. At the same time, Jesus shows that the institutional religious leaders are still in the dark because they claim to see. John's gospel presents the religious peoples' refusal to acknowledge their equality with blind "sinners" as the primary obstacle to true vision.

Finally, the location of preacher and parishioner, Jesus and the blind man both outside the institutional church is hardly a hopeful image for pastors, priests, and rabbis today. Yet while Jesus' focus is on the blind man, the bulk of the text recounts the interface between the newly seeing man, the disciples, and the religious authorities embodied by the Pharisees. John's gospel shows both a brutally honest assessment of the religious barriers to Jesus' ministry of proclamation and liberating presence and a modeling of what it might take for disciples and Pharisees to join Jesus' redemptive ministry without restraints–outside of the bounds of the institutional church.

Obstacles to the Empowering Word

My work with inmates and with others on the margins has given me a unique perspective on the barriers to the efficacy of the spoken word to empower. People's perception that they are inferior and unworthy (or that they are viewed that way) may be more clearly visible in a jail setting than in a middle-class congregation. However, mainstream people also perceive themselves as insignificant and even radically lacking–feelings that may be especially present when they find themselves "before God" during Sunday worship. Too often the very physical location, setting, and protocol of Christian worship, together with the manner of dress of the preacher and delivery of most liturgies and sermons subvert the highest espoused objectives.

The Preacher's Persona

As spokesperson for God, the minister inevitably reinforces or subverts the helpful or unhelpful images of God through her/his dress and demeanor. If parishioners are to learn to anticipate respectfully Jesus' presence and voice in the hungry, thirsty, foreigner, naked, sick, and prisoner (Mt. 25:31–46) or among those who are not wise, powerful, or nobly born but are foolish, weak, low, and despised (1 Cor. 1:26–29), should not these characteristics be incarnated in our very presence and demeanor?

When week after week parishioners hear the scriptures read and proclaimed from white-gowned clergy with colorful stoles or pastors in the black robes of judges or academics,[10] the opposite message may be inadvertently given: that those called as God's spokespersons are the pure, holy, wise, powerful, and nobly born.[11] A sports coat and tie may reinforce prejudices that associate clergy with professional classes or the elite, supporting the fallacious view that business dress makes one appear more successful, more worthy of trust and respect. Titles such as reverend, doctor, professor, or father further distance clergy from the common people, disempowering those of lower social standing through reminding them of their perceived inferior, dependent status. Rather than wearing the trappings of the institutional church (robes, albs, fancy crosses, clerical collars) that reinforce hierarchical power structures, today's preachers should perhaps experiment with preaching in jail uniform and handcuffs, hospital gowns, an apron, or rags.

Jesus' scathing critique of some of the professional religious leaders of his time must be heard freshly and heeded if the people are to take to the streets with liberating words and actions:

> "They do their all deeds to be seen by others; for they make their phylacteries broad and their fringes long. They love to have the place of honor at banquets and the best seats in the synagogues, and to be greeted with respect in the marketplaces, and to have people call them rabbi. But you are not to be called rabbi, for you have one teacher, and you are all students. And call no one your father on earth, for you have one Father—the one in heaven. Nor are you to be called instructors, for you have one instructor, the Messiah. The greatest among you will be your servant. All who exalt themselves will be humbled, and all who humble themselves will be exalted." (Mt. 23:5–12)

Preachers desirous of engaging congregants in lives committed to social justice and works of mercy do better to imitate Christ's humble posture as suffering servant. Yet the fanciness of our places of worship and apparent holiness of their religious décor exert their pressure on parishioners and clergy alike to dress appropriately for the out-of-the-ordinary setting.

The Location and Pedagogy of Preaching

Jesus' call to *go out* into the whole world to preach the good news is most convincing when given on the streets—or anywhere but the comfortable confines of most churches.[12] Most churches and synagogues have a formal (sometimes sterile) and otherworldly aura that hardly illustrates the scenes of most of Jesus' deeds and teaching. The single-file pews place congregants seated and facing the front—the perfect posture for passive reception of a monologue.[13]

Paulo Freire critiques what he calls the "banking method" of communication—which corresponds in many ways with the religious system embodied by the Pharisees in John's gospel. According to the banking method, knowledge or information is disseminated to passive recipients in ways that reinforce comfortable and oppressive patterns of dependency:

Instead of communicating, the teacher issues communiqués and makes deposits which the students patiently receive, memorize, and repeat. This is the "banking" concept of education, in which the scope of action allowed to the students extends only as far as receiving, filing, and storing the deposits. They do, it is true, have the opportunity to become collectors or cataloguers of the things they store. But in the last analysis, it is people themselves who are filed away through the lack of creativity, transformation, and knowledge in this (at best) misguided system. For apart from inquiry, apart from the praxis, people cannot be truly human. Knowledge emerges only through invention and re-invention, through the restless, impatient, continuing, hopeful inquiry people pursue in the world, with the world, and with each other.[14]

Freire argues that people on the margins have internalized the oppressor mentality, which is conveyed through nearly every means of communication. In contrast to the banking method, a truly liberating pedagogy happens best using a dialogical approach. The pedagogue must deliberately subvert the system of dependency. This is done by creating an environment of trust whereby the voices of the "voiceless" are sought after and elevated–a first step in education for a critical consciousness and empowerment. While parishioners in mainstream churches are hardly the voiceless poor, banking-style education certainly has led to a noticeable passivity that must be deliberately combated if middle-class Christians are to be empowered for life-giving, active service. According to Freire the vertical, teacher-student (read professional clergy-parishioner) contradiction must be reconciled,[15] replaced with a dialogical, problem-solving pedagogy:

> Whereas banking education anesthetizes and inhibits creative power, problem-posing education involves a constant unveiling of reality. The former attempts to maintain the submersion of consciousness; the later strives for the emergence of consciousness and critical intervention in reality.[16]

According to a dialogical, problem-solving model, a circle of chairs or benches and a smaller group of participants as in the jail Bible study are clearly superior to rows of pews and large numbers of people. Many clergy understandably feel trapped by the buildings, pews, and traditions they have inherited, lacking the resources needed for the ideal overhaul.[17] However, church leaders must be courageous in their championing of new places and forms of worship as important ingredients to help achieve the desperately needed empowerment of people for mission.[18]

Does the church have the courage to be the church outside of the church–the body of Christ with and for "the damned"? Deliberate moves away from hierarchical models of leadership will help move congregations from passive receptors to active subjects in mission. Dialogical sermons, small group Bible studies, new forms of participatory liturgies, and attempts to bridge the gap between comfortable places of worship and harsher realities of the streets and people's lives all will contribute to empowering people for social justice. However, more importantly than any technique is the genuine humility born out of struggle and encounters with the humble God of the scriptures. This God comes to us stripped of all means of power— a vulnerable one whose authenticity is disarming. This God is a respecter of persons in ways that inspire trust and invite authenticity. This God-with-us is finally the only teacher, rabbi, and father who can lead us down the narrow path, causing us to become "fishers of people" as we humbly follow. Without this continual divine mentoring, even the most revolutionary pedagogy is futile.

30

"From the Lips of Foreigners"

VICTOR MCCRACKEN

Then Amaziah, the priest of Bethel, sent to King Jeroboam of Israel, saying, "Amos has conspired against you in the very center of the house of Israel; the land is not able to bear all his words. For thus Amos has said,

> *Jeroboam shall die by the sword,*
> *and Israel must go into exile*
> *away from his land.'"*

And Amaziah said to Amos, "O seer, go, flee away to the land of Judah, earn your bread there, and prophesy there; but never again prophesy at Bethel, for it is the king's sanctuary, and it is a temple of the kingdom." (Am. 7:10–13)

The underbelly of San Antonio is a nice place to be.

Certainly more so than the underbelly of most cities. That four-mile stretch of river that draws so many million tourists to our fair city every year. Those fine Mexican and Italian restaurants, the pubs, the Rivercenter Mall—a virtual Mecca of consumer delight. I was reminded a few weeks ago while standing in line for my four-dollar ice cream cone how utterly at home I am on the river. Is it not a sign that you have truly become a native of San Antonio when you can give the lost tourist directions to Casa Rio from any point on the Riverwalk? Yes, call me a native.

Now we natives know many things about San Antonio. We know where to find all the fine restaurants. We know proper etiquette for visiting the Alamo (Remove your hat! Control your kids! Don't touch the walls!). We know that you're not supposed to stop traffic on the Riverwalk, especially on those narrow stretches of sidewalk where traffic moves in both directions. So you can imagine my consternation several months ago while walking toward La Villita when I was stopped by a thirty-something Hispanic man asking me for spare change. You've seen him before. You know, that worn leather backpack sits next to him on the ground. Unshaven, with holes in those dirty denim pants. He spoke to me in broken English, asking if I could spare him a dollar or two. And I did, feeling just a little less guilty as I made my way to the bourbon chicken I had already decided on for my noontime meal.

We natives know that beggars don't belong on the Riverwalk. They belong about fifteen feet upward, street side, sitting next to the bus depots alongside the street preachers shouting hellfire and brimstone at the passersby. Certainly they don't belong on the Riverwalk! Not on this stretch of consumer paradise. This is supposed to be one of the unspoken luxuries of the Riverwalk, knowing that one faces little risk of being accosted by the local homeless beggar.

I've been thinking a lot about that homeless man lately. I've been unable to avoid this growing sense that there is something just not right about a world where our stock portfolios are busting at the seams while families live in cardboard-box homes. Amos has a way of doing that to us. Amos has quite a bit to say about poverty and wealth, justice and oppression. Let's admit that most of us are not familiar with Amos. His collected oracles reside somewhere in that canonical void between the psalms of David and the Sermon on the Mount. If our schedule of scripture readings in worship has anything to say about our religious affections, I would say that Amos hasn't fared well in our church. No, we like Paul, and we like Jesus. But Amos? No, Amos is an odd voice to most of us.

Amos, a shepherd from the southern kingdom of Judah, proclaimed the word of the Lord in the northern kingdom of Israel during the reign of Jeroboam II. This was a time of peace and prosperity in Israel. The 401(k) plans were growing. The borders were secure. The churches were full of people effusive in their praise for the Lord, thanking the Lord God for blessing beyond measure. The air was full of the aroma of religious sacrifices, a true sign of the piety that pervaded the lives of so many.

Amos certainly must have stuck out like a sore thumb in Israel. The economy is booming, the sanctuaries are full, and up steps this strange shepherd—not even an Israelite, no, a foreigner from Judah—shouting for all to hear that things are *not* all right. "Hear this word, you cows of Bashan, you who oppress the poor and deny justice to the weak. God's judgment is coming by way of an invading army that will take you into exile, marching single file through the broken walls of your city, tied together with rings in your noses. This same God whom you think you're worshiping every week with all of your pious-sounding words in your gated communities and cloth-padded pews is about to appear by way of a clattering army that will ravage your lavish homes! The day of the Lord that you proclaim with joy and hope is coming, but for you it will be a day of darkness and despair! This is the word of the Lord."

Listen a while to the prophet Amos, and I think you'll agree that he was a complete idiot or a madman or both. I picture Amos standing on top of the Market Street Bridge raining down God's judgment on all the families eating Tex-Mex next to the glistening river. Or let us picture him stationed outside the entrance to our church building, just in front of our ushers, yelling at all of us scurrying into our sanctuary that God loathes what is going on inside these stone-veneered walls, that the God we claim to worship is more concerned with how we care for the poor than with how well orchestrated is our liturgy. People aren't supposed to say these kinds of things. This is the kind of sermon that could get one removed from the Riverwalk in handcuffs.

This is the kind of unscheduled homily that would have us ministers scrambling on the phone to get the intruder removed from our premises.

This is the kind of behavior that gets prophets expelled from foreign lands, as concerned Amaziahs work to protect God's people from the mad rantings of simple men.

As a minister who is expected to protect and nurture this church, I have some empathy for Amaziah, the Israelite priest forced to deal with Amos. Who can blame Amaziah? He's merely doing his job. Let's not assume that Amaziah bears any ill will toward Amos. One wonders if Amaziah might not be doing as much to protect Amos as he is to protect the sanctuary. After all, Jeroboam will not take kindly to any sermon that ends with the vivid image of him impaled on a sword. "Go, flee away to the land of Judah, earn your bread there, and prophesy there; but don't come back to Bethel," warns Amaziah. "This is the king's sanctuary. It is a temple of the kingdom." If Amos stays in Israel, *he* may be the one facing the sharp edge of the sword. No, I don't think that Amaziah is the bad guy of the story. He's merely doing what the community expects of him: to stand up for the community against the intrusive words of foreigners. What is wrong with that? Is this not what is expected of every minister?

I want to believe that we can feel safe and protected from this sort of speech. I would like to believe that were Amos to make an unscheduled appearance in my office, he would speak for God, thanking me for my compassionate care for the homeless and dispossessed, the manner in which I as a minister have helped our church embody that care in our life together.

But for the life of me I can't get that homeless beggar on the Riverwalk out of my mind, my indignation toward this stranger's intrusion into my ordered world. I still wonder—were Amos to visit us, would we have the courage to welcome him to this podium rather then discreetly usher him from the premises?

After all, it is so much more natural being an Amaziah in church. Let's face it, Amos hasn't really mastered the art of homiletical finesse. He'll have a hard time making his bread and butter preaching like this. "It is because of your lack of compassion for the poor that God will soon send the bank creditors to repossess your $14 million sanctuary and turn it into a shopping mall and dance club. You think God is on your side, but God is really about to bring judgment upon you for the way your religion has become self-serving, your way of manipulating God for your own ends." Who would dare preach *that* sermon today? And who would have ears to hear?

All the way around there doesn't seem to be much good news in this story. Amos will return to Judah a failure. Israel will become vassal to the Assyrian Empire. This is certainly not the sort of uplifting story we have come to expect in our worship! However, I think after we get over the shock of the spectacle, we can get along with Amos. We can look back, feeling relieved that we weren't present to experience God's judgment enfleshed in a horde of sword-clad pagans. We can accept Amos's harsh metaphors and doomsday attitude. This seems like something out of a Star Wars movie: "A long time ago in a galaxy far, far away." We can sit up next to our Bible with a warm cup of cappuccino and peruse Amos on our way to the more soothing tones of Philippians.

And just a few miles from here Larry sits in front of an abandoned theater picking his guitar in hopes that kind natives will spare him some change so he can eat. A forty-seven-year-old Vietnam veteran and an alcoholic, Larry is not allowed to visit the Alamo, because the police view him as a threat and an eyesore to the local tourist industry. And maybe that is just what he is. Larry has recently befriended a twenty-three-year-old named Rick. Rick has been homeless for only about a month, has a backpack full of books about Tarot cards and the occult, and is deeply suspicious of churches, believing Christians to be more concerned about money than about spirituality. And maybe he is right. Maybe our worship has become just another way of appeasing our self-centeredness. But we preachers aren't supposed to say these kinds of things. No, sometimes the word of the Lord can come only from the lips of foreigners.

My confession: I don't like visiting with people on airplanes. I think it has something to do with the cramped space, or maybe it's because we ministers spend so much of our time speaking that airplanes have become one of the few places of reprieve. Give me a pillow so I can sleep, or let me read a good book. But don't force me to talk to someone whom I've never met.

Last week I was on a plane from St. Louis to San Antonio, returning from a Christian education conference. I sat down at my window seat anticipating a flight unhindered by noise when a heavyset man with crooked glasses told me that the flight was full and he would be sitting next to me. His name was Karl. It quickly became obvious that Karl *loved* to talk. As we began the flight he told the woman on his other side all about his wife, his children, his grandchildren, how he had just moved from Alabama to San Antonio, how his job requires him to travel around the country much of the time, how he is adjusting to his new life in our city. Karl is my nightmare-come-to-life: a talkative man who loves strangers and doesn't mind sharing his opinion about politics or morality or any other topic you might not care to discuss. I tried to sleep through the banter until I heard him start talking about religion, and then curiosity got the better of me.

Karl was talking about his pastor when I asked him where he went to church. "My wife and I are members at Leon Spring Baptist Church," he replied. I then informed him that I was a minister of the Oak Hills Church of Christ. "Oh, yes. That's that large church up on I-10 on the northwest side, right? I've seen your church before." Karl spoke that last sentence with a bit too much weight, like there was something he wanted to say but knew he shouldn't. As is common convention among ministers these days, I invited Karl to come visit our church sometime. I find that visitors are often quite impressed with our facilities, and if Karl didn't eventually decide to place membership at our church, at least a visit would make him appreciate all that God is doing in this place. But I got the strange feeling that he wasn't interested.

Karl and I spent the remainder of the flight talking religion. I listened for the most part, because as I said, Karl loved to talk. In the broader theological spectrum Karl resides somewhere to the right of the fundamentalists, one of the few Baptists I've ever met who believes that the Southern Baptist Convention has become too liberal. For the next hour Karl explained to me why the *King James Version* of the Bible is preferable to modern translations. He enlightened me with stories of dark portent– how Applebee's corrupted one rural Alabama town by bringing liquor into the city limits, how America has been taken over by secular humanists and the church corrupted by those who doubt biblical inerrancy. Theologically, Karl and I are worlds apart, but the last thing I wanted to do was start a religious debate twenty-four thousand feet over Oklahoma, so I kept my peace. I was pondering the finer points of the *King James Version* debate when our conversation took a sudden dramatic turn.

"You know, sometimes I wonder if some of us Christians have lost sight of what's important," he said. "I see so many churches that spend so much of their time and money building large elaborate buildings." *At this point, I began to bristle.* "We spend our energy trying to outdo one another so that we can get larger, appear more successful." *At this point I was about to object, "You don't understand; we built our new sanctuary in Crownridge so we could minister to more people!"* He continued, "We want to be acceptable to the world, so we spend our time trying to make people feel better about the lives they're already living." *I reacted inside, "Karl, that's not fair! Parenting and stress-management classes are our church's way of speaking the language of the world so that they will come to church!"* "And we wonder why the church isn't having an influence on our culture! We look so much like the world that people wonder why they should become Christians in the first place!"

Amaziah was becoming a more sympathetic figure by the second.

"My church isn't a very large one," he continued. "We may not look successful or powerful. But one Friday night a month some of us volunteer down at the local SAMM shelter. We provide homeless men and women a place to sleep and a warm meal. You remember that homeless woman who died under that bridge a few months ago?"

"Yes, I remember the news reports," I replied.

"Our church worked at the shelter two nights before she died. *I tell you, down there you really learn what's most important.*"

Silence.

The word of the Lord, from the lips of a foreigner. I doubt that we'll be inviting Karl to Oak Hills anytime soon to entertain us with his prophetic pleasantries, but then again maybe this is a good sign that Karl is indeed a prophet for us. There are times when God's word to his people is "repent!" Change your ways and love what God loves the most. "Let justice roll down like waters, and righteousness like an ever-flowing stream" (Am. 5:24).

But can an Amaziah really say that? Or must we keep our eyes open for those discomforting foreigners among us who shatter our comfortable complacency and threaten our security?

> And will we have ears to hear when those foreigners *do* come
>   among us,
> beckoning Riverwalk natives to look upward,
> street side; where homeless drunks seek good news unaware;
> where illegal aliens come begging for a meal;
> where single mothers bring McDonald-land paychecks to street
>   corners,
> where children spend after-school hours scanning the classifieds for
>   affordable housing?

The word of the Lord, from the lips of foreigners.

31

"Lazarus Who?"

Luke 16:19–31

STEVEN EGLAND

We gathered around the grave. It was easy to distinguish between rich and poor. The truly impoverished wore cloth that draped from their backs like rags hung out to dry. Deep creases lined their faces, and drooping eyes no longer saw the light of day these are the birthmarks of those born in a world that will not care.

The wealthy, too, were standing there. Many came robed in beautiful kangas hailing their traditional roots. Others wore dresses; men wore shirts all in honor of the events unfolding.

As the service began, all eyes bowed to the ground. For some reason, I remember the feet. Some people were barefoot, while others wore sandals carved from old motorcycle tires. These were tired feet, dusty feet that had traveled miles over dirt roads, feet made beautiful because of the stories they told.

Then there were the feet that came garbed. Brightly washed tennis shoes, black patent leather—shoes that insulated the one who wore them from the poverty of the past...a poverty to which they would never return.

But this day would be different. No amount of pageantry could shield those who gathered from the common roots they shared. This was a day all of humanity would stand together and mourn the death of three children. The total who had died that week from measles now rose to sixty-seven. The disease knew no class distinction; it struck both rich and poor.

I sat alone at my desk waiting to go home once all the busyness of the day came to rest. No thoughts could penetrate my rumination. Then, from outside my office, the voice of a woman interrupted my silence. Through the door she shuffled with cloth draped from her back. Her appearance was gaunt—deep creases, drooping eyes, bare feet. As she entered the room she kicked up the dust that permeated the old cement floor of my six-by-eight foot space.

I motioned for her to sit on a wooden chair that tilted slightly to the left. She had traveled far—her feet told me that. After a moment of silence that set the stage for the seriousness of her visit she took a deep breath, leaned across my desk, drawing her face within inches of my own, and opened her mouth to speak. I could smell her breath. She had gone too long without food. When she spoke, she whispered, catching me off guard, "What do you think of Lazarus?"

My mind quickly scanned the growing list of children who had died that week. I didn't recall a Lazarus.

"Lazarus?" I repeated. "Do you mean the Lazarus from the Bible?"

"Yes, Lazarus."

I could feel a growing discomfort. I needed time to think, so I asked, "Do you mean the one who died?"

"Yes."

And she waited.

The woman may have been poor, but one thing you learn about people of faith who are poor is that their faith runs deep. No trite answer would do, nor could I delay. She demanded my answer, so I said the first thing that came to mind, "I believe in the resurrection."

"Do you really?" she fired back.

I was trapped. What does she want? What does she know? Is she mocking me? Should I be honest with this woman, who has most likely traveled miles to bury a child? Dare I be honest with this woman and tell her that just before she came into my office I wasn't sure? Dare I be truthful and tell her, "On most days, yes, I believe in the resurrection—but right now I really don't know what to believe. Children are dying, and God doesn't appear to stop it." Dare I be honest?

In an attempt to regain my composure I began to explain, "We've seen children die all week, but an image that sticks with me now is that at Lazarus's grave Jesus wept. I have to believe that God has the same compassion for the children who are dying now."

For the first time during the course of our conversation the woman gave me room to breathe. Laughing, she threw her head back with such abandonment that she nearly knocked her head against the brick wall. I could see her rotting teeth beaming at me as though she were at a party. There was no haughtiness in her laughter; it was a laughter born of stress relieved.

When she finished laughing, she leaned back across my desk with a friendliness not before expressed and said, "Not that Lazarus. I mean the Lazarus who lay at the rich man's gate full of sores. It's in the gospel of Luke. Look it up."

Then she rose from her chair, shuffled through the dust, and left the room. I never saw her again.

Luke's story (in Lk. 16:19–31) is about a rich man. The rich man wasn't evil; he didn't chase the poor off his porch. He just ignored the fact that the poor went through his garbage. Catch what you can; at least it's something. You've seen this happen at the garbage bins of restaurants.

It's a story about two deaths. The poor at the resurrection rest in God's abundance. The rich suffer torment. Even the final resting place doesn't come as a surprise, for it is a common thread running through Jesus' message.

What might come as a surprise, however, is the denial of the rich man's request to return and warn his brothers. It's a sobering thought, given the fact that we, in the twenty-first century, still have the prophets, and we have had one come back from the dead, yet we still ignore the Lazaruses lying at our doorsteps as we toss them our garbage, hoping they don't break into our homes. Jesus was right. Each new generation will not be convinced.

But the matter that causes me the most sobriety is the woman. What was she asking? Did she see me as the rich man in the midst of poverty wondering what my role was going to be? Or did she come that day because she saw in her child a resemblance to Lazarus–hungry and full of sores– simply wanting to hear words of encouragement that her child was now lying whole and content in the midst of God's grace?

I never asked her if she had come to the funeral. *Who* was she? Was she one of the poor at my doorstep? Or was she the rich man come back from the dead?

I've come to this conclusion: I see her now as the Christ who once again rose from the dead and appeared to me in the form of a stranger, a woman with rags on her back, rotting teeth, bare feet that shuffled, and with the smell of hunger on her breath. Yes–Lazarus visited me.

We are all people on a journey accompanied by a host of strangers along the way. We have enjoyed the company of our God, but have lost the habit of responding to the needs at our doorsteps. We overindulge and ignore the needs of the poor who line our streets.

If nothing else, let this be a cry to the Lazaruses of our world: Keep knocking, Lazarus! And keep begging to return, you rich men and women, from your eternal resting place. For as long as the poor remain, they will continue to haunt us and appear in the most unplanned ways.

We beg you to come...so *we* might be saved!

"The Gift of Anger"

John 2:13–22

ANN R. PALMERTON

It's been said that *anger* is just one letter short of *danger*. And, based on my experience, that really can ring true. Who among us hasn't felt uncomfortable around anger? Who hasn't heard an argument begin and felt one's stomach wrench and concentration fade?

If anger makes us uncomfortable, it probably has something to do with the fact that we live in a culture that virtually mandates "niceness." In addition to being friendly, polite, and thoughtful, being nice means never appearing upset or even irritated, never "letting 'em see you sweat."

And if we were taught to be nice anywhere, we had it drilled into us to be downright angelic at church. In Sunday school we learned about a "gentle, sweet" man named Jesus. We learned that being angry upset our teachers, parents, ministers, and thus by extension God. Our experience confirmed what the church in the Middle Ages preached, that anger is one of the seven deadly sins.

And then along comes today's gospel lesson, and we hear Jesus screaming, "Take these things out of here! Stop making my Father's house a marketplace!" Could anyone hear these words from John 2 and doubt that Jesus felt anger? Imagine the chaotic impression that the wild scene must have burned into the disciples' minds. A passionate rabbi with a whip of cords suddenly moves against money changers and merchants, driving them from the temple courtyard. Tables overturn with a crash, pigeons flutter loose, oxen bray, sheep bleat, coins clang and roll around on the floor, animals scatter, people shout, and the whip flies. Shocked gasps escape from the crowd. Jesus was angry.

Psychologists tell us that anger is a "secondary" emotion. It is what you feel after you feel something else, something that hurts, something that is askew. Anger then moves in and covers up the hurt we feel at first.

The hurt that Jesus felt had to do with what was going on in the temple. This was his Father's house! He saw the money changers and the merchants profiting from the Jewish sacrificial law. He saw the Gentiles crowded out of even the outer court, the only place that non-Jews could access worship and the lowest rung on the religious ladder. It was reserved for the non-Jew, persons with deformities, and women. Jesus saw how inaccessible worship and thus God had become for people on the margins. He saw how the powerful kept God at a "safe" distance from the riffraff. And it made him mad. It made him really, really mad.

If we've believed all our lives that Christians should not feel anger or express it, we are uncomfortable with a red-faced, steam-coming-out-of-the-ears Jesus image. Preachers and commentators throughout the centuries have tried to airbrush this and other gospel texts to soften Jesus' portrayal. One commentator has called these

> desperate attempts...to tone it down and edge out this incident...because they feel unhappily that it will not fit into their preconceived idea of what Christ should do and be; that here somehow he acted for once out of character, and fell inexplicably below himself, forgot his own law of life, lost his head and his temper.[1]

Well, it seems to me that Jesus didn't lose his temper; he found it. And thank God. I know from personal experience that anger is a terrible thing to lose—lose, that is, to the point of not knowing that you have it.

I was reared to be nice. It has taken me years to believe that my capacity for anger can be a gift from God. My early experiences in home and church and school reinforced in me the idea that "good" Christians should not show anger and that the "best" Christians would not even feel anger. I was in my mid-twenties before I realized that everyone feels—at least *should* feel—the emotion of anger. I remember the moment vividly. I was in seminary, attending a workshop on being a woman in ministry. One of the discussion groups was on anger. We were asked to describe what made us feel anger and what we did when we were angry. As my peer group went around the room, I was dumbfounded. Not only did people describe a depth of emotion that was foreign to me; they described a whole range of ways they creatively coped with angry feelings—individually, in relationships, and before God.

When it came my turn, all I could offer was that I didn't feel angry very often and that when I was angry I chewed gum. I could remember times when I really chomped on that gum. But the point *is* that I certainly wasn't expressing those feelings to anyone, let alone to God. That was a first step for me in exploring the frozen places within myself that needed thawing.

Given our inadequacies in dealing with anger, the scriptures are refreshing in their honesty about it. The Bible takes for granted that our capacity for anger is part of our God-created nature. In Ephesians 4:26–27 we are even *commanded* to be angry: "*Be angry* but do not sin; do not let the sun go down on your anger, and do not make room for the devil." Anger can lead to sin, but in and of itself it is morally neutral. Scripture criticizes destructive expressions of anger, but anger, like pain, is a vital capacity without which we wouldn't be fully human.

In *Madeline,* the story of ten little girls in two straight lines, Miss Clavel wakes in the middle of the night, sits bolt upright in bed, and declares, "Something is not right." Anger is that signal within the soul that something is not right. It's almost never the first thing we feel, which means that it's important for us to lift the lid on our anger and see what's underneath it. What has been hurt?

As a danger signal, anger functions as an early warning system indicating that something is threatening. Anger challenges us to be aware of those relationships and situations and organizations that would keep us immature, dependent, and alienated.

I believe one reason for the church's historic reluctance to be a champion of justice lies in our aversion to anger. The phrase *frozen chosen* was given to followers of Calvin for a reason! We must ask ourselves some hard questions: Are we willing to give up Stoicism as a Christian virtue? Are we willing to be vulnerable enough to be hurt? And if we do feel hurt, are we secure enough in our identity as God's children to work for greater justice and not just for personal defense? More often than not, I believe, we don't take action because we don't allow ourselves to feel pain and hurt: our own or that of others.

There are people in this city who experience oppression from institutions that many of us experience as benign and therefore don't question. Take housing as an example. When I hear one of Columbus's leading developers say that economic and racial segregation in Columbus is at a forty-year high, I listen. That is not the kind of city I want for my family. We live in a relatively safe neighborhood in a comfortable home. But it matters to me that there is a shortage of low- to moderate-income housing in Franklin County. It matters to me that the number of new homes selling for less than $100,000 dropped from 1,200 in 1992 to 52 in 1997. It matters to me that over a twenty-year period federal government funding for low-income housing dropped from $85 billion in 1977 to $16 billion in 1997. The results of this are that low-income housing increasingly has been concentrated in older, inner-city Columbus. And in the meantime, suburban communities have enacted restrictive zoning ordinances that keep developers from building low- and moderate-income housing.

The comfortable don't often speak out on behalf of the uncomfortable. I am grateful to be part of a church that has taken risks to respond to those at the margins of our city. Closing our eyes and ears, sitting still is not an option for us. When we listen and see, may we allow ourselves to feel anger at what is not here in our cities and suburbs. May we step out in faith to work for change and renewal.

Anger is just one letter away from *danger*. But our greatest danger may be in our suppression of healthy anger–the impulses from God that tell us: "Something is not right!" This kind of anger fuels reform for justice. This anger is dangerous, but it's the kind of danger the world needs.

Family Promise

Who We Are

Family Promise is an interfaith, nonprofit organization committed to helping low-income families nationwide achieve lasting independence. We help families accomplish this by providing shelter, meals, and support services for homeless families and through programs designed to redress the underlying causes of homelessness. Family Promise was founded on the belief that Americans are compassionate people who want to make a difference. Our promise has been to link those in need with those who want to help. Fourteen years and ninety thousand volunteers later, our pledge is ever broader and deeper.

What We Do

Family Promise focuses on four program areas:

1. *Interfaith Hospitality Network (IHN)*–Networks of congregations and volunteers providing shelter, meals, and comprehensive support services to homeless families.

2. *Family Mentoring*–A homelessness-prevention initiative, training volunteers to act as advisers to and community advocates for at-risk families, helping the families achieve goals and maintain self-sufficiency.

3. *Just Neighbors*–A multimedia interactive educational program that raises awareness of poverty and homelessness and their root causes as the first step in establishing community-based responses to a national problem.

4. *Community Initiatives*–Fostering local IHN outgrowth programs such as transitional housing, housing renovation, job training, healthcare services, childcare, and literacy.

Interfaith Hospitality Network

People of faith and religious communities want to respond to the needs of their homeless neighbors, but often lack a vehicle to focus their efforts. What can we do to help? Where do we begin? How do we become part of the solution?

The Interfaith Hospitality Network (IHN) provides a way. IHN enables religious groups to unite hearts and hands to provide shelter, meals, and compassionate assistance for homeless families. By uniting eight to thirteen congregations, plus day centers and social service agencies, an IHN program can do what individuals alone cannot do.

Because IHN programs are formed primarily from existing resources, they can be implemented quickly, without major startup costs. Programs vary from community to community, reflecting local needs and resources.

In the IHN program, a host congregation furnishes clean, safe, overnight lodging and nutritious meals for three to five families (up to fourteen guests) for one week every two or three months. During the host week, other congregations may provide additional volunteers to support the host group.

Volunteers in the IHN program provide homeless families with basic human needs in a spirit of warmth and hospitality. They provide both the "people power" to get the jobs done and the personal support and compassion that homeless families need. In addition to furnishing meals, overnight hosting, and other program requirements, volunteers do simple but immeasurably important things. They talk to guests. They listen to them. They treat them with respect. Volunteers can be a source of hope when hope has been lost.

The IHN works. More than 70 percent of the families who participate in IHN programs find permanent housing; guests without jobs often find them or enter job-training programs.

For many congregations, helping those in need fulfills a biblical, traditional mission. Thousands of volunteers and hundreds of religious communities already participate in IHN programs and have helped homeless families attain more stable lives. Congregations have found that the IHN provides an effective way to be involved in a hands-on outreach program that serves the poor, and it also fosters congregational unity and interfaith cooperation.

Many clergy and laity attest to the IHN program's ability to invigorate a congregation. "Getting involved in IHN served as a turning point in our ministry," said a pastor from Houston. "We were ingrown…IHN expanded our vision." A Minnesota minister wrote: "In twenty-four years of pastoral ministry, no human care ministry has so touched the hearts of the people I serve. Of all the outreach ministries of our church, IHN fills up soonest with volunteers. After all, it's biblical. The spiritual gift of hospitality means nothing less than, literally, 'a love of strangers.' It's real love in action, broadening perspectives on poverty and homelessness, and allowing singles and whole family units an opportunity to be servants and to make new friends at the same time."

Just Neighbors

Family Promise created *Just Preaching* because we know that clergy can be powerful voices for justice. Preaching can provide the inspiration, but congregations also need information—opportunities for study and education that can lead to action.

Just Neighbors is a way to help your congregation follow one of scripture's most basic teachings: to love your neighbor as yourself.

It is an interactive multimedia curriculum, an engaging and inspiring educational experience. Its purpose is to get your congregation involved in helping their neighbors who are living in poverty.

Just Neighbors introduces congregations to some of their neighbors who are in need. It offers insight into the neighbors' daily struggles. It points the way to greater understanding—not only of problems but of solutions. It inspires people of faith to act on what they've learned.

Just Neighbors has three goals:

- to educate your congregation about poverty in the United States
- to spur them to greater service to families in poverty
- to send them forth as advocates for neighbors in need

Just Neighbors leads your congregation to examine in depth the pervasive issues at the root of poverty. More importantly, though, *Just Neighbors* will inspire your group to do something about them.

The format of the curriculum is flexible and easily tailored to your congregation's unique needs. *Just Neighbors* sessions include readings of scripture, interactive exercises, and engaging videos and discussions. Each session ends with ideas for putting faith and knowledge into action.

You can use *Just Neighbors* to

- provide an exciting program for adult education classes
- recruit volunteer support for congregational activities
- involve an inwardly focused congregation in the community
- gather support for a new initiative
- engage the congregation in social justice issues

The *Just Neighbors* program includes nine interactive multimedia sessions. It is designed as a series, but has a flexible structure that you can adapt to meet your congregation's needs and interests. Each session is designed so that a group can complete it in one hour (though the final session may take considerably longer if the group uses it to plan a course of action that extends beyond the program). Depending on your purposes, your group may decide to complete the entire program or any number of individual sessions—even only one.

Session 1: Who Is My Neighbor?

People of faith have a responsibility to love all neighbors—not just those next door, but anyone in need. In this session, participants are introduced through a video to some of our neighbors—three families living in poverty. They see the obstacles that the families face each day and discuss how, as people of faith, we are called to help.

Session 2: Making Ends Meet

Living in poverty means maintaining a constant financial juggling act, a never-ending struggle to make ends meet. In this session, participants watch a video about a family, and then try to balance the family's budget, experiencing the nearly impossible financial decisions that low-income families must make on a daily basis.

Session 3: What Would You Choose?

Is it better for Annie, a single mother struggling to care for her children, to move to a cheaper but less safe neighborhood or to spend more hours working away from her children so they can stay where they are? In this session, participants make the tough decisions that Annie faces and feel the stresses and struggles of life below the poverty line.

Session 4: Does Working Work?

Even full-time employment does not guarantee a successful climb out of poverty. In this session, participants consider the lives of three working families who struggle to meet their basic needs as they seek to understand how trends and changes in employment and wages affect the families who make up the "working poor."

Session 5: Housing Matters

The word *home* evokes images of safety, warmth, and love, but for millions of Americans, a decent and affordable home is an impossible dream. In this session, participants examine the nation's housing crisis and commonly believed myths about housing. Through a video, they learn about ways in which communities are responding to the need for housing.

Session 6: Prejudice, Privilege, and Poverty

Race and poverty have been closely linked throughout the history of the United States. In this session, a thought-provoking video provides the basis for the group's discussion. Participants explore the ways that racial discrimination affects education, employment, and economic opportunities.

Session 7: Our Children, Our Future

Childhood should be a time of innocence and joy, a time free from worry and fear, but that is not the case for the one in six American children who lives in poverty. In a moving video, children show photographs that they have taken of their lives and tell of the harsh realities of growing up poor. And in a creative activity, participants identify the essential elements all children need to thrive.

Session 8: Justice for All?

Over the last several decades, the gulf between the rich and the poor in America has widened. In this session, participants take on the roles of people of different economic status and grapple with the differing ways they are affected by economic trends reflected in the news of the day.

Session 9: Stepping Out in Faith

For groups that have completed more than one *Just Neighbors* session, this session is a springboard for further action. Some groups will identify volunteer opportunities and consider ways of becoming involved. Others will develop a plan of action and concrete goals for service or advocacy.

The *"Just Neighbors* ToolKit" contains all the components you'll need for a successful program—from video to audio, from playing cards to die-cut blocks. A member of your congregation will be fully prepared to lead the workshops after reviewing the material in the facilitator's guide.

To learn more about *Just Neighbors,* please contact Family Promise:

71 Summit Avenue
Summit, New Jersey 07901
908-273-1100
info@familypromise.org
www.familypromise.org

Notes

Introduction

[1]A similar story can be found in Fred B. Craddock, *Craddock Stories,* ed. Mike Graves and Richard F. Ward (St. Louis: Chalice Press, 2001), 52–53.

[2]Abraham J. Heschel, *The Prophets* (New York: Harper & Row, 1962), 1:198.

[3]Ibid.

[4]Ibid.

[5]Ibid., 199.

Chapter 1: Preaching in the Face of Economic Injustice

[1]This reflects the "self-sufficiency standard"–a measurement of how much income is needed for a family of a given composition in a given place to adequately meet its basic needs without public or private assistance–for Bergen County, New Jersey. Data from Diana Pearce and Jennifer Brooks, *The Real Cost of Living in 2002: The Self-Sufficiency Standard for New Jersey* (Edison, N.J.: Legal Services of New Jersey Poverty Research Institute, 2002), 49.

[2]Marvin A. McMickle, "The Prophet Amos as a Model for Preaching on Issues of Social Justice," *The African American Pulpit* (Spring 2001): 6–10.

[3]Ibid., 6.

[4]Ibid., 7.

[5]Cf. Beard, *Economic Interpretation of the Constitution of the United States;* and Susan Previant Lee and Peter Passell, *A New Economic View of American History* (New York: Norton, 1979).

[6]Cf. "Giving Life to a Living Wage: Facts and Resources for Living Wage Campaigns," National Interfaith Committee for Worker Justice, 1020 West Bryn Mawr, 4th Floor, Chicago, IL 60690-4627; telephone: 773-728-8409; Internet: www.nicwj.org.

[7]Beard, *Economic Interpretation of the Constitution of the United States,* 157.

[8]Marvin A. McMickle, *Preaching to the Black Middle Class* (Valley Forge, Pa.: Judson Press, 2000), 99–108.

[9]James H. Cone, "The Servant Church," in *The Pastor as Servant,* ed. Earl E. Shelp and Ronald H. Sunderland (New York: Pilgrim Press, 1986), 63–64.

Chapter 2: Preaching's Purpose: Thoughts on Message and Method

[1]Charles Campbell, *The Word Against the Powers* (Louisville: Westminster John Knox Press, 2002).

[2]This was in a class that Nichols taught at Princeton Theological Seminary for which I was a teaching fellow. Cf. J. Randall Nichols's two books on preaching: *Building the Word: The Dynamics of Communication and Preaching* (San Francisco: HarperCollins, 1981) and *Restoring the Word: Preaching as Pastoral Communication* (San Francisco: HarperCollins, 1987).

[3]Hans-Georg Gadamer, *Truth and Method,* ed. Joel C. Weinsheimer and Donald G. Marshall (New York: Continuum, 1990).

[4]Cf. Charles Wood, *Vision and Discernment* (Atlanta: Scholars Press, 1985).

[5]Cf. Thomas G. Long's incisive critique of the bridge-building metaphor for preaching in "The Use of Scripture in Contemporary Preaching," *Interpretation* 44 (1990): 341–52.

[6]I do not presume to speak for everyone in this book on the precise definition of preaching's core message. Since this book represents thirty-two authors with theologies and faith commitments quite diverse from one another, I can only assert my conviction here about preaching's core message. However, I would argue that every author herein operates in the same way: each preacher's understanding of what the core message of preaching is functions as the mediator between scripture and sermon.

[7]The tracks of God in this process are untraceable, at least from a post-Enlightenment scientific perspective. I trust that God does infuse this discerning process, but do not know how to map it out heuristically.

[8]A helpful guide for developing eyes to see the revelatory in human experience is Mary Catherine Hilkert, *Naming Grace: Preaching and the Sacramental Imagination* (New York: Continuum, 1997).

⁹Thomas G. Long's *Witness of Preaching* (Louisville: Westminster/John Knox Press, 1989), esp. chaps. 4–5, remains a useful guide to sermon construction. Cf. too, Paul Scott Wilson's *The Four Pages of the Sermon* (Nashville: Abingdon Press, 1989) and Ronald J. Allen's *Interpreting the Gospel: An Introduction to Preaching* (St. Louis: Chalice Press, 2001) for helpful guides for building the sermon.

¹⁰A useful guide here is Wood's *Vision and Discernment.*

Chapter 3: "Faith Plus Persistence Pays Off"

¹This reflects the "self-sufficiency standard"–a measurement of how much income is needed for a family of a given composition in a given place to adequately meet its needs without public or private assistance–for Bergen County, New Jersey. Data from Diana Pearce and Jennifer Brooks, *The Real Cost of Living in 2002: The Self-Sufficiency Standard for New Jersey* (Edison, N.J.: Legal Services of New Jersey Poverty Research Institute, 2002), 49.

Chapter 4: "The Torah's Personal Responsibility Act"

¹United States Department of Health and Human Services, Office of Family Assistance, *Temporary Assistance for Needy Families (TANF): Fifth Annual Report to Congress* (Washington, D.C.: United States Department of Health and Human Services, 2003).

²Bread for the World, "TANF 101: An Introduction to the Program" (Washington, D.C.: Bread for the World, 2002).

³The United States Conference of Mayors, *A Status Report on Hunger and Homelessness in America's Cities: 2002, A 25-City Survey* (Washington, D.C.: United States Conference of Mayors, 2002), ii.

⁴Data from United States Department of Agriculture, Food and Nutrition Service.

⁵United States Bureau of Labor Statistics, "Employment Situation Summary: February 2003" (Washington, D.C.: United States Bureau of Labor Statistics, 2003).

⁶Kevin Carey and Iris J. Law, "States Are Cutting Low-Income Programs in Response to Fiscal Crisis: Less Counter-Productive Options Are Available" (Washington, D.C.: Center for Budget and Policy Priorities, 2002).

⁷Children's Defense Fund, *The State of Children in America's Union: A 2002 Action Guide to Leave No Children Behind* (Washington, D.C.: Children's Defense Fund, 2002), 14.

⁸Babylonian Talmud, *Sanhedrin* 86a, *Kiddushin* 29a.

⁹Babylonian Talmud, *Pesachim* 113a.

¹⁰Babylonian Talmud, *Shabbat* 118a, which permits eating fewer than the prescribed three Sabbath meals rather than become dependent upon others.

¹¹Aaron Levine, *Economics and Jewish Law: Halakhic Perspectives* (New York: Ktav, 1987), 127.

¹²Ibid., 117.

Chapter 6: Enabling Grace

¹E. L. Doctorow, *City of God* (New York: Random, 2000), 44–45.

²Daniel C. Maguire, *Sacred Energies* (Minneapolis: Fortress Press, 2000), 72.

³For another treatment of this twofold theme, see my book *Preaching Justice: The Ethical Vocation of Word and Sacrament Ministry* (Harrisburg, Pa.: Trinity Press Int'l., 2000), 17–30.

⁴Willi Marxsen, *New Testament Foundations for Christian Ethics,* trans. O. C. Dean Jr. (Minneapolis: Fortress Press, 1993), 180ff.; and Victor Paul Furnish, *Theology and Ethics in Paul* (Nashville: Abingdon Press, 1968), 224–27.

⁵Furnish, *Theology and Ethics in Paul,* 225–26.

⁶Ibid., 225 (italics mine).

⁷E. C. Blackman, "Justification, Justify," in *The Interpreter's Dictionary of the Bible,* ed. George Arthur Buttrick, vol. 2 (New York: Abingdon Press, 1962), 1027–30.

⁸Furnish, *Theology and Ethics in Paul,* 224.

⁹Helmut Thielicke, *Theological Ethics,* ed. William Lazareth, vol. 1 (Philadelphia: Fortress Press, 1966), 51–52.

[10]Martin Luther, "The Freedom of a Christian," in *Luther's Works,* vol. 31, ed. Harold Grimm (Philadelphia: Muhlenberg, 1957), 329–77.

[11]Ibid., 344.

[12]Ibid., 367–68.

[13]Ibid., 367.

[14]Martin Luther, "Lectures on Galatians 1519," in *Luther's Works,* vol. 27, ed. Jaroslav Pelikan, trans. Richard Jungkuntz (St. Louis: Concordia, 1964), 325–26.

[15]Jan Milic Lochman, *Signposts to Freedom,* trans. David Lewis (Minneapolis: Augsburg, 1982), 18–20.

[16]George Wolfgang Forell, *History of Christian Ethics,* vol. 1 (Minneapolis: Augsburg, 1979), 146–53.

[17]Ibid., 149–51.

[18]Augustine, *Sermons on the Liturgical Seasons,* trans. Mary Sarah Muldowney, Fathers of the Church, vol. 36 (New York: Fathers of the Church, 1959), 120–21.

[19]Ibid., 323.

[20]Robert McAfee Brown, *Unexpected News: Reading the Bible with Third World Eyes* (Philadelphia: Westminster, 1984), 157–61.

[21]Ibid., 93–94.

[22]For some inspiring examples see Nile Harper, *Urban Churches Vital Signs: Beyond Charity toward Justice* (Grand Rapids: Eerdmans, 1999).

Chapter 7: "The Politics of Compassion"

[1]"The Politics of Compassion" is reprinted from William Sloane Coffin, "The Politics of Compassion," from *The Heart Is a Little to the Left* © 1999 William Sloane Coffin. Reprinted by permission of University Press of New England.

Chapter 8: "Sitting Down to Eat or Standing Up to Life"

[1]*United Nations Report* (June 27, 2000): 135.

[2]President William Clinton's 2000 State of the Union address, available online in March 2003 at www.fas.org/news/usa/2000/000127-sotu-text.htm.

[3]*New Republic* (May 17, 1999): 23.

Chapter 9: "Not Innocent or Perfect, Just Faithful"

[1]Jacqui James et al., *Weaving the Fabric of Diversity: An Anti-Bias Program for Adults* (Boston: Unitarian Universalist Association, 1996), 21–23.

[2]The current sermon was one of a series on "isms."

[3]This principle and the ones that follow are those of the Unitarian Universalist Covenant.

[4]Peggy MacIntosh, "White Benefits Checklist," was used earlier in the service as a meditation.

Chapter 10: Ancient Utterance and Contemporary Hearing

[1]Patrick D. Miller, "Deuteronomy and Psalms: Evoking a Biblical Conversation," in Miller's *Israelite Religion and Biblical Theology: Collected Essays,* Journal for the Study of the Old Testament Supplement 267 (Sheffield: Sheffield Academic Press, 2000), 318–36, has seen most clearly how the cry of the Psalms connects to the requirements of Torah.

[2]The normative work on God's pathos is Abraham J. Heschel, *The Prophets,* 2 vols. (New York: Harper & Row, 1962).

[3]The data on the scribes have been usefully summarized by Philip R. Davies, *Scribes and Schools: The Canonization of the Hebrew Scriptures,* Library of Ancient Israel (Louisville: Westminster John Knox Press, 1998).

[4]See Walter Brueggemann, *The Prophetic Imagination* (Philadelphia: Fortress Press, 1978; 2d ed., Minneapolis: Fortress Press, 2002).

[5]See Walter Brueggemann, "An Imaginative 'Or,'" in Brueggemann's *Testimony to Otherwise: The Witness of Elijah and Elisha* (St. Louis: Chalice Press, 2001), 5–25.

Chapter 11: "The Prophet's Sons and Daughters"

[1]"The Prophet's Sons and Daughters" is reprinted from "The Prophet's Sons and Daughters" by Patrick D. Miller, *The Princeton Seminary Bulletin,* Volume 22, no. 3 (2001), pages 27–284, with permission of *The Princeton Seminary Bulletin.*

[2]James L. Mays, "Justice: Perspectives from the Prophets," *Interpretation* 37 (1983): 16.

Chapter 12: "Two Fingers under the Door"

[1]T. S. Eliot, "Journey of the Magi," in *The Complete Poems and Plays, 1909–1950* (New York: Harcourt, Brace & World, 1971), 68.

[2]Ibid.

[3] Meister Eckhart, in *Meditations with Meister Eckhart,* ed. Matthew Fox (Santa Fe, N.M.: Bear, 1983).

[4]Anne Lamott, *Operating Instructions: A Journal of My Son's First Year* (New York: Pantheon, 1993).

Chapter 14: Poverty and Homelessness in the United States

[1]The United States Conference of Mayors, in their 1998 survey of hunger and homelessness, reported that one in four homeless persons in the thirty cities surveyed was a child. Since that time, the proportion of family homelessness in cities has increased, and the proportion of family homelessness is apparently greater in rural areas than it is in cities.

[2]The United States Conference of Mayors, *A Status Report on Hunger and Homelessness in America's Cities 2002: A 25-City Survey* (Washington, D.C.: United States Conference of Mayors, 2002), 61; Yvonne Vissing, *Out of Sight, Out of Mind: Homeless Children and Families in Small Town America* (Lexington: University of Kentucky Press, 1996), 8–9.

[3]The Better Homes Fund, *Homeless Children: America's New Outcasts* (Newport Centre, Mass.: Better Homes Fund, 1999).

[4]In 1999, there were only forty units of affordable and available housing for every one hundred extremely low-income households wishing to rent. The federal standard for housing affordability is that it costs no more than 30 percent of household income. United States Department of Housing and Urban Development, *A Report on Worst Case Housing Needs in 1999: New Opportunity Amid Continuing Challenges, Executive Summary* (Washington, D.C.: United States Department of Housing and Urban Development, 2001), 8.

[5]Center for Housing Policy/National Housing Conference, *America's Working Families and the Housing Landscape 1997–2001*(Washington, D.C.: Center for Housing Policy, 2002).

[6]Maria was earning $7 an hour. Consider a minimum-wage worker, earning $5.15 an hour, who would have to work more than one hundred hours per week to afford the nationwide median Fair Market Rent for a two-bedroom apartment. In no state, county, or metropolitan area is the prevailing minimum wage adequate to afford the Fair Market Rent on a two-bedroom apartment. National Low Income Housing Coalition, *Out of Reach 2002: Further Out of Reach than Ever* (Washington, D.C.: National Low Income Housing Coalition, 2002).

[7]Cushing Dolbeare, *Changing Priorities: The Federal Budget and Housing Assistance 1976–2006* (Washington, D.C.: National Low Income Housing Coalition, 2001), 14.

[8]Data from Joint Center for Housing Studies, Harvard University.

[9]United States Department of Housing and Urban Development, *Worst Case Housing Needs in 1999,* 5.

[10]See Barbara R. Bergmann, "Deciding Who's Poor," *Dollars and Sense* (March/April 2000).

[11]For comparison of the average annual cost of childcare for a four-year-old in an urban childcare center with the average cost of public college tuition, see Karen Schulman, *Issue Brief: The High Cost of Child Care Puts Quality Care Out of Reach for Many Families* (Washington, D.C.: Children's Defense Fund, 2000).

[12]Joseph Dalaker, United States Census Bureau, Current Population Reports Series P60-214, *Poverty in the United States: 2000* (Washington, D.C.: United States Government Printing Office, 2001), 8.

[13]More than half, 58.2 percent, of minimum-wage workers are women. Lawrence Mishel, Jared Bernstein, and Heather Boushey, *The State of Working America 2002/2003* (Ithaca, N.Y.: Cornell University Press, 2003), 195.

[14]Data from United States Bureau of Labor Statistics, "Real Earnings in January 2003" (Washington, D.C.: United States Bureau of Labor Statistics, 2003).

[15]See the National Priorities Project, *Working Hard, Earning Less: The Story of Job Growth in America* (Northampton, Mass.: National Priorities Project, 1999).

[16]Lawrence Mishel, Jared Bernstein, and John Schmitt, *The State of Working America 2000/2001* (Ithaca, N.Y.: Cornell University Press, 2001), 245.

[17]Data from United for a Fair Economy.

Chapter 15: *"Tikun Olam"*

[1]Keary Kincannon, *Building on Faith: Models of Church-Sponsored Affordable Housing Programs in the Washington D.C. Area* (Washington, D.C.: Churches' Conference on Shelter and Housing, 1989), ii.

[2]*Pirke Avot* 1:14.

Chapter 16: "Bring Forth Justice"

[1]Henri Nouwen, *Reaching Out* (New York: Doubleday, 1986), 47.

[2]Loren Mead, *Transforming Congregations for the Future* (Bethesda, Md.: Alban Institute, 1994), 44–45.

Part 5: Children, Poverty, and the Just Word

[1]Jennifer Egan, "To Be Young and Homeless," *The New York Times Magazine* (March 24, 2002): 34.

Chapter 19: "God's Justice and America's Sixth Child"

[1]Children's Defense Fund, *The State of Children in America's Union: A 2002 Action Guide to Leave No Children Behind* (Washington, D.C.: Children's Defense Fund, 2002), 15.

[2]Ibid.

[3]Children's Defense Fund, *The State of America's Children: Yearbook 2000* (Washington, D.C.: Children's Defense Fund, 2000), xiv–xv (emphasis added).

[4]See ibid., xiv. The source of these figures is the Office of Research, Evaluation, and Statistics, Social Security Administration, Social Security Programs throughout the World, 1999, Summary Table and Individual Entries.

Chapter 21: The Word Off Center

[1]See Fernando F. Segovia, *Decolonizing Biblical Studies: A View from the Margins* (Maryknoll, N.Y.: Orbis, 2000). Segovia expresses some uncertainty about the appropriateness of the terms, saying that although he continues to use them, "in employing all such categories, one continues to view the reality and experience of the periphery…with reference to the center and hence in terms of external intervention, domination, and oppression. As a result, the role of the center continues to be privileged over that of the periphery" (134–35).

[2]For example, all dancing, which was "immoral"; the Christmas creche, which was "idolatrous"; or the gift-bearing Three Kings, who were "Roman Catholic."

[3]For example, Thanksgiving Day, Mother's Day, the Christmas tree, and Santa Claus.

[4]R. Douglas Brackenridge and Francisco O. García-Treto, *Iglesia Presbiteriana: A History of Presbyterians and Mexican Americans in the Southwest* (San Antonio: Trinity University Press, 1974, 1987).

[5]Segovia, *Decolonizing Biblical Studies,* 128.

[6]Casiodoro de Reina's translation was first published in 1569, Cipriano de Valera's revision in 1602. Other revisions were published in 1862, 1909, and 1960.

[7]R. S. Sugirtharajah, *The Bible and the Third World: Precolonial, Colonial, and Postcolonial Encounters* (Cambridge: Cambridge University Press, 2001), 61–73, lists the "marks of colonial hermeneutics" as "inculcation" (the use of the Bible for inculcating European–or North American–customs), "encroachment" (introduction of values alien to a "primitive" culture under the cover of "biblicization"), "displacement" (replacement of local values by "biblical" ones), "analogies and implication" ("juxtaposition of biblical and secular history as a convenient weapon against those who dare to resist colonial intervention"), "textualization" (the written

word is privileged over oral forms; reading is essential), and "historicization of faith" (i.e., of the Christian faith as represented in the Bible; other religious traditions are dismissed as myths).

[8]Segovia, *Decolonizing Biblical Studies,* 128–29.

[9]See, for example, Joerg Rieger, *God and the Excluded: Visions and Blindspots in Contemporary Theology* (Minneapolis: Fortress Press, 2001).

[10]Virgilio Elizondo, *Galilean Journey: The Mexican-American Promise* (Maryknoll, N.Y.: Orbis, 1983), 54.

[11]Ibid., 54–55.

[12]Ibid., 70.

[13]Ibid.

[14]Ibid., 124–25.

[15]Roberto Goizueta, *Caminemos con Jesus: Toward a Hispanic/Latino Theology of Accompaniment* (Maryknoll, N.Y.: Orbis, 1995), 16.

[16]Ibid., 17.

[17]Ibid., 37.

[18]Ibid., 186–87.

[19]Harold J. Recinos, *Who Comes in the Name of the Lord? Jesus at the Margins* (Nashville: Abingdon Press, 1997), 39.

[20]Ibid., 54–55.

[21]Ibid., 141.

[22]Elizondo, *Galilean Journey,* 91.

[23]Ibid., 92.

[24]Ibid., 124.

[25]Goizueta, *Caminemos con Jesus,* 184.

[26]Ibid., 195.

[27]Recinos, *Who Comes in the Name of the Lord?* 155.

Chapter 22: "Give to Everyone Who Begs from You"

[1]See the classic lampoon of this notion by Robert Lupton, "The Truly Worthy Poor," in his *Theirs Is the Kingdom: Celebrating the Gospel in Urban America* (San Francisco: Harper & Row, 1989).

Part 7: "Affluenza"

[1]Erich Auerbach, *Mimesis: The Representation of Reality in Western Literature,* trans. Willard R. Trask (Princeton, N.J.: Princeton University Press, 1972).

Chapter 25: Preaching a Just Word in Privileged Pulpits

[1]John de Graaf, David Wann, and Thomas H. Naylor, *Affluenza: The All-Consuming Epidemic* (San Francisco: Berrett-Koehler, 2001), 2.

[2]John de Graaf, Vivia Boe, and Sheila Espinoza, *Affluenza,* ed. Cleven Ticeson (Oley, Pa.: Bullfrog, 1997), videocassette.

[3]Michael Novak, "Wealth and Virtue: The Development of Christian Economic Teaching," in *The Capitalist Spirit: Toward a Religious Ethic of Wealth Creation,* ed. Peter L. Berger (San Francisco: Institute for Contemporary Studies, 1990), 57–66.

[4]Cornel West, "Black Theology and Marxist Thought," in *Black Theology: A Documented History,* vol. 1: *1966–1979,* ed. James H. Cone and Gayraud S. Wilmore (Maryknoll, N.Y.: Orbis, 1993), 410.

[5]Cornel West, "Black Theology of Liberation as Critique of Capitalist Civilization," in *Black Theology: A Documentary History,* vol. 2: *1980–1992,* ed. James H. Cone and Gayraud S. Wilmore (Maryknoll, N.Y.: Orbis, 1993), 417–18.

[6]J. Mark Thomas, "The Quest for Economic Justice," in *God and Capitalism: A Prophetic Critique of Market Economy,* ed. J. Mark Thomas and Vernon Visick (Madison, Wisc.: A-R Editions, 1991), 2.

[7]Peter L. Berger, *The Noise of Solemn Assemblies: Christian Commitment and the Religious Establishment in America* (Garden City, N.Y.: Doubleday, 1961), 39–41.

[8]Ibid., 47.

[9]See Dale P. Andrews, *Practical Theology for Black Churches: Spanning the Chasm between Black Theology and African American Folk Religion* (Louisville: Westminster John Knox Press, 2002).

[10]George M. Marsden, "Preachers in Paradox," in *Individualism and Commitment in American Life: Readings on the Themes of Habits of the Heart,* ed. Robert Bellah, Richard Madsen, William M. Sullivan, Ann Swidler, and Steven M. Tipton (New York: Harper & Row, 1987), 341.

[11]See Philip Kenneson and James L. Street, *Selling Out the Church: The Danger of Church Marketing* (Nashville: Abingdon Press, 1997).

[12]Robert N. Bellah, Richard Madsen, William M. Sullivan, Ann Swidler, and Steven M. Tipton, *The Good Society* (New York: Knopf, 1991), 93–94.

[13]Ibid., 206–11.

[14]See de Graaf et al., *Affluenza,* part 1: "Symptoms."

[15]Peter L. Berger, *A Far Glory: The Quest for Faith in an Age of Credulity* (New York: Anchor, 1992), 48–49, 172–73.

[16]Parker J. Palmer, *The Company of Strangers: Christians and the Renewal of America's Public Life* (New York: Crossroad, 1981), 72.

[17]Barbara Rumscheidt, *No Room for Grace: Pastoral Theology and Dehumanization in the Global Economy* (Grand Rapids: Eerdmans, 1998), 112.

Chapter 26: "Famine in the Land"

[1]"Famine in the Land," is copyright 1999, Barbara Brown Taylor. All rights reserved. Reprinted from *Home by Another Way* by Barbara Brown Taylor; published by Cowley Publications, 907 Massachusetts Ave., Cambridge, MA 02139. www.cowley.org (800-225-1534).

Chapter 29: Preaching Outside the Lines

[1]Paulo Freire, *Pedagogy of the Oppressed,* trans. Myra Bergman Ramos (New York: Seabury Press, 1970); idem, *Education for Critical Consciousness,* trans. Myra Bergman Ramos (New York: Continuum, 1974).

[2]See Freire's account of the empowerment of marginal communities through their reading the gospels under the military dictatorship in Brazil in the 1970s in Paulo Freire and Antonio Faundez, *Learning to Question: A Pedagogy of Liberation,* trans. Tony Coates (Geneva: WCC Publications, 1989), 63–64.

[3]I use the consonants of the Hebrew tetragrammaton to specify the personal God of the First Testament, often referred to as Lord, *Adonai,* or *hashem* (the name).

[4]The determined "heart of the matter" in a text is best held lightly. The "heart" or "good news" of the text from the perspective of the margins is often quite different than what is visible from a mainstream perspective. Often in the midst of a dialogical Bible study, I witness a shift in my own perception. Most of this paradigm shift is initiated by an untrained reader's reaction to the story. Gerald West goes into great detail regarding the "hidden transcript" of marginalized readers—interpretations that are disclosed only in an environment of total trust. See Gerald O. West, *The Academy of the Poor: Towards a Dialogical Reading of the Bible* (Sheffield: Sheffield Academic Press, 1999).

[5]When I begin with issues I seek to address among my parishioners or with their spontaneous questions, knowledge of the scriptures becomes especially important. The more you know the Bible, the more ready you are to choose the appropriate text for your particular context. Once a text is selected that appears to address a given contemporary situation, the leader can explore the group's questions before inviting them to look at the selected scripture.

[6]"Homes" is standard gang slang for "homeboy," the modern equivalent for comrade or brother.

[7]Juan used the term *bitch* for *woman.*

[8]This is not to say that the men have no responsibility for their actions. Their very presence in the jail is a constant reminder that they are being held responsible for their offenses and paying the price by doing time. Today in North America the ideology of free choice and personal responsibility reigns supreme, affecting disproportionately those who

lack the resources to pay for a private attorney who can prove their innocence (and thus lack of personal responsibility). Jesus moves the discussion to a higher level by refusing to affirm the dominant retributive model of justice. Jesus' grace-filled approach looks at calamity not as deserved punishment but as an occasion for life-giving action on behalf of the undeserving.

[9]The exact location of this miracle is not completely clear. The mention of Jesus' "passing by" (9:1) and his spitting on the ground (9:6) support the thesis that this encounter occurred outside. At any rate the blind man received his sight upon washing in the pool Siloam (9:7).

[10]The symbolism of "putting on Christ" by putting on a white robe is certainly appropriate dress for one who emerges from the cleansing waters of baptism. The white robe or alb also can be a valuable reminder that the pastor occupies an "office" and functions not on her or his own but as a representative of Christ's church. However, this symbolism is often lost on people to whom it is rarely explained, becoming instead a uniform connoting a distancing otherworldly separation or presumed perfection. In contrast, the black robe's symbolic reminder of human sinfulness is usually eclipsed by the robe's more commonly understood association with the judge or academic—hardly pastoral images.

[11]Women, people of color, and sexual minorities sometimes claim that robes, stoles, clerical collars, and such give them more credibility. The Mormon Church certainly espouses this view, as do many impoverished churches in rural Honduras who attract members by their "dressing for success." By using the means of the powerful and successful, might we be promoting the dominant culture at the expense of the saving power manifested in the weakness of Christ crucified?

[12]See Stanley P. Saunders and Charles L. Campbell's excellent apologetic for this street reading and preaching in *The Word on the Street: Performing the Scriptures in the Urban Context* (Grand Rapids: Eerdmans, 2000).

[13]Paulo Freire, *La educación como práctica de la libertad* (Santiago, Chile: ICIRA, 1969); and idem, *Pedagogy of the Oppressed.* See also Freire and Faundez, *Learning to Question.*

[14]Freire, *Pedagogy of the Oppressed,* 58.

[15]Ibid., 59.

[16]Ibid., 68.

[17]Many new-church development leaders who seek to minister to professional and middle-class people argue that churches must be user-friendly, comfortable places. The tendency to tailor a church to the comfort level of more privileged people may well set up these churches for failure when it comes to ministries of social justice and transformation. Professional, middle-class people stand to benefit from a theology that emphasizes God's coming in weakness and brokenness and a deliberate learning from and dialoguing with those on the margins of their community right from the start.

[18]This is especially true for churches where the majority of parishioners attend only the larger, weekly Saturday or Sunday services. Many churches organize their larger congregations into smaller "home" or "cell" groups that meet during the week and gather on Sundays in a larger and more traditional setting for "corporate" worship. Some of these models are proving to be an effective way to empower individuals in larger churches.

Chapter 32: "The Gift of Anger"

[1]Arthur John Gossip, "Exposition of John," in *Interpreter's Bible,* ed. George Arthur Buttrick, vol. 8 (New York: Abingdon Press, 1952), 497–98.